William Adair Bernoudy, Architect

William Adair Bernoudy, Architect

Bringing the Legacy of Frank Lloyd Wright to St. Louis

Text by Osmund Overby

Photographs by Sam Fentress

Foreword by Gyo Obata

University of Missouri Press   Columbia and London

♾™ This paper meets the requirements of the American National Standard for Permanence of Paper for Printed Library Materials, Z39.48, 1984.

Design and Composition: Kristie Lee
Printer and Binder: The Stinehour Press
Typefaces: Bembo and Frutiger Ultra Black

Unless otherwise indicated, all of the photographs were taken by Sam Fentress between 1994 and 1996, and all of the architectural drawings are by Robert J. Lippert.

Frontispiece portrait of William Bernoudy, photograph 1982 by Karen Elshout, courtesy *St. Louis Post-Dispatch.*

Library of Congress Cataloging-in-Publication Data

Overby, Osmund, 1931–
    William Adair Bernoudy, architect : bringing the legacy of Frank Lloyd Wright to St. Louis / text by Osmund Overby ; photographs by Sam Fentress ; foreword by Gyo Obata.
        p.   cm.
    Includes bibliographical references and index.
    ISBN 0-8262-1224-7 (alk. paper)
    1. Bernoudy, W. A. (William Adair), 1910–1988—Criticism and Interpretation.   2. Organic architecture—Missouri—St. Louis.
3. St. Louis (Mo.)—Buildings, structures, etc.   4. Wright, Frank Lloyd, 1867–1959—Influence.   I. Bernoudy, W. A. (William Adair), 1910–1988.
II. Title.
NA737.B475O83   1999
720' .92—dc21

                                                          99—11930
                                                          CIP

The University of Missouri Press offers its grateful acknowledgment to the Trustees of the Gertrude and William A. Bernoudy Foundation for their generous contribution in support of the publication of this volume.

Contents

Foreword

This book is about William Bernoudy, his life, his education to become an architect, and his architectural practice in St. Louis. In telling Bernoudy's story, the author details the experiences of a fellow at Frank Lloyd Wright's school at Taliesin and the intimate life there, which centered on Wright and his philosophy. In addition, we learn the interesting history of architecture and society in St. Louis and this country during the transition from the industrial age to the modern.

Bernoudy was a fellow at Taliesin for only three years, but those years and his continuing relationship with Wright made an indelible mark on his life and his practice as an architect. I believe Bill learned the following principles from Wright:

1. Respect for the site and its natural conditions.
2. Sensitivity to materials, particularly brick, wood, and glass.
3. Understanding of the interrelationship of each area to the whole, with an openness and flow of one space to another.
4. Awareness of the extension of the interior to the exterior, particularly of residential spaces to the garden.

In addition, we learn that Bill Bernoudy was a warm, sensitive person who listened to his clients' needs. He created architecture, therefore, that fulfilled those needs aesthetically as well as emotionally. From Wright's influence he went on to develop his own interpretation of organic architecture, which included a more active partnership with his clients and, interestingly, an acknowledgment of history, particularly American idioms of the earlier century. Bernoudy, unlike Wright, did not reject the past outright but incorporated his awareness of the past into a modern language.

The Pulitzer pavilion is a fine example of Bernoudy's creativity. The house melds into the site. The masterful relationship between the main living spaces and the beautiful pool is articulated at every level. A restrained use of materials and a minimum of formal manipulation achieve a dramatic effect for a relatively small building. Bernoudy's own compact house on a restrictive site also shows his genius for achieving high impact with restraint. The interior spaces flow out into the garden and beyond and demonstrate how the disposition of building to site can harmonize the relationship between the two. In many ways, Bernoudy was "green" before the term came in vogue.

Bernoudy was a rare individual in St. Louis for his time, where competence in architecture was not in demand. He built a body of residential work that exemplifies an ease of living in harmony with the local climate and terrain. St. Louis has a history of traditional residential architecture but few good examples of the modern home. Residential architecture of merit is not built in this area because residential builders control the market and its aesthetic. If a prospective family looks to build a new home, they would do well to study the work of Bill Bernoudy. Perhaps his work can inspire a level of quality and sensitivity to the environment in this community, and elsewhere.

Gyo Obata

Acknowledgments

We are grateful for the privilege of working together on this study
of such wonderful examples of modern architecture and of their talented architect, William Bernoudy. We would also like to pay tribute to
Gertrude Bernoudy, who first conceived this book and who herself is a
subject of it to the extent we believe her life played an important role
in the development of her husband's career. She was determined that
this book would ultimately be published, even when it was clear in her
last years that she lacked the energy to see it through herself. But by
virtue of generous provisions through her estate she made it possible. We
want to thank the Trustees of the Gertrude and William A. Bernoudy
Foundation, Edwin B. Meissner Jr., John D. Schaperkotter, William P.
Stiritz, and Stuart Symington Jr., and Linda M. Dougherty of Bank of
America, who originally asked us to produce this work and have given
us extraordinary support and assistance from the beginning.

A continuing legacy of Bernoudy's architectural career is the affection
and respect with which he and Gertrude are remembered by a large
group of friends, former clients, and owners of the houses he designed.
We have especially enjoyed meeting them, and they have been unfailingly
kind and generous in sharing their recollections and inviting us into their
homes. There are far too many for us to list them all here, but we want
to emphasize that this book could not have been completed without
their cooperation and assistance.

■　■　■

For me as author, it has been a great pleasure—personal as well as professional—to work with Sam Fentress. Because he started on the project
first, establishing the catalog of Bernoudy's works in large part fell to
him. This would normally have been my job, and I am grateful for his
major help with it. As architectural historians know, the interpretation
of buildings in a project like this depends as much on the images of the
photographer as on the words of the historian, and I could not have
wished for a better collaborator.

A number of prominent individuals in our professional fields have
been especially helpful. Ed and Elsa Mutrux and Hank and Ann Bauer
shared their memories with me as generously as Mutrux and Bauer
shared their talents with Bernoudy as his partners. Esley Hamilton, an
authority on the architecture of the St. Louis region and its architects,
could not have been more generous with that knowledge. Henry Herold,
a native of St. Louis, a friend of the Bernoudys, an apprentice at Taliesin
in the 1950s, and subsequently an architect in Tiburon, California, has
special insight on Bernoudy's responses to the Wright tradition, which he
shared most generously. Other members of the architectural community
have stepped forward to provide additional information and insights
throughout this process.

The majority of the Bernoudy office records are preserved at the Missouri Historical Society in St. Louis, where the private files and correspondence of the Bernoudys have also been lodged. These are identified in the notes as William Bernoudy papers and Bernoudy Trust Archive, respectively. Kirsten Hammerstrom, Associate Curator of Architectural Collections, and Eric Sandweiss, Director of Research, were especially helpful to me. A collection of drawings is preserved at Washington University's School of Architecture together with microfilm of nearly all of the drawings produced by the Bernoudy firms. We are grateful to Associate Dean Jim Harris for making these available and for sharing his recollections about the Bernoudys.

The correspondence between Bernoudy and Frank Lloyd Wright and others at Taliesin was essential for this study. These letters are preserved in the Frank Lloyd Wright Archives at Taliesin West in Scottsdale, Arizona, and are readily accessible through a microfiche copy at the Getty Center for the History of Art and Humanities in Los Angeles. I am grateful to the staffs at both institutions for their help. The files on St. Louis architects that have been assembled over many years by the librarians of the Fine Arts Department of the St. Louis Public Library are an invaluable resource. It is a pleasure to acknowledge the usefulness of these files once again and the friendly assistance of the present librarian, Mary S. Frechette. Materials at the State Historical Society of Wisconsin at Madison about Frank Lloyd Wright and Taliesin were made available to me, the Collected Papers of John H. Howe being most important for this project. John O. Holzhueter of the staff there was especially generous with his help and intimate knowledge of the Taliesin Fellowship. Letters from Bernoudy to George and Helen Beal are preserved in the Taliesin Collection in the Department of Special Collections of the Kenneth Spencer Research Library at the University of Kansas, Lawrence. Alexandra Mason, Spencer Librarian, was most helpful in making these available.

While this book was in preparation, I was invited to offer a class at Washington University on the theme "Modernism and St. Louis Architecture." I am grateful to professor Mark S. Weil, Chairman of the Department of Art History and Archaeology at Washington University, for making this opportunity possible and for the indulgence of the Trustees in permitting me to devote a portion of my time to this related project. The class provided a lively, informed, and critical audience as the main themes of the book developed, and several students wrote research papers for that course that are specifically cited herein. One member of the class, Robert Lippert, in addition to his paper for the course, prepared a detailed index of the microfilm drawings and brought his extraordinary computer graphic talents to bear in the preparation of the plan drawings included in this book. He is now finding an outlet for his intimate acquaintance with Bernoudy's architecture as a partner in Lippert Cannon Design, Inc.

Throughout the publication process we and the Trustees have been guided by the experienced staff of the University of Missouri Press. Its Director and Editor-in-Chief, Beverly Jarrett, and other personnel, including Dwight Browne, Jane Lago, and Kristie Lee, have made numerous helpful suggestions. I feel especially fortunate to have had the benefit of Jane Lago's copyediting. The completion of this book is due in no small part to their efforts.

On a personal level I want to thank my wife, Barbara, for her interest and unfailing support. Years ago she shared my early enthusiasm for Frank Lloyd Wright and modern architecture, and together we have visited innumerable wonderful buildings—Wrightian ones and every other sort too—over the years. Our daughter, Charlotte Overby, gladly offered to serve as my first editor on this book, and I want to acknowledge what a great help that was.

Osmund Overby

■ ■ ■

The opportunity to explore a wonderful group of modern homes through twelve seasons, with their varying foliage and angles of light, was unique in my career as an architectural photographer. William Bernoudy and his associates were masters at nestling a home artfully into its surrounding landscape. The beauty and maturity of that landscape made documenting their work a very engaging challenge.

Working with Osmund Overby has been a rare treat and a privilege. His humility, wry wit, and constant good humor made collaborating on this project a joy. I would like to pay tribute to Gertrude Bernoudy for originally conceiving this book and to the Trustees of the Gertrude and William A. Bernoudy Foundation for their confidence in my ability to work in various roles as researcher, art director, and photographer. I would like to thank Eugene Mackey and Eliot Smith for telling the Trustees about me before the project began.

The owners of Bernoudy homes deserve special thanks for their willingness to endure the many inconveniences of architectural photography. It was a pleasure and a privilege to meet them, and I will always remember their countless acts of kindness.

Michael Jacob, born in Germany and trained there by a master photographer, helped me on almost every photo shoot throughout the project, and I am very grateful for his assistance. He provided many useful suggestions regarding camera placement and lighting.

My wife, Betsy, knew of Bernoudy before I did because of visits with her friend and fellow bibliophile Marian Tichvinsky, who as Mrs. Clarence King had commissioned one of our favorite Bernoudy houses many years before. I want to thank Betsy for her encouragement and good spirits throughout this project. More than anyone else she has taught me what a house and home should be. My deepest appreciation goes to her and to my children, Madeleine, Clare, Jane, Paul, Sam, and Joseph, for their patience at home while I traveled across town and country photographing Bernoudy houses.

Sam Fentress

William Adair Bernoudy, Architect

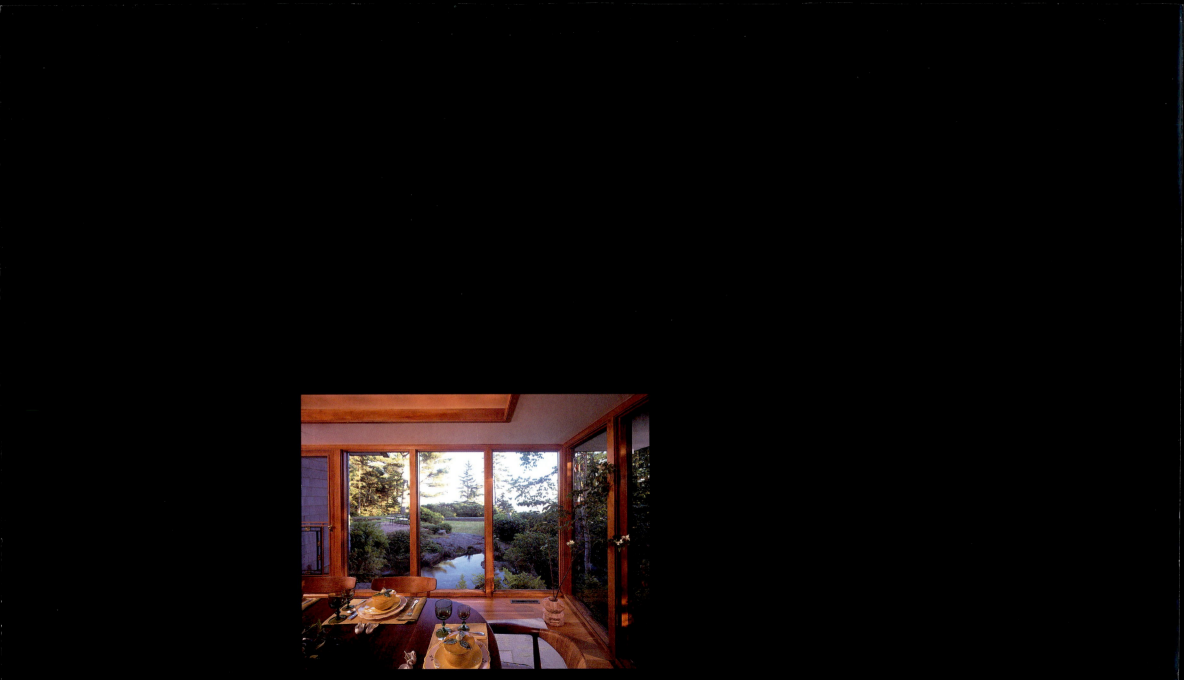

Introduction

When Frank Lloyd Wright opened the Taliesin Fellowship in October 1932, William Adair Bernoudy of St. Louis was among the forty charter apprentices. Three years later, back in St. Louis to stay, he became the leading advocate for Organic Modern architecture in the region, giving voice to what he had experienced and learned at Taliesin. Speaking to architectural students soon after his return, he explained, "Frank Lloyd Wright has made his principles articulate just as he has made the Taliesin Fellowship possible. It is suffused with his spirit. All activity there has direction and purpose under his leadership. Without his inspiration there would be no apprenticeship or no fellowship."

Frank Lloyd Wright's influence on twentieth-century architecture is second to no one's, and quite unlike that of anyone else. In his extraordinarily long and productive career, Wright, who began designing buildings before 1890 and was still active at his death in 1959, left behind a great body of architectural work that has inspired generations of architects in many different ways. In his voluminous writing and his lectures, he argued the cause of modern architecture persuasively and in great detail, drawing on intellectual traditions very different from those that fed other main theories of modern architecture. And in his own dramatic life, he defined a captivating role for the architect in the life and culture of our times.

Many modern architects, while they might have admired Wright, found the message of his life and the example of his work irrelevant to their own careers, especially in the middle decades of the twentieth century. Yet he would not go away. One always had the feeling that he would once again have his day. In terms of scholarly interest in the last decades of the twentieth century—a period often called postmodern—that day has come, for certainly no single individual in the history of art is prompting the sheer volume, if nothing else, of publication.

Wright, with his forceful personality, has seemed such a towering figure that it has been hard to focus on those who were his willing followers, especially the apprentices in the Taliesin Fellowship. Often misunderstood, they seemed to be pale imitations of the original. That towering figure, long after his death, was always diffidently referred to by this group as "Mr. Wright," while he in turn addressed them by their first names or by nicknames, even ones he coined. William Bernoudy was always Billy. Although it was clear who was master of these apprentices, we are beginning to learn about the creative ways in which the stronger apprentices developed their own styles, not just following in the shadow of Mr. Wright but also moving on with his illumination.

William Adair Bernoudy's life was one sustained response to this powerful figure. Inevitably, his career was shaped both by his own circumstances and personality and by the opportunities that came to him and the people he met. Like Wright, but much more openly and democratically, he found professional partners who held similar points of view about modern architecture, and they built a successful practice together. Bernoudy left behind a host of admirers, particularly in the St. Louis region. His buildings, especially his houses, wedded so sensitively to their sites in the suburbs that grew in the postwar decades, are treasured and continue to give joy to their owners.

When the opportunity came to me to write this study of Bernoudy, there was no question about doing it. When I was a child in the 1930s, my parents built a modern house in southern Minnesota, and from then on I just assumed that architecture would be my career. This idea began to take on substance in college, where I became a close friend of Robert Warn, just back from his three-year apprenticeship with Wright. The ideas and designs that I have encountered researching this book have been familiar to me from those talks and visits to buildings with Bob. When I graduated from college in 1953, if the Korean War and the draft had not intervened, I might very well have followed Bob—and Bill Bernoudy— to Taliesin as an apprentice.

I was discharged in 1955. With the meager professional prospects of my friend Bob Warn in mind, and on the advice of others, I decided to put off the idea of an apprenticeship to Wright and to work for a professional degree in architecture first. When I finished in 1958, Wright, who seemed then as if he would live forever, was in fact ninety-one years old and less than a year from his death. But more significant for me, in the course of studying architecture, I had discovered architectural history. William Bernoudy has given me, after his death, the opportunity to go back and experience again those passions for the Organic Modern architecture that is Wright's continuing legacy.

As Bernoudy explained to the architectural students, the Taliesin Fellowship "is not an architectural school or an institution. It is a voluntary group of apprentices, led by a great master, that hopes by way of an organic life to learn the principles of an organic architecture." This idea about the interconnectedness of life and architecture is fundamental to architects such as Bernoudy. That is why this book is not simply a study of Bernoudy's architectural works; if we are to understand those works fully, we need to consider his life as well.

The book, then, falls naturally into two sections. Chapters 1 and 2 trace Bernoudy's life from his birth in 1910 to the end of World War II. By then he had been to Taliesin, knew Frank Lloyd Wright well, and was a committed advocate of Wright's Organic Modern architecture. He had also laid the groundwork that would make a career in architecture possible and had found his first partner, Edouard Mutrux.

In Chapters 3, 4, and 5—richly illustrated with photographs and drawings—the focus is on the buildings Bernoudy designed and built following the war until shortly before his death in 1988 and their architectural evolution. This evolution corresponds with changes in the organization of Bernoudy's firm, reflected in the different names given to it. These provide the titles for chapters 3, 4, and 5: Bernoudy-Mutrux, Bernoudy-Mutrux-Bauer, and Bernoudy Associates.

In 1955 William Bernoudy and Gertrude Lenart were married. She was as important to his life and career as Olgivanna Wright was to Frank Lloyd Wright's, but in very different ways, in spite of striking similarities between the two women. From the time of his marriage, it is not possible to fully understand Bernoudy's architecture and career without considering Gertrude's role in his life. Together the Bernoudys played an important part in the cultural life of the community. For these reasons we will also focus on the influence of this talented and remarkable woman in parts of the last two chapters.

The great interest in Wright as seen in the vast number of publications about his work that have appeared in the past decade has its parallel in a growing interest in those who were his apprentices. In 1988, the year of Bernoudy's death, a group of Wright's apprentices established Taliesin Fellows. Conscious of their own important role in the cause of organic architecture, they define their mission as one of networking, publishing, and education. The *Journal of the Taliesin Fellows* regularly publishes articles about architects with backgrounds and careers similar to Bernoudy's, and this literature joins a growing list of books on the same subject. Bernoudy would certainly have happily joined in the work of the Taliesin Fellows, and that same spirit lies behind this book as a record of his great legacy to the cause.

Chapter 1   "How I Might Study Architecture"

The letter is undated, but it must have been in early September 1932 that William Adair Bernoudy first wrote to Frank Lloyd Wright:

> For a number of years I have pondered how I might study architecture under the tutelage of someone whose ideas about the subject were in harmony with yours. Yesterday I received the very excellent news that you were forming an "apprenticeship school" and am tremendously anxious to avail myself of the opportunity to attend this fall.
>
> Will you please let me know how I can matriculate, entrance requirements, fees and any other information that will be of interest and help to a prospective apprentice.[1]

Much later, Bernoudy said that a friend—not named—had shown him an article about the Taliesin apprenticeship program in 1932 when Wright announced it. Bernoudy remembered it being in *Time* magazine, which ran a sarcastic—typical of the magazine's treatment of Wright then—and not very informative report in its September 5, 1932, issue.[2] More useful would have been the detailed article in the *New York Times* on August 19, 1932, headlined "F. L. Wright to Open a Bookless School." In any case, Bernoudy received a prospectus for the program and an application form, which he promptly completed and sent back with the required application fee of $135. In turn, he received a reply from Karl E. Jensen, Wright's secretary, dated September 19, 1932: "Here is Mr. Wright's receipt. We shall enroll you as an apprentice in the Taliesin Fellowship and will send you further information in the near future."

Bernoudy's apprenticeship with Wright was the foundation of his career. Many years later, when he was interviewed about his years at Taliesin, he usually said that he was seventeen when he went, once he even said that he was sixteen, and that he stayed for four years, although once he said five years. In fact, he was twenty-one, nearly twenty-two, in that fall of 1932, and he stayed at Taliesin for just under three years.

William Adair Bernoudy was born in St. Louis at 11:00 A.M. on Sunday, December 4, 1910, to Elizabeth and Bauduy Bernoudy, at the family's home at 5974 Julian Avenue.[3] He was the second of two Bernoudy children. His older brother, Jerome Francis, was a leap-year baby, born on February 29, 1908, when the family lived at 1221 Montclair Avenue, in the same neighborhood (Fig. 1–1). By all indications, the Bernoudys were a happy, middle-class family. While William was growing up, the family always called him Billy, and this was Wright's name for him, too, even

though everyone else by then was calling him Bill. In 1917 the Bernoudys bought a house at 7033 Lindell Avenue, immediately west of the Washington University campus.[4] Recently built by the Laage Real Estate and Investment Company in a mildly arts and crafts style, the house was two stories high with stucco walls and a low-pitched hip roof. Billy was to live here with his parents until he was forty years old, except for his years at Taliesin and his wartime service in the navy.

Elizabeth Stone Maddox and Jerome Bauduy Bernoudy had been married in New York on November 21, 1906.[5] He came from an old St. Louis French family, used his middle name, and was called Baud by his friends. She was called Liz or Beth by Baud and came from an old Kentucky family from Shelbyville, a more prominent family than the Bernoudys. Her parents were living in New York for business reasons at the time of her marriage, and the wedding took place in the Maddoxes' house on the Upper West Side, 502 West 143d Street. It was performed by a Presbyterian clergyman and friend of the Maddox family, the Reverend L. M. Bates. The wedding made the papers in New York, St. Louis, Shelbyville, and Cincinnati. Liz and Baud honeymooned in Washington, D.C.,

1–1. William Adair Bernoudy and Jerome Francis Bernoudy, ca. 1915. Bernoudy Trust Archive, Missouri Historical Society, St. Louis.

staying at the Willard Hotel and going to plays and concerts. Baud Bernoudy was employed by the Railway Steel Spring Company in St. Louis, and he kept a detailed record of the honeymoon trip as the couple traveled by train from New York, to Washington, to Shelbyville, and finally home to St. Louis.

Baud Bernoudy's diaries from 1927 and 1929 through August 27, 1940, survive and offer a glimpse into the activities of the Bernoudy family during those years.[6] All four Bernoudys frequently attended concerts, operas, the picture shows, and lectures, either as a family or separately with friends. The family—including the boys until they were twenty-one—also went to church almost every Sunday, and the parents often took part in Wednesday evening Bible classes. There were many friends and much entertaining back and forth, and the boys' friends often were welcomed for dinner at the Bernoudy home. The Bernoudys were especially close to Elizabeth Bernoudy's family in Kentucky; it was in honor of her unmarried sister, Adair Maddox, who often came for extended visits to St. Louis, that Billy was given his middle name, Adair. The Bernoudys often visited the Maddoxes, and a week or two in Shelbyville was the usual summer vacation. The parents also attended church conferences in different parts of the country nearly every summer. As Billy grew older, he traveled to Shelbyville on his own and seems to have felt more comfortable with the Anglo-Southern culture of the Maddoxes than with the Mississippi French traditions of the Bernoudy family.

The Bernoudy home still stands on Lindell, in the suburb of University City immediately adjacent to the city of St. Louis. Jerome and Billy attended University City High School, at that time something of a preparatory school for Washington University, and both went on to attend Washington University. Jerome graduated from high school in 1925. He completed a degree in business at Washington University in 1929 and went on to a business career in St. Louis. After graduation from the university, he continued to live with his parents and his brother.

A small group of drawings of buildings and ships that Billy did as a five year old survive among the family papers. Bernoudy liked to remember them as the earliest evidence that he would grow up to be an architect and a naval officer. School was another matter. Billy followed Jerome to University City High School and Washington University, but he was much less successful as a student.[7] He entered ninth grade at University City High School in 1925, taking the usual academic course of English,

1-2. William Bernoudy's high school graduation portrait, 1929. Photograph by Van-Miller Studio, Bernoudy Trust Archive.

Latin, mathematics, science, and history. He earned mostly D's and C's, had to repeat several courses, and made up for failed courses by attending two summer sessions. He finally received his high school diploma following the summer session in 1929 (Fig. 1–2). His most successful work was in four semesters of art, for which he consistently earned B's.

The summer following his sophomore year, Billy spent two months at a camp in Colorado. But most satisfying must have been his extracurricular musical activity. In the tenth grade, he played in the high school band, which performed at a baseball game (the St. Louis Cardinals lost to the New York Giants, 10–5) and traveled as far as Columbia, Missouri, for a music festival. In his senior year, Billy sang in a two-hundred-voice mixed glee club and also in a more select boys' glee club of thirty-one voices. A lavish production of the popular musical comedy *The Prince of Pilsen,* with lyrics by Frank Pixley and music by Gustav Carl Luders, first published in 1902, was staged by these combined high school musical groups and was the highlight of the year. As described in the University City High School yearbook, the *Dial,* for 1929, the boys' glee club "sang the male choruses exceptionally well, and gave proof of their versatility by performing several dance numbers." Friends joined the Bernoudy family to see the performance on Friday, April 12; after the opera, according to his father's diary, Billy went to a social affair, not returning home until after 2:00 A.M. The member of the University City High School class of 1929 who went on to become a great celebrity in the theater, Tennessee Williams, does not seem to have taken part in *The Prince of Pilsen*. The following summer of 1929, while Bernoudy was finishing up the last credit for his high school diploma, he was also ushering almost every night at the Muny Opera in nearby Forest Park. As preparation for the Taliesin apprenticeship, the musical and theatrical experiences would have been as relevant as any of the academic work in high school.

In spite of his weak academic record from high school, Bernoudy was admitted to Washington University in the fall of 1929. He placed in the lowest third on the entrance examinations. He enrolled in pre-business administration, taking general courses including history, English, geology, and French. He earned one C, in English, three D's, and five F's. His academic career ended in the spring of 1930 after only two semesters.[8] Years later, he explained to a dinner companion when the subject of dyslexia came up that he had suffered from it.[9] He felt that if he had been born later, an architectural career would not have been possible for him because of the expectation of academic degrees and the requirement for passing written examinations to become a registered architect. He once described some aspect of his problem, if that is what it should be called, by saying, "In accordance with a peculiarity of my nature, I have always associated images with names."[10] Whatever his learning disabilities, they never hindered his ability to write elegant, persuasive letters, give public lectures, attract clients as well as friends, and design beautiful buildings.

In June 1930, following his dismissal from Washington University, Bernoudy and a friend, Everett Davis, set off in Davis's car for Memphis. From there they planned to drive on to New Orleans, where they hoped to land jobs on a lumber steamer bound for Europe. Four days after leaving St. Louis, Bernoudy sent a telegram home saying they had arrived safely in New Orleans. But somehow the dream of a job on a lumber steamer fell through; after visiting several southern points, they were back in St. Louis three weeks later. It would be another quarter century before Bernoudy was able to travel to Europe. In St. Louis, Bernoudy continued to take advantage of activities at Washington University and even remained active in a fraternity with Jerome. A part-time job in the Wash-

ington University library seems to have been his main employment until he left for Taliesin two years later.

Important friendships find mention in his father's diaries. The name of Charles Van Ravenswaay, two years younger than Bernoudy and an undergraduate at Washington University, begins to appear in the fall of 1930 when the senior Bernoudy reports that Bill and Charles visited the Van Ravenswaay home in Boonville for a weekend. Van Ravenswaay already was developing the deep knowledge and love of Missouri history that eventually led to his distinguished career, first as the director and principal author of the WPA Writers' Program for Missouri, work that resulted in the 1941 publication of *Missouri: A Guide to the Show Me State*, and then after World War II as director of the Missouri Historical Society for sixteen years, during which time the size and quality of its museum collections were vastly enhanced. Increasingly, Bernoudy was spending weekends and even longer periods with friends in the country, which was not necessarily that far away in those days, but sometimes these excursions included canoe trips and camping along Ozark streams. Andy Bakewell was the most frequent partner for these trips. A sentimental document, hand lettered by Bernoudy in an affected alphabet, entitled "Certificate of Eternal Friendship," and signed by Alexander McNair Bakewell and William Adair Bernoudy on August 28, 1932, survives among the Bernoudy papers. Andy's father, Edward Bakewell, was one of the men Bernoudy listed as a reference on his application to Taliesin in 1932.

The Great Depression does not seem to have had much impact on the Bernoudy family and its activities. The tone of family life is suggested by a note written to Billy by his father on December 4, 1931, his twenty-first birthday.

My dear Billy:—

You may be sure that precious mother and I share with you the joy this day brings to you. You have meant a world of happiness in our lives. And so, by this same token we are hoping and wishing for you, that all the coming years will be filled, each one to the very brim, with real happiness that neither time nor adverse circumstance can dim or obstruct. And since only the great Heavenly Father bestows such good fortune we pray for His favor upon you, being confident He will bless you.

Affectionately, Dad[11]

Recalling the summer of 1932 before going off to Taliesin, Bernoudy much later remembered it as a time of floating along Ozark streams, trying to catch some vision of his future. By the end of the summer, he would no sooner return from a few days in the Ozarks than he would turn around and go back, with Andy as his most frequent companion. There was an increasingly frantic quality to the pace of this getting away on float trips and fishing jaunts. With his twenty-second birthday approaching in December, with the possibility of following in the steps of his older brother closed for academic reasons, and with his love for the arts and a strong inclination that architecture was where his heart lay, Bernoudy was ready for Taliesin.

Bernoudy's letter to Wright, in which he described the person under whom he might study architecture as "someone whose ideas about the subject were in harmony with yours," suggests that he had some understanding of the issues facing young architects at that time. The School of Architecture at Washington University remained a conservative bastion of eclectic architecture, rooted in the Beaux Arts curriculum, under the authoritarian leadership of Gabriel Ferrand. But there was a dissenting minority, led by an Italian member of the faculty, Paul Valenti, and modernism was a contentious issue among the faculty and students.[12] One student who would go on to a distinguished career as a pioneer of the modern movement in architecture and design, Charles Eames, had left Washington University as early as 1928 because his interest in the work of Frank Lloyd Wright received no support, except from Valenti.[13] Even though he was no longer a student after the spring of 1930, the young Bernoudy was on the Washington University campus almost daily. With his growing interest in architecture, Bernoudy must have followed this modernist controversy.

Bernoudy probably knew quite a bit about Frank Lloyd Wright, too, since Wright's work and his writings about architecture had been published regularly for many years in professional journals. Working in the Washington University library, he may have seen Wright's Princeton lectures, *Modern Architecture, Being the Kahn Lectures for 1930.* And Bernoudy might well have seen Wright's extraordinary autobiography, which Wright began at his wife's suggestion in 1926. The work was finally published in the spring of 1932 and sold out its first printing of twenty-five hundred copies almost at once, to everyone's surprise. *An Autobiography* received wide attention and merited a half column in the *New York Times* of

March 30, 1932. The *New Republic* gave it three-quarters of a page on June 29.[14]

The application fee of $135 that Bernoudy sent to Taliesin was to cover the tuition for a first month as a "tentative apprentice." Upon full acceptance, an additional tuition fee of $270 would be due, and after half a year another $270, for a total cost of $675 for the first year. In April 1930, Jerome and Billy had received inheritances from a relative's estate.[15] Jerome, who was twenty-two years old at that time, used his inheritance to buy a Ford Tudor Sedan, which the whole family enjoyed. But Billy was still nineteen, and his father was named guardian of his inheritance. That inheritance, Bernoudy remembered years later, was available for the Taliesin tuition that first year and must have been just about the right amount.

Wright's secretary, Karl E. Jensen, wrote again from Taliesin outside Spring Green, Wisconsin, on October 11, 1932.

> My dear Mr. Bernoudy: We are asking those who have been accepted as eligible to the Taliesin Fellowship to defer their arrival a few days. October 25th we will be able to make all comfortable and find plenty of work for everybody.
> We will use the quarters already established at Taliesin temporarily. Work will be transferred to the new buildings, in the building of which all will have a share, so soon as the first units are finished and ready.
> The weather here is likely to be cold and warm sports clothes will be the most comfortable wear here in the country. Overshoes and warm underclothing are necessary as we often have to make our way through snow and slush. You should bring your drawing instruments. A T-square, triangles and such other equipment as you may have. It would also be well to bring a pair of blankets and a comforter for your bed.[16]

September and October 1932, the last months before Bernoudy headed off to Taliesin, were filled with the usual activities at the Bernoudy house. Bernoudy did not join the others on the customary August holiday to Shelbyville, but he welcomed them back on September 2 to a clean house with flowers in every room. Charles Van Ravenswaay arrived at the Bernoudy house on September 19 and stayed on as a paying lodger, providing a welcome bit of additional income. The usual canoe trips and social events filled the weeks, and on October 5 both of the Bernoudy boys attended the Veiled Prophet Ball. The meticulous record of their father's diary tells us that Billy returned home at mid-

1–3. Frank Lloyd Wright in the Taliesin Courtyard, ca. 1934. Photograph probably by William Bernoudy, Bernoudy Trust Archive.

night, but Jerome not until 4:30. It also tells us that Billy's mother took him shopping on Monday, October 17, and that at 7:30 on Sunday, October 23, Billy caught the bus for Chicago "en route to school at Spring Green, Wisconsin." It was probably on October 25 or the next day that Mr. Wright and Billy, as they forever after addressed each other, met (Fig. 1–3). Four weeks later, on November 21, a letter arrived from Bernoudy to let his parents know that he had been accepted as a regular apprentice at Taliesin.[17]

The young William Bernoudy was one of forty on the official list of the original group of apprentices that was published with a new brochure about the fellowship on January 1, 1933. A few who had been part of Taliesin earlier were called Taliesin Men on the role. Two foreign members had already returned home, and three who were identified as Honor Fellows played little if any role in the fellowship. One of the Honor Fellows, Mendel Glickman, was a structural engineer who had a long connection to Taliesin as a consultant. Counting the Taliesin Men, thirty-five apprentices composed the first group. Seven were women. All but three had some college experience, but only seven had baccalaureate degrees. Bernoudy was identified as coming from Washington University.

Among those with no college experience was Svetlana Wright, Frank Lloyd Wright's stepdaughter. They must all have had rich expectations for their apprenticeships, but they could hardly have known what to expect. The brochure said that they were "at work in temporary quarters . . . taking part in the construction of the Fellowship buildings under the direct leadership of Frank Lloyd Wright." Taliesin has always been a work in progress.

The story of Frank Lloyd Wright's extraordinarily dramatic life has been told often, but some aspects of it need to be considered in detail for their influence on Bernoudy. Wright himself told the story first in his autobiography, which Bernoudy, like others of the new apprentices, could well have read shortly before journeying to Taliesin. But they would not have had the benefit of the several subsequent retellings, which range from the highly personal version of his son John, *My Father Who Is on Earth,* to the recent, detailed biography by Meryle Secrest.[18] Nor, of course, could they have had the benefit of recent accounts of the Taliesin apprenticeship.[19] They probably did know something about Wright's career and the dramatic way his personal life resonated with it. They probably knew something, too, about Taliesin, Wright's home, office, and farm complex near Spring Green, Wisconsin, to which they were headed. And they knew from Jensen's letter setting the date for arrival that the physical facilities were not ready and that the apprentices would be working on that project first.

Frank Lloyd Wright began to build Taliesin in 1911 on a hillside overlooking the beautiful Wisconsin River valley. This ancestral land had been settled by his mother's family, the Lloyd Joneses, beginning in 1864, twenty years after they came to the United States from Wales to join a farming community in the Welsh community of Ixonia near Oconomowoc. The site was not far from the progressive Hillside Home School, founded in 1886 by Wright's aunts Nell and Jane Lloyd Jones. Wright had spent extended periods of time in this valley as a child, working on his uncle's farm. In 1886, while working for the architect J. Lyman Silsbee in Chicago, he participated in the design of Unity Chapel, built for the Jones family in the valley, and in 1902 he designed a new building for his aunts' school, which was built the following year.

Wright abruptly broke off his brilliant early career in Chicago in 1909, leaving his wife, Catherine Tobin Wright, and their six children in Oak Park. He headed to New York for a rendezvous with Mamah Borthwick Cheney, the wife of a former client, and the two sailed for Europe. They spent a year traveling between Florence and Berlin, where Wright participated in the preparation of a lavish portfolio of his work published by Ernst Wasmuth. This portfolio firmly established his reputation in Europe and made possible his influence on the evolution of early modern architecture there. When Wright returned to Chicago in 1910, he set in motion his plans for moving his practice and himself with Mamah Cheney to a new complex he called Taliesin—Welsh for "shining brow" and also the name of a mythical Welsh hero. The newspapers made the most of the marital scandal, and the idea of Wright's building a new hideaway for his mistress outside the small Wisconsin town of Spring Green did not go over well there.

That first Taliesin was the scene of a grisly tragedy when, on August 15, 1914, a household servant set the house on fire and brutally murdered Mamah Cheney, her two children, and four other members of the household. Wright was in Chicago checking on his Midway Gardens project at the time. The most moving account of this terrible event is in Wright's autobiography, including a description of the burial of Mamah Cheney in the graveyard adjoining the small Unity Chapel. Although the fire was devastating, the general form of the house—laid up in native stone—survived and was incorporated into a new building. The second Taliesin also burned—an electrical fire, this time—and the house was rebuilt again and enlarged in 1925. It was the third Taliesin that welcomed the new apprentices in 1932. In an evolved form, this is the Taliesin one visits today.

The marital scandal in 1911 resulted in a serious decline in enrollment for the aunts' Hillside Home School. This decline coincided with other financial problems in the Lloyd Jones family, and in 1915 the school closed. Title to the property passed to Frank Lloyd Wright for a nominal sum in exchange for his commitment to care for and support his aunts. The aunts, together with Wright's mother, Anna, created, in Wright's words, "a perfect hell" at Taliesin, but by 1919 both aunts had died. Hillside quickly fell into serious disrepair, but Wright envisioned it as the home for the Taliesin Fellowship, and its remodeling and restoration became a major project for the new apprentices in 1932.

In December 1914, five months following the first fire at Taliesin and the murder of Mamah Cheney, Wright received a letter of sympathy and commiseration from someone he did not know, Miriam Noel. Wright was fascinated by and soon fell in love with this strange and deeply troubled woman. His work on the great Imperial Hotel project in Tokyo kept Wright in Japan for much of the time from 1916 to 1922, and Miriam was always with him. They were taken for husband and wife in Japan, though in fact they were not married until November 1923, when the divorce that Catherine Tobin Wright had finally agreed to became final. Six months later Miriam left Frank, and after much acrimony their divorce became final in 1928.

Olgivanna Lazovich entered Frank Lloyd Wright's life shortly after Miriam left him, and by early 1925 she was living at Taliesin. A Montenegrin with an exotic background, fluent in several languages, and thirty-one years younger than Wright, she was to play a major role in his life and career and keep him productive for another thirty-five years. When she met Wright, Olgivanna was married to a Russian architect, Vlademar Hinzenberg, with whom she had a daughter, Svetlana, born in 1917. By then she had met the mystic and student of esoteric knowledge Georgi Gurdjieff. She soon became part of his entourage, which fled the Near East during the turbulent years in the Caucasus following the Russian Revolution and the collapse of the Ottoman empire. They finally settled safely in France, at Fontainebleau outside Paris. In 1922 Gurdjieff created the Institute for the Harmonious Development of Man at the Prieuré of Avon at Fontainebleau. Dance was central to the institute's activities, and Olgivanna was soon both a star of the troupe and one of six instructors at the school. The troupe's performances attracted wide interest and led to a U.S. tour. But in 1924 Gurdjieff disbanded the operation, and that fall he urged Olgivanna to return to the United States, where divorce proceedings begun by her husband were underway. She and Wright met almost immediately, beginning a relationship that continued the public scandal of his life until the divorce from Miriam became final in 1928, allowing another marriage. By then, Frank and Olgivanna had a child, Iovanna, born in 1925, his seventh child and her second.

Wright's brilliant early works, done as leader of the Prairie School, were in large part complete upon his flight to Europe with Mamah Cheney in 1909.[20] These works would have been well known to the new apprentices, if not through their lavish publication by Ernst Wasmuth in Berlin in 1910 and 1911, then through their treatments in American professional publications. Built mostly in the Chicago area and the Midwest, these buildings were visited easily and frequently by Bernoudy during his stay at Taliesin or when traveling to and from St. Louis. Wright's Imperial Hotel and other works in Japan could not be seen firsthand, but Wright's deep and complex relationship with Japanese culture and art became a vivid part of the apprentice experience at Taliesin. Wright's California work in the 1910s and 1920s would also have been difficult for the apprentices to see. And for Bernoudy, at least, such examples of it as the Hollyhock House, built for Aline Barnsdall in 1916–1921, with its unusual evocation of Mayan architecture, seem to have been of little interest. On the other hand, Wright's exploration of low-cost housing and prefabricated materials, as in the American System-Built Houses he designed for the Richards Company in 1915–1917, or the concrete textile block houses built in Southern California in the 1920s, lay behind two ideas that became major focuses for the first apprentices: the Broadacre city project and the idea of the Usonian house. Like other formative figures in modern architecture, Wright had developed an ideal vision of the city of the future and had written about it. The model of Broadacre City would present his ideas in striking visual form and in great detail. The residential zones of this ideal city were filled with Usonian houses, a term Wright coined for these radically new, modestly priced houses.

Architecture is a sensitive index of the economy, and the crash of 1929 and the Great Depression virtually stopped activity in Wright's office. Wright's almost psychotic inability to manage his own financial affairs caused him to depend on friends, clients, admirers, even apprentices, for help of every kind. Finally, even his continued ownership of Taliesin fell into serious question. It was in those circumstances that the Wrights learned that lectures and writings could provide a financial alternative. Their strained financial circumstances must also have entered into their decision to form the Taliesin Fellowship with tuition-paying apprentices to provide a steady source of annual income.

When Wright took over the Hillside Home School property in 1915, he promised his aunts and his mother that he would somehow revive the school. The idea stayed with him, but eventually it evolved into the Hillside Home School of the Allied Arts. The Progressive Era was a time for experimental schools and colleges, and among them were many likely models for a revived Hillside school. The Arts and Crafts movement, which advocated arts training and production in a community setting, had figured significantly in Wright's early career. C. R. Ashbee, the English architect, craftsman, and follower of William Morris, became a close friend of Wright's, probably as early as 1896, and wrote an introduction for the German publication of Wright's work in 1911.[21] In the late 1880s, Ashbee created the Guild of Handicraft, one of the most experimental of the Arts and Crafts workshops. In 1902 he moved the workshop to Chipping Campden in Gloucestershire, where Wright visited in 1910.

Wright also knew Elbert Hubbard, a principal proponent of the Arts and Crafts movement in the United States.[22] Hubbard, too, had met William Morris and been influenced by him. In 1895, Hubbard formed the Roycroft Press in East Aurora, New York; four years later, he started Roycroft Industries, which became a sizable and widely known craft community. Louis Sullivan had visited there, as did Olgivanna and Frank Lloyd Wright shortly before founding the Taliesin Fellowship. Like Wright, Hubbard was an impressive figure, and the communities they created had important parallels in the number of arts and crafts that flourished there and in the emphasis on the joy of work.

The Cranbrook Art Academy, together with the complex of children's schools that Eliel Saarinen designed in the late 1920s and early 1930s at Bloomfield Hills, Michigan, is another likely model. Saarinen also served as president of the Cranbrook Academy beginning in 1932, and the Arts and Crafts ideal of collaboration among the fine and applied arts permeated the institution. The proper role of the modern machine in the production—even the mass production—of craft objects or artworks, if any, had long been an issue for proponents of the Arts and Crafts movement. While some argued for the exclusion of machines altogether and the use of only traditional hand methods of fabrication, Wright had argued for making use of modern machines as early as 1901.[23] As the Bauhaus evolved in Germany under Walter Gropius in the years following World War I, machine-made works and materials were integrated into an Arts and Crafts context stressing the interaction of the arts and crafts within a community of masters and students. The Bauhaus, too, in spite of Wright's utter disdain for Gropius, was in place as a model for the Taliesin Fellowship. An ideal of community life was common to all of these models. Olgivanna Wright brought quite another dimension of this ideal from her background with Gurdjieff. In a number of ways, life in the fellowship at Taliesin came to parallel the life Olgivanna had known at Gurdjieff's institute, and Gurdjieff was an occasional visitor.

Wright's own ideas about the revived Hillside school that ultimately became the Taliesin Fellowship began to take form in 1928 when he proposed establishing the Hillside Home School of the Allied Arts. He elaborated the program in his 1930 lectures on modern architecture at Princeton. In this version, Wright envisioned seven centers, each specializing in a branch of the industrial arts. Wright proposed that each center could attract support from established industries and reciprocal benefits would result from the interaction between sponsors and centers. Each center would have forty students studying and working under an experienced artist or craftsman. The centers would be located away from cities, with sufficient land so that the students could experience farmwork, too, and each center would become as self-sufficient as possible. Work was the essential experience. After three hours on the farm each morning, the students would spend seven hours in the workshops, where they would produce beautiful and marketable objects. Wright predicted that the quality of their products would inspire and enhance industrial design and that American life would benefit.

If those first apprentices had read the Princeton lectures when they were published in 1931, they would have had a good idea of what lay in store for them at Taliesin. Many of these ideas were repeated, as well, in the announcement sent out in the summer of 1932, which was reported in detail in the *New York Times* article that Bernoudy probably saw. The students would learn through hard work—quarrying stone, hewing timber, spending time in the machine shops—as well as through work at the drawing board. Firsthand experience was to take the place of textbooks. Three hours of work a day would be required on the grounds and the farm to ensure a supply of food, and meals would be taken in common. The other arts, including theater and music, would be a part of the experience, all within a fixed schedule. Students would be called apprentices and the school the Taliesin Fellowship.

In the Princeton lectures, Wright had proposed affiliation with nearby universities to make available additional courses in architecture, archaeology, and the history of art. Wright had ties with the nearby University of Wisconsin, and he knew about the University's Experimental College created by Alexander Meikeljohn in 1925. With that as something of a model, Wright's 1928 proposal envisioned the Hillside Home School as a university program but located at Taliesin. Negotiations collapsed at the end of 1929, and by 1932 Meikeljohn's Experimental College had come to an end. But the 1933 University of Wisconsin annual carried an illustrated four-page report about the Taliesin Fellowship with a vigorously argued justification for its pedagogical approach.[24]

Wright had not intended to head the Taliesin Fellowship. The post was offered to several people, most seriously to H. T. Wijdveld, a Dutch architect who was the founder and editor of the architectural magazine *Wendingen*. In 1925 *Wendingen* had published Wright's work in serial form, and those articles had subsequently been reprinted as a book.[25] The *Wendingen* publication served to bring European architects up-to-date about Wright's work since the Wasmuth publications of 1910 and 1911, something for which Wright was always grateful. But in the end, Wijdveld, like the others, turned down the offer, and it fell to the Wrights to take charge. Mr. Wright's domain was the drafting room. Mrs. Wright was in charge of the daily routine and ran a tight ship, giving out work assignments and monitoring the apprentices' performances and attitudes.

But the new apprentices could hardly have been prepared for the bizarre events that followed almost immediately upon their arrival. C. R. Secrest and his wife had been employed at Taliesin, and like many who had business dealings with Wright at this time, they had not been paid and were owed $282. On Monday, October 31, not quite a week after the apprentices assembled at Taliesin, Wright and Secrest met on the street in

Madison. Words led to blows between the two, and Secrest's son and a Wright apprentice broke up the fight. Wright's nose was injured and required a large bandage; he claimed it was broken. Reprisal followed. That night five apprentices broke into Secrest's house and horsewhipped him until he chased them out with a butcher knife. Warrants were issued against the five and against Secrest. There was much news coverage in Madison. In Superior Court a week later, on November 7, five apprentices faced punishment for their attack on Secrest—Karl Jensen, Wright's secretary, from Copenhagen, Rudolph Mock from Basle, and Sam Ratensky from New York were each fined $150 and costs, and William Beye Fyfe and William Wesley Peters, who "stood by," were each fined $50. Poor Secrest, meanwhile, languished in jail pending his trial.

In the meantime, a self-styled "committee of vigilantes" mailed a threat from Madison on November 4 that was received at Taliesin the next day. The group demanded money, threatening that if it was not paid Wright would be abducted and held for ransom. On November 16 an article in the *Wisconsin News* reported that detectives had been on the case for ten days, and students at Taliesin were maintaining an armed guard. The Wrights were in New York.[26]

The contrast between these events and the high-minded announcements of the opening of the fellowship must have tested the apprentices in unexpected ways. Wright probably did not deliberately make it all happen, but one can imagine the famous twinkle lighting up his eyes as he enjoyed the improbability and outlandishness of it all. Certainly it gave the fellows something to talk about as they settled into the heavy work of reconstruction at the Hillside School and the make-work in the studio where there were no commissions needing attention.

Five weeks later, on December 21, Bernoudy returned to St. Louis for a twelve-day holiday, immediately plunging into his old whirl of activities—concerts, picture shows, trips to the country, visits from friends, or going out with friends for lunches and dinners. A note in his father's diary from a few weeks later sheds light on the affectionate relationship that developed between Wright and some, if not all, of the apprentices. On Sunday, February 26, Wright called the Bernoudys from Union Station in St. Louis, where he had some time between trains. "He came out and spent time with us until 1 pm when he took the train for Texas." It was the first of several times that Wright was the guest of the Bernoudys. Holidays in St. Louis for Bernoudy came regularly. In 1933,

after having been at home for the prior Christmas, he was back on June 6–16, September 6–15, and November 24–December 5.

During the last of these holidays, a letter postmarked November 29 arrived from Taliesin from Edgar Tafel, an apprentice from New York City. Bernoudy, with his Missouri and Kentucky background, from farther south in the United States than any of the other apprentices, seems to have represented southern culture in the group. The salutation in Tafel's letter reads: "Well well Massah!" The letter closes with wishes to "Col. Banoudy from his slaves." Bernoudy already had a following for his beaten biscuits, which he made when it was his turn to do kitchen duty. Discipline at Taliesin must have been lax; the letter confesses that it is 10:30 A.M. on a Tuesday and Tafel has just climbed out of bed. He passes along the Taliesin news: there were some possible architectural commissions, Karl Jensen had "taken some initiative and cleaned up the studio, rearranging everything, so that nothing can be found," and John Dewey and Alexander Woollcott were expected for visits.[27] Philip Holliday, another of the charter apprentices and one who became a close friend of Bernoudy's, also wrote him in St. Louis on November 29. He, too, refers to the "beaten biscuits and other things for which you all are known down South. Did you know that St. Louis was on *our* side in the War of '61?"[28]

The big project that first year had been the reconstruction of the Hillside School. It says something about the Wrights' vision for the fellowship that the first focus was on the conversion of the old gymnasium to a theater. The Taliesin Playhouse opened on November 1, 1933. For an admission of 50 cents for adults and 25 cents for children, the public could join the fellowship on Sunday afternoons at 3:00 for "picture-plays with appropriate interpretation, music by way of integral sound, cup of coffee by the fire." Foreign films were shown frequently. In his November 29 letter Edgar Tafel indicated that the film the previous Sunday had been *The Road to Life* from the USSR, written and directed by Nikolai Ekk, in which street children in Moscow are rounded up and reformed. Tafel thought it was fair, but all propaganda, and noted that there were no paid outside admissions that day. At coffee following, Mrs. Wright poured.

Sometime in the fall of 1933, James Watrous visited Taliesin. Watrous was a graduate student in art history at the University of Wisconsin, where he received a Ph.D. in 1939 with a dissertation on mural painting in the United States. His report on the construction work was published in the December issue of *American Magazine of Art*. "About thirty Fellowship apprentices have worked with skilled laborers to build the units that they will soon occupy." The theater, which was nearly finished, caught his attention. "The original values of the stained woods in beams and walls have been retained," he wrote, "but in contrast to them the colorful decorations in the seats and curtains impart theatrical atmosphere. Strong coloration in the powerful reds, greens, blues, and purples, set off by blacks and the deep-stained woods, gives the tenor of the designs for the curtains and the seats. Furnishings for the theater were designed and made by students." He noted with approval the designs for the large drafting studio and the adjoining living quarters for apprentices, but added that the majority of the apprentices still resided at Wright's home.[29]

Bernoudy spent Christmas 1933 at Taliesin. A woodcut Christmas card he sent home, which he must have made, shows a strong silhouette of Taliesin in a wintery, snowy setting with leafless trees (Fig. 1–4). It carries the message "Greetings from Taliesin" and is similar to a Christmas card created that year by another of the apprentices, William Beye Fyfe.[30] The original design was most likely Fyfe's, and the variations that he created on it came to serve as a signature for Taliesin for several years.[31]

Fyfe came from a family with both professional and personal connections to Wright and became one of Bernoudy's close friends at Taliesin (Fig. 1–5). With the opening of the fellowship, Wright complained that he had too many Bills. William Beye Fyfe, whose middle name was his mother's maiden name, was thereafter known at Taliesin as Beye. William Wesley Peters, who became the Wrights' son-in-law after his marriage to Svetlana and remained at Taliesin as a senior member of the fellowship for the rest of his life, was always known as Wes. Wright separated Bernoudy from the other Williams by always calling him Billy, even long after everyone else took to calling him Bill.

1–5. Elizabeth (Bitzie) Enright Gillham, Frank Lloyd Wright's niece, with **William Beye Fyfe and William Bernoudy, ca. 1934. Photograph in the Bernoudy Trust Archive.**

1–4. **Taliesin Christmas Greeting, 1933. William Bernoudy papers, Missouri Historical Society, St. Louis.**

At the beginning of 1934, the Wrights apparently felt it necessary to firm up discipline. A memorandum signed by Frank Lloyd Wright and dated January 4 reads:

1. We are here at Taliesin to work and to work hard. A day of hard work requires rather more than the normal eight hours of sleep. Adequate sleep is as essential to a healthy psyche as fresh air and good food. The curfew will ring therefore at ten minutes of ten o'clock. All member[s] of the Fellowship are requested to promptly turn in at this time. Those unable or unwilling to conform in spirit to the letter of this regulation will be invited to leave Taliesin.

2. The rising bell will ring fifteen minutes before breakfast at seven o'clock. With sufficient sleep everyone should be willing and able to appear promptly at the breakfast table every morning. On Sundays breakfast may be had anytime up to ten o'clock.

3. Members of the fellowship are requested not to seek the town for relaxation. If relaxation of this sort is necessary some quality that should be present in work and fellowship is missing. The seeking of such relaxation in the circumstances set up at Taliesin will prove this. Either the life at Taliesin will be for the purpose of membership here, complete, or the member "town-relaxed" will be invited to return to the life of the town where, manifestly, he belongs.

4. But to avoid drawing hard lines for the present, exceptions may be made to the above regulations on appeal to Mrs. Wright or Mr. Wright for special occasions.

5. In the light of past experience it appears that the less the life of the private room and the town is practiced and the more the Fellowship foregathers on common ground the richer the quality of our social life will be for all concerned in this endeavor.

6. The outside work day begins at Taliesin promptly at eight o'clock—one hour being allowed each apprentice for breakfast and the upkeep of his room. The outside day at Taliesin ends at fifteen minutes to four o'clock when members will wash and appear at the studio for tea, thereafter working on studio projects until the supper bell rings at six o'clock. Such work as may particularly interest the apprentice can be carried on there after supper. The more the studio life is a feature of fellowship evenings the better.

FINALLY. Man is essentially an appetite. Only as then [sic] satisfactions of appetite tend to uplift the individual and do not tend to sink him is there culture. Life at Taliesin is seeking earnestly for a natural basis for a natural culture. I hope all will be too much in earnest to put up long with thoughtlessness or willful disregard of the limitations fixed to ensure the growth of that life as a whole.[32]

Modifications to Taliesin and further construction work on the Hillside complex, along with farmwork and household chores, kept the apprentices busy during 1934. Construction work included quarrying stone and felling trees and sawing them into lumber, as well as assisting the resident craftsmen in building (Fig. 1–6). The Hilltower wing at Taliesin, which had been prepared for the apprentices just before the opening of the fellowship, with a dining room and dormitories, received further changes. Major work continued at the Hillside School following the completion and opening of the theater in the fall of 1933. Because Wright was not able to leave well enough alone, the theater got its share of improvements too. The long-range plan was for Hillside to be the principal quarters for the fellowship, but in 1934 work was just beginning on the new dining room wing and the stone paving for the new large drafting room.[33] Every two weeks an apprentice took a turn as chief, with two other apprentices as assistants, to see that Mrs. Wright's directions were carried out and that everyone was kept busy.

1–6. Bernoudy at Taliesin, May 12, 1934. Courtesy the Frank Lloyd Wright Archives, Scottsdale, Arizona.

1–7. The studio at Taliesin with renderings of earlier projects by Wright. Photograph probably by Bernoudy, ca. 1934, Bernoudy Trust Archive.

The one architectural commission underway in the studio—the old drafting room at Taliesin—was the redesign of a house for Malcolm and Nancy Willey of Minneapolis. An earlier version from 1932, which proved too costly, was scaled down and redesigned in 1933 and early 1934. Mrs. Willey visited Taliesin in 1934, going home with the revised drawings on March 1. Numerous drawings of construction details and furniture designs followed, dated from August and September. These clearly were done by several different apprentices—presumably putting in their time between tea and dinner—and clearly some of the apprentices were still beginners at architectural drawing.[34] A small snapshot among Bernoudy's papers shows the studio set up with drawings and models of earlier projects by Wright (Fig. 1–7). Repair and reworking of these was the more usual activity in the studio.

The heavy work schedule gave way to other activities on the weekends. These are chronicled in great detail in an extensive series of newspaper articles entitled "At Taliesin," which were written by the apprentices or by Wright and made available to several Wisconsin newspapers. They

began to appear in February 1934 and continued through 1937, by which time 285 columns had been published.[35] The 3:00 Sunday open house at the theater became a major focus of fellowship and community life. The international range and quality of the films shown were impressive, especially for the 1930s. On Sunday mornings the fellowship gathered in the old Lloyd Jones family chapel, Unity Chapel. Speakers representing many different faiths and philosophical persuasions were invited to lead the service. Reverend Holloway, a Unitarian from Madison who explored the relationships among architecture, art, and religion and espoused an organic religious philosophy—simple and honest—was the favorite of the apprentices.[36] Sometimes Wright or an apprentice would speak, and there was always music provided by visitors or the apprentices. In good weather, a picnic lunch outside the chapel sometimes followed the morning service.

There were often weekend guests at Taliesin, and Sunday evenings would conclude with a formal dinner and a gathering in the Wrights' great living room. There would be further entertainment, discussion provided by a guest, or often a musical performance, depending upon who was there and ready to perform. Georgi Gurdjieff visited in July 1934. Wright described him as "something of a Walt Whitman in Oriental terms." The "At Taliesin" column reporting on his visit observed, "His powerful personality affected us all strangely. It seemed as though we had an oriental Buddha come to life in our midst." There were readings of Gurdjieff's works and a performance of his music. Gurdjieff was not a trained musician, but he did enjoy composing simple melodies and improvising settings for them. A young Russian composer, Thomas de Hartmann, had joined Gurdjieff's group in Russia at about the same time that Olgivanna Lazovich Wright did. The music was a collaborative effort with de Hartmann taking Gurdjieff's simple melodies and creating sophisticated settings for them that reflected the musical traditions of the period.

Bernoudy had been home in St. Louis on a holiday from March 29 to April 8, where he jumped right back into his familiar round of social activities, concerts, and picture shows. In June, back at Taliesin, he began to keep a journal, but he made entries for only five days, with one more entry in September. On Monday, June 18, he wrote:

1–8. Bernoudy in the kitchen garden at Taliesin, ca. 1934. Bernoudy Trust Archive.

> Awake early. Awake but depressed, why even arise, another day of fitful ennui and malaise. . . . Alone, barefoot, shirtless; clad only in my blue shorts inspecting my lettuce and spinach rows. Too wet to work so with pen and paper I found myself sketching cows. . . . A glorious barefoot race through the recently plowed and deliciously muddy corn field atop the hill. . . . At the kitchen I took a knife and pan and went out to gather a pail-full of greens, after that a pan of asparagus for Mr. Wright's lunch. And now following the unresistible desire to run I found myself again in the muddy field on the hill. . . . I went to my room. Soon Phil came and then Beye. We played Beethoven's Quartet 132—not much moved at the time. Good gravy and bread at noon.

He goes on to explore his malaise, "thinking and wondering what the future holds for me." The stream in the valley below Taliesin was dammed to power a generator, and the dam and the generator both were constant sources of trouble. Both the millpond and the nearby Wisconsin River were good places for swimming, and later that same day, Bernoudy helped save another apprentice from drowning—an event that gave a sharp edge to his entries about his anxiety about the future. "After supper John, Mary-Bud, Hank, Helen and George came up to my room and I played them my Bach Passacaglia. That did me a great good."[37]

He spent all of the next day, Tuesday, apart from a brief swim before lunch, weeding and cultivating the garden (Fig. 1–8). After dinner a few friends visited him in his room. They cranked up the record player—it must have been a hand-cranked machine, since the power was out and the room is described as enchantingly illuminated with one candle—and listened to Bach's Second Brandenberg Concerto. "The Chorale is a magnificent structure and, to be banal, rips something out of me each time I play it," he wrote in his journal.[38] "I think one cannot appreciate Bach in a profound emotional degree until he has approached his work intellectually."

A small group of drawings by Bernoudy from the summer of 1934 survive among his papers.[39] They are mostly simple line drawings in pencil on eight-and-one-half-by-eleven-inch sheets of white paper, a few rendered with charcoal or watercolor. The drawings include figure studies of other apprentices and flower studies. There are no cows, but one drawing, titled *La vie de Bohème,* shows two figures reclining on a bed and listening raptly to Bernoudy's hand-cranked record player, which is shown alongside the bed.

Wednesday, June 20, was a rainy day, and Bernoudy seems to have had nothing more to do than swing in a hammock and soak up the beauty of the changing light and color. He wrote, "Life would be simple if it were enough merely to love nature. Perhaps I have never really loved but it seems that the peace and satisfaction that comes from contact with nature must surely transcend any mortal love."

Thursday after lunch Mrs. Wright sent Bernoudy to Dodgeville for groceries. He took along another apprentice, Philip Holliday. They took time from their errand to have "ice-cream cones and two glasses of beer" and to walk "up some of the side streets, glimpsing a few quaint little houses." In his malaise, Bernoudy seems to have carried on an internal dialogue about friendship and love. "Phil is the nearest to a friend I have at Taliesin. . . . Life is much fuller and is fun to face when one has a friend." He goes on about another apprentice, "Yvonne [Wood] is so kind but I cannot take what she offers me. I do not love her and consequently should not wish to be obligated to her. Will she understand?"

We also learn from the journal that, on this Thursday, George Beal—a professor in the department of architecture and architectural engineering at the University of Kansas who, with his wife, Helen, was taking part in the Taliesin Fellowship for just the summer of 1934, an exception to the usual term of a year—was injured in an automobile accident. Beal remained unconscious for twenty-four hours but eventually recovered fully from the accident. He was one of the few young progressive academics interested in modern architecture, and he and his wife and Bernoudy became good friends and corresponded for several years. The day ended with more music on the record player, and the diary entry ends with an aphorism of a Wrightian sort: "Man's greatest works are never the image of a pre-conceived idea: they are creations that have sprung naturally from a germ and in the process of growing have achieved perfection."

On Friday, after coming in from hoeing his lettuce, Bernoudy made a short entry before setting aside his journal for three months, "Work is my only salvation these days, yet somehow these very days I think will mean a great deal to me. It seems to be the kind of chaos from which something new and stronger will issue." The tone is even bleaker in the final entry in September, when he says he has not been true to himself, is selfish, and is plagued by an insidious demon, laziness. "I see and understand it now, but how shall I overcome it?"

In his journal, Bernoudy mentions playing Franck's A Major Sonata for violin and piano on his record player and seeing Wright in the Taliesin court listening to the music coming from Bernoudy's room. This indicates that Bernoudy, along with most of the apprentices, was living in the Hill-tower wing of Taliesin, where the kitchen, dining room, and dormitory for the fellowship were located while work slowly progressed on the rebuilding of the old Hillside Home School. Bernoudy may have been moved to other quarters later. Herbert Fritz, an architect who—as the son of one of the Wright draftsmen who survived the tragic murders and fire at Taliesin in 1914—had a long association with Taliesin going back to his childhood, remembers that Bernoudy lived in another building called Tan-y-Deri, Under the Oaks.[40] This was a cottage built in 1907 by Wright for his sister Jennie (Mary Jane Wright) and her husband, Andrew Porter, above the Hillside school complex, between it and Taliesin, and next to the celebrated Romeo and Juliet windmill, which Wright designed in 1896 to supply water for his aunts' Hillside School. Andrew Porter, a Canadian with an import business in Montreal, became business manager of the Hillside School in 1907 at the time of a financial crisis involving Wright's uncle James Lloyd Jones.[41] The Porters had a home in Oak Park, Illinois, but during the summers spent time at Taliesin. Their cottage provided a welcome retreat for the apprentices on Thursday evenings when there was lighter music on the record player and dancing on the porch.

As the number of summer visitors increased at Taliesin, Wright made an effort to separate the invited and seriously interested visitors from the merely curious. Beginning on May 20, 1934, the merely curious were invited to pay fifty cents for a tour through Taliesin and the fellowship buildings. The apprentices took on the duty of serving as guides. As "At Taliesin" explained to the public, "All the details of the work going on will be explained by a guide familiar with the details. This seems to be the best way to acquaint the people of Wisconsin of an important cultural enterprise which is developing in their midst and protect the work from casual interruption by too many curious and irresponsible strangers."[42] Jerome Bernoudy came for a visit at the end of June, and he must certainly have received the insider's tour.[43]

Reconstruction of the old Hillside School continued slowly, with two new galleries—the Dana Gallery for architectural exhibits and the Roberts Gallery to display works from Wright's Japanese collection—completed and put into use in July. Wright had collected Oriental art for many years and had amassed one of the largest and finest collections of Japanese prints in the United States. The fascinating history of Wright's collections is tied in large part to his tortuous financial affairs, and he had already parted with portions of them to settle debts or secure loans. On July 31, Wright began the practice of lecturing informally to the apprentices on Tuesday evenings in the Dana Gallery. Bernoudy took careful notes, which he wrote up as an article that he gave to Wright for his review before it was published in the "At Taliesin" column on September 19. On Sunday, September 30, an exhibition of prints from Wright's collection by the Japanese painter Ando Hiroshige opened to the public in the Roberts Gallery, drawing some forty people from Madison. The exhibition had been hung that morning by two apprentices under Wright's direction.

Bernoudy did not see the Japanese print exhibition, because he had returned to St. Louis the previous Friday. He immediately resumed the busy social schedule of prior visits home. On November 2–4, he spent a long weekend in Ste. Genevieve, but he was one week too late for the fall art show organized by the Ste. Genevieve artists' colony and summer school of art, even though he must have had friends among that group.[44] In a letter he wrote to the Beals just before leaving Taliesin he said that he was going home, "perhaps to stay. I shall be in St. Louis for at least a month in any case."[45] An important reason for the trip was that the anniversary of the opening of the fellowship was coming up and there would be another tuition bill to pay. The tuition for the second year had been $1,100, and it would be that much again for the third year. A letter written to the Beals from St. Louis about two weeks after Bernoudy's arrival there seems to refer to that tuition and the difficulty of raising it: "Thus far all arrangements for returning to Taliesin have been unsuccessful but I am still trying."[46] He also confessed in the letter that he had designed a sign for a real estate firm; although he was not proud of this work, it was a paying job and therefore welcome.

Eugene Masselink, who had joined the fellowship in 1933, succeeded Jensen as Wright's secretary and remained at Taliesin for the rest of his life. He and Bernoudy became good friends, and he wrote to Bernoudy in St. Louis on October 20. Along with all of the gossip from Taliesin came the news that Edgar Kaufmann Jr. had arrived as a new apprentice. He was the son of the couple who would underwrite the Broadacre City project, just beginning, and who would commission Fallingwater the next year. The younger Kaufmann also became a good friend of Bernoudy's. He would later commission Bernoudy to design a garden for his New York town house and consult with him about projects he was responsible for at the Museum of Modern Art.

Bernoudy must finally have raised enough money for tuition, because on November 13 he headed back for a third year at Taliesin. He arrived just in time for an important weekend. Kaufmann's parents from Pittsburgh and Mr. and Mrs. George S. Parker of Janesville, Wisconsin, owners of the Parker Pen Company, joined the fellowship for the Sunday activities on November 18. Wright himself wrote the "At Taliesin" article about their visits. Before the weekend was over, the elder Kaufmanns had agreed to underwrite the preparation of the model of Broadacre City, certainly the most architecturally significant effort that Bernoudy was able to participate in during his time at Taliesin. Like other formative figures in modern architecture, Wright had developed an ideal vision of the city of the future and had begun writing about it in his book *The Disappearing City,* published the same year as his autobiography, 1932.[47] The model of Broadacre City would present Wright's ideas about city planning in visual form and in great detail and was to be ready in time to be shown in the Industrial Arts Exposition in the Rockefeller Center Forum in New York beginning the following April 15. The wooden model was to be twelve feet by twelve feet and represent four square miles of land surface. Suddenly the fellowship had a major project and an early deadline. Work began on it right away.

Bernoudy had one distraction: his turn to lead the Sunday morning service in Unity Chapel came up on December 9. Wright often assigned the topics for the sermons, picking topics he thought represented weaknesses in the character of the speaker. Edgar Tafel reported on the service the following week in "At Taliesin": "William Bernoudy led chapel services last Sunday and preached on the difficult topic 'Purpose.' The service was well arranged and Bill quoted from Emerson and Thoreau to substantiate his own views. Next Sunday John Lautner will officiate on the topic of 'Energy.'"

Wright decided that the fellowship should pack up all of the work on the Broadacre City model and move the entire operation to the Arizona desert in January 1935. Wright knew the region well from two projects he worked on in the late 1920s, the Arizona Biltmore Hotel, 1928–1929, a clouded commission not formally given to Wright, and a project known as San Marcos-in-the-Desert. Designed for Dr. Alexander J. Chandler, San Marcos-in-the-Desert was envisioned as a luxury resort hotel near Chandler, Arizona, just south of Phoenix. It was a particularly creative project but unfortunately was never built due to the stock market crash and the onset of the Great Depression. While working on it, Wright moved his office force—a party of fifteen—to Arizona in the winter of 1929. They built a wonderful desert camp on Chandler's land, which they named Ocatillo, and lived and worked there for five months. Ocatillo was a prevision of Taliesin West, the permanent winter camp that would begin to take form a decade later. As the Wrights grew older and the Wisconsin winters harder and more costly to endure, the idea of a winter camp in Arizona grew ever more attractive. Wright had kept in touch with Chandler, who still had hopes of reviving the San Marcos-in-the-Desert project, and in early 1935 Chandler offered the fellowship a ranch complex, originally a polo stable, named La Hacienda.

The trek was amazing. Wright purchased a large red truck, and it was packed ten feet high, not just with the unfinished model and all the building supplies, but also with great quantities of food. The truck and a small fleet of automobiles filled with passengers and their luggage left Taliesin on January 23. After stopping at the homes of friends along the way, the caravan arrived at Chandler on January 29.[48] La Hacienda lent itself well to the needs of the group, with enough horse stalls converted to bedrooms to accommodate all the apprentices, an apartment for the Wrights, and sufficient space for other activities, all arranged around a grassy courtyard where the building of the model took place (Fig. 1–9).[49]

One stop on the trip out had been at the home of Helen and George Beal in Lawrence, Kansas. Bernoudy wrote to them from La Hacienda soon after arriving there. He had been surprised by a week of very unusual rainy weather but was amazed and energized by the desert landscape, a theme also echoed in the "At Taliesin" articles sent back to Wisconsin. Bernoudy wrote to the Beals: "La Hacienda is just outside

1–9. From the left, Edgar Kaufmann Jr., William Bernoudy, and Frank Lloyd Wright with a Broadacre City model, La Hacienda Courtyard, Arizona, ca. February–April, 1935. Courtesy the Frank Lloyd Wright Archives, Scottsdale, Arizona.

Chandler, in the lush green fields of the irrigated section in the valley. All around us are emerald green fields, many of them filled with sheep. There are great areas devoted to citrus groves and everywhere are palms, tamaris, eucalyptis, iron-wood, palo-verdi, and pepper trees." He was learning the plant names, if not yet quite how to spell them all. He continued: "La Hacienda itself resembles a stage set. There is a large central patio covered by a high gable roof which also embraces a large living room on one side and the dining room on the other. This patio opens out upon a large open grass court with a long series of rooms on each side having a covered walk in front of them. . . . We have been living off of wonderful fruits and vegetables since we have been here. . . . The only thing that mars a complete Utopia is the rain and that can't last much longer."[50]

In early March the fellowship took a break from work on the Broadacre City project, regrouped the caravan of cars, and went to Los Angeles to see a number of buildings that Wright had designed during the 1920s. These buildings were quite different from those the apprentices knew from the Midwest and were also some of Wright's most recent works at that time because of the long hiatus in building caused by the depression. Best known are the Millard House, La Miniatura, and Hollyhock House, which was built for Aline Barnsdall. They also visited the Freeman house, the Ennis house, and the Storrer house, all of which were built of concrete and showed Wright's imaginative innovations with concrete block. Bernoudy went along and took snapshots of these buildings.[51]

The Broadacre project expanded upon earlier city planning ideas such as the decentralization and low density of the Garden City movement but saw them in relation to the American landscape and in the social and economic context of the Great Depression. It envisioned features that have become familiar in later suburban development and was to some extent like the suburbs in which Bernoudy would later find himself working. Dependence on the automobile was a given. With that came a differentiation between major arterial roads, secondary arterial roads, and feeder roads, with bridges for grade separation at intersections. Institutional and commercial activities found their places within the total scheme. The plan called for a mixture of single-family dwellings and small apartment buildings, but the density was kept low and most people were envisioned as living on enough land to be able to reach some measure of self-sufficiency through gardening. The most revolutionary and

philosophical idea accompanying the plan grew out of Wright's conviction that fundamental change to our social and economic system was necessary if the United States was to recover from the Great Depression. He proposed to abolish the concept of rents and held that all citizens were entitled to hold land and make use of it.

A number of smaller models to show the various buildings at a larger scale were also included in the Broadacre project. The large model required dozens of small houses in various configurations. In this context Wright was working out his idea for what he would call the Usonian house. Important elements of that idea were present in the Willey house, the one project underway at Taliesin during the first two years of the fellowship, which was completed in Minneapolis just as the group headed for Arizona. The idea of the Usonian house was further explained in a publication venture that became a project of the fellowship in the summer of 1934. It was titled *Taliesin*—a magazine, or "monograph" as the fellowship called it—and the first issue, devoted in large part to the subject of a small house costing between $3,500 and $5,000, appeared toward the end of the year.[52] The first structures identified as Usonian houses were not built until after Bernoudy left the fellowship, but he was well grounded in the ideas that produced them while still at Taliesin and followed their development closely. Bernoudy's first architectural project with his partner Edouard Mutrux in 1938–1939 is a mature example of the Usonian house (see Figs. 2–4 through 2–11).

The large Broadacre City model and other exhibition materials were finished on schedule on March 31 and sent to New York in the red truck on April 1. Six days later the remaining work was finished, and the cars were packed for the trip back to Wisconsin. The members of the fellowship did not travel in a caravan on the return trip, and it took them between five and ten days to complete the journey, depending on their various routes, the weather conditions, and the time needed to repair mechanical breakdowns. The Broadacre City project was exhibited in New York from April 15 through May 15 before moving to the State Historical Society Gallery in Madison from June 5 through June 14, the Auditorium of Kaufmann's Department Store in Pittsburgh from June 18 through June 28, and the Corcoran Gallery in Washington, D.C., from July 2 through July 21. It then returned to Taliesin to be set up in the unfinished drafting room at Hillside. After a showing at the Iowa County Fair in Mineral Point from September 7 through September 10, where it was deemed the outstanding attraction of the fair, it was returned to Taliesin and set up in the fellowship's living room.[53]

Henry Herold, a later apprentice in the Taliesin Fellowship who was also from St. Louis and was a close friend of the Bernoudys, had the impression that Bernoudy often was assigned to chauffeur Wright and even served as a valet. At 4:00 A.M. on Sunday, May 26, 1935, Bernoudy and another apprentice from Taliesin arrived at his parents' house in St. Louis. They had been sent to meet Wright, who arrived in St. Louis at 8:30 A.M., presumably by train; by 10:00 A.M. they had all left to return to Taliesin. Bernoudy's father, probably having offered to make use of his railroad connections, arranged refunds on unused railroad and parlor car tickets and forwarded the checks to Wright on June 15, with a note: "We enjoyed very much your all too brief visit."[54]

Bernoudy's brother, Jerome, was at this time employed by Scruggs-Vandervoort-Barney, a leading department store in St. Louis. He wrote to Wright on July 11, saying how much they all had enjoyed his recent visit. He added that Mr. Mayfield, the president of the department store, was keenly interested in exhibiting the Broadacre City model. A month later Eugene Masselink answered for Wright, explaining that the delay was due to Wright's waiting to decide about letting the model travel again. A number of department stores had inquired, and it was being offered to them on the same basis it had been shown at Kaufmann's in Pittsburgh. The rental fee would be $300 for the first week and $100 for each additional week, with an additional charge of ten cents per mile for transportation and $25 a week for two "expositors." These were apprentices who would travel with the exhibition, set it up and take it down, and be present during the hours it was open to the public to protect it and answer visitors' questions. Their expenses were to be paid by the sponsor. Broadacre City did not come to St. Louis.

As the summer of 1935 wore on, Bernoudy was weighing the pluses and minuses of staying on at Taliesin. A long "At Taliesin" column on July 6, 1935 was devoted to eating. "Meals at Taliesin are a three-a-day delight . . . our two cook-apprentices, stimulated by the comments and criticism of the eaters, are continually in friendly rivalry seeking to present old familiar dishes in new and pleasurable forms."[55] In a letter from Taliesin to the Beals dated August 16, Bernoudy explains he has not had time to write because the cook has left and "I have been doing the cooking for the Taliesin Fellowship three days a week, can you be-

lieve it? I have become irascible, mean, selfish, all those things which cooking here turns one into. I have worked hard and saved myself from monotony by employing my imagination as freely as possible. I have in a measure succeeded I think. Everyone apparently is pleased with the results so I have not worked in vain: though long enough for me as I plan to leave sometime next month for St. Louis for an extended vacation if not for good. I have never mentioned this work to my parents for many reasons: chiefly they would never understand why I would do it. Often I wonder too but beneath it I know that Taliesin is much greater than its many petty irritations and so I have stayed on usually content to give myself to the rich flowing life here though I don't understand its nature clearly."[56]

On September 10, Bernoudy arrived home in St. Louis, never again to return to Taliesin as an apprentice, only as a visitor. He almost immediately found a position in the same department store where his brother worked, Scruggs-Vandervoort-Barney. In letters both to the Beals and to the Wrights he put the best possible face on the job, explaining that he was working in the fabric department, which gave him the opportunity to learn all about fabrics, something he needed to do if he was to be an architect. Mrs. Wright struck back: "I must tell you right away, how much I dislike the idea of you being in a stuffy silly Dept. Store! . . . We miss you here so much. You represent such a definite style & character. . . . Why don't you throw away everything and come here?"[57] Feeling freer to be frank with the Beals, Bernoudy admitted that he was just a stock boy, that the pay was terrible, the routine deadly, and the whole experience very disagreeable. He begged them, "Write to me everything you know. I am so lonesome at times I think I'll lose my mind."[58]

A note from Eugene Masselink just before Christmas informed Bernoudy that George Parker, Wright's friend and client, whom Bernoudy had met at Taliesin, had slipped on the ice and broken a leg. Bernoudy wrote him and received a long, friendly answer in return that reflects the good impression Bernoudy made on everyone. "Billy, you made a great impression on both Mrs. Parker and the writer. Your gentlemanly qualities, your tact and your interest in life generally appealed to us very strongly. Never shall we forget the courtesies you extended to us in Arizona as well as at Taliesin. I think that one of the things that Mrs. Parker admired about you in some of the drives we took down in Arizona was the absolute confidence you exhibited in yourself to know the country and know what to do and then did it."[59] Parker went on to quote Olgivanna Wright: "Billy is a lovely boy." This was surely a pleasant letter to receive, but it would also have reminded Bernoudy that among his duties at Taliesin was serving as a driver not only for the master but also for the master's guests.

Their father's diary makes clear that both of the Bernoudy sons were keeping up their usual round of activities, going out about every other night. The elder Bernoudy notes that Bill did not return home from the Veiled Prophet Ball, one of the social highlights of the year in St. Louis, until 4:00 A.M. The Wrights invited Bernoudy to Taliesin both for the annual Halloween party and for Christmas. He did not go to either, but he did send the Wrights a Christmas gift, a set of glasses, which was very well received. Mrs. Wright wrote for most of a two-page letter about how nice they were, describing how they were opened under the Christmas tree so the whole fellowship could participate and what a sensation they made with everyone.[60] She went on to say how often they talked about him, how much they missed him, that he should be there with them getting ready to go to Arizona, and that she could not "understand how you can stand to be without us!" In an undated letter written that fall, Bernoudy wrote to Wright that he intended to stay in St. Louis only long enough to "beg, borrow, or steal the necessary money to enable me to stay another year at Taliesin."[61] That may have been the official line, but it seems to have been only half true, at best.

Bernoudy saved among his papers a copy of an article Wright published in 1936 entitled "Apprenticeship-Training for the Architect," in which Wright described life at Taliesin as Bernoudy would have known it.[62] He emphasized the importance of the experience of working with building materials, of actually planning and actually building. He ridiculed the standard architectural education in the schools for its textbooks and attention to the history of architecture. Rather, America needed an organic architecture where "experience furnishes the only data and inspiration furnishes the only interpretation." The relationship in which an apprentice seeks experience under the inspired leadership of a master was the way to achieve this. In this situation, work—hard, absorbing, unremitting work—would become a way of life. Without knowing this transforming way of life, Wright believed, the would-be architect would never be able to create an organic architecture. He described the building projects undertaken by the fellowship at Taliesin and the caravan

to the Arizona desert for the winter months. The winter after Bernoudy left Taliesin, the fellowship had repeated the trip to Arizona, working on additional furnishings for Broadacre City. In his article, Wright stated that the fellowship would move to Russia for the winter of 1936–1937 and the next year, maybe, to Japan. Nothing came of these plans for foreign residency. The fellowship remained in Wisconsin in 1937 and in 1938 began the development of Taliesin West in Arizona. Since then, the community has returned to Taliesin West every winter.

Bernoudy had his own chance to explain the Taliesin Fellowship when he was invited to address the Scarab Honor Society of the School of Architecture at Washington University on February 27, 1936. He was only twenty-five years old, closer in age to students than to the faculty, yet his lecture displays a mature judgment worthy of an experienced architect. The full text survives:

> This evening I have been requested to tell you about the Taliesin Fellowship. Before I enter into a discussion of it I should like to explain that it is not an architectural school or an institution. It is a voluntary group of apprentices, led by a great master, that hopes by way of an organic life to learn the principles of an organic architecture. Since the life of this endeavor is inspired and made possible by its master, Frank Lloyd Wright, it appears natural that some explanation be made of the circumstances that led Mr. Wright to conceive of the Taliesin Fellowship.
>
> Attending University Mr. Wright was oppressed by the system and felt in it a lack of something essential. To him, the procedure was unrelated to reality and so with graduation a few months away, he, longing for experience, some first hand contact with his chosen work, left the University and went off to Chicago against the advice and warnings of his mother and uncle.[63]
>
> In Chicago he became associated with the architectural firm of Adler and Sullivan and served in the position of apprentice to Louis Sullivan. The idea grew in his mind during these years of apprenticeship that he served to a master that this was the way for youth to acquire knowledge. And when in a few years he opened his own studio it was his intention to give what he had to offer to others in the way that he had learned.
>
> As the years passed it developed that he did have a great deal to offer and from distant parts young men came, unsolicited, to work under his guidance. And seeing them work with him he remembered how he had as a young man worked with a master and had seen ideas grow from sketches into great buildings. But his experience then and subsequent incidents convinced him that this working in an office, while more fundamental

than an academic procedure was in itself insufficient. Architecture appealed to him as something more than office designing: it was an art intimately associated with life and living and he realized the importance of nature as a source of inspiration.

Later when he moved his studio to the country he planned to some day have a spontaneous group there with him and by way of a simple life show them the tie-up between nature and living and architecture. There in the country these young people might have an opportunity to discard the false standards that a vicarious life had given them and learn by living a simple and natural life, a philosophy based on principle. For to live simply was to think and hear and see simply and perhaps to create simply. That was one of the goals.

Nature was to be the research laboratory of this enterprise: it would be the source of inspiration, the prescribed reading for the course. There could be no better beginning for the students of an organic architecture. Until embryo architects understood this process of organic growth there could be no issue. This precept was paramount. Within the comprehension of this principle an understanding of the nature of materials was vital, in fact, without an understanding of one there could be no apprehension of the other. These, then, were concepts an architect must have before he could create. They were notes in the architectural scale on which he composed.

These factors determined logically that the study of architecture must be preceded by a thorough understanding of the ways of nature. Hence the Taliesin Fellowship has as its setting the rocky and wooded hill country of Southern Wisconsin, four miles from the nearest village, in the valley where Mr. Wright played as a youngster and grew into manhood. It is not an escapist, back to the land movement as many have thoughtlessly labelled it.

On the brow of a low hill Mr. Wright first built Taliesin in 1910. Taliesin is a Welsh word meaning "shining brow." The low rambling house has seen two disastrous fires and out of the ruins of each a new Taliesin has grown each time to be a part of the same hillside. The house is wrapped about several courts and the hill top rises from these to be a beautiful garden.

And so from a mere drafting-room apprenticeship the Taliesin Fellowship has expanded until it has become in itself a complete life retaining the apprenticeship relationship, where life and work are synonymous.

Early in his career Mr. Wright began to realize the necessity of understanding the nature of materials. He saw that materials if used sympathetically had qualities and textures peculiarly their own and that ornament applied to their surfaces or covering them was deceitful aside from being an unnecessary waste of materials and labor. His apprentices then, before they might ever think of becoming architects, must have a knowledge of the nature of materials so that they might use them to full and honest advantage. And at Taliesin an introduction is promptly made to materials and the student is left free to pursue the acquaintance and understanding for himself.

During the first winter of the Fellowship every alternate day was spent in the woods chopping and sawing trees. There would be a brief interval for a pick-up lunch in a shack at noon before we resumed our work. Late in the afternoon the long tramp home through the snow would begin. Sometimes the supper bell would ring across the valley before we had climbed the hill to Taliesin. In the Spring these logs were hauled down to the side of the Fellowship buildings. This group of buildings is on the same land about half a mile from Taliesin and has as its nucleus the old Hillside Home School buildings that Mr. Wright built in 1900. The old buildings are being remodeled and new ones are being added by the apprentices. Here the great logs were sliced in boards and timbers of all dimensions and laid on frames in the sun and rain to weather.

And while this was going on, other apprentices were working in the sandstone quarries a mile or more away, picking out great blocks of soft, pink and green sandstone which when weathered turned to the hardness of granite and resembled it in color. The shapeless blocks were piled on the truck and hauled down to the building site. There under the skilled direction of Charlie Curtis, an aged stone craftsman, apprentices learned to cut and finish rock.

Nearly five miles away in a deeply wooded and hilly region there was another quarry: this one offering a limestone rock that loosened in long flat slabs colored a sandy yellow. An old lime kiln had been built near the base of the quarry hill and the limestone slabs were hauled down to the kiln and built carefully into the dome-shaped structure. At the base of the kiln was an opening for draft and on top was another opening. A piece of sheet metal served as the furnace door. For six days and nights apprentices kept the fires roaring with cord wood. At night the flames would rise in a great column through the roof opening. At the end of the week we let the fires go out and returned again a week later to extract the crumbling masses of lime. This was hauled to the building site where apprentices slaked it and under guidance mixed it with the proper proportions of sand and water for mortar.

And now with the logs that had been made into boards and beams we built trusses and laid floors and put them together in buildings that had been designed in the drafting room with Mr. Wright's direction. The stone we had quarried and shaped was laid with the mortar we had made from our lime and built into walls and piers. We had followed a sequence, had seen three raw materials in their original growth and had translated them into another kind of growth remembering the original nature of each.

Remodeling the gymnasium of the Old School Buildings into a theatre of glowing beauty was the first work set before us. There was a gala opening night to celebrate its near completion just one year after the official opening of the Taliesin Fellowship. A fire burned in the old stove fireplace set deep beneath the low wood balcony. The theatre was illuminated by the soft glow of indirect lighting that picked out the brilliant pattern and colors of the heavy curtains. The low apprentice-made benches were arranged so that their pattern tied in to the design of the room. They were covered with rust-colored cushions made by the female members of the Fellowship. The new sound and movie equipment worked flawlessly and advantage was taken of the pattern cast by the sound track on a red panel edging the screen.

During a generous intermission our guests wound up the old stone stairs to a corridor above, which led them into the uncompleted living room which was the library of the old School. Though unfinished the room breathed an atmosphere and the firelight illuminated the old Druid motto carved in the wood balcony above, "Truth against the World." From this room the corridor bridges the driveway and merges into the great drafting room where at the far end a huge fire was roaring in the mammoth fireplace. A whole roast pig was turning over the flames and apprentices were carving another one recently come from the same fire. Seven trusses span the width of the large room built to accommodate seventy drafting tables. Above each truss are windows extending the width of the truss to admit north light to the tables.

The guests filed back to the theatre after the barbecue and the program was concluded. Outstanding pictures of the world have been shown in succession since that opening night. Every Saturday evening the Fellowship enjoys a private showing and on Sunday afternoons the public is admitted to enjoy the theatre with the Fellowship.

Sunday evening the group and its guests have supper in the living room of the home. Two apprentices plan and prepare what there is to eat for the occasion—everyone taking his turn at it. Apprentices wash their faces and dress for supper on this night and remember that there are manners to be practiced. After supper the guest of the evening, whether it be Alexander Woollcott, Childen Cheney, or a professor from the University at Madison tells us about his special interest. Or perhaps it turns out to be an evening of music—invariably it is time pleasantly and profitably spent.

During the winter the old family chapel that was built by Mr. Wright's forefathers who lived in the wide valley, is used by the Fellowship. Each Sunday morning a different apprentice must speak on a subject assigned him by Mr. Wright. Some of the subjects discussed have been "Self-confidence," "Purpose," "Generosity," and "Humility."

In the summer Sunday picnics are substituted for the chapel services. The Fellowship starts out shortly before noon with Mr. Wright in the lead car. Often he drives so fast that we lose him before we find a stopping place but when we are successful in keeping up with him he invariably takes us to an ideal setting for a picnic. Usually there is a discussion after our hunger has been satisfied but we always prefer to listen to Mr. Wright philosophize and watch the gestures of his expressive hands as he talks. When it is hot he naps a little in the shade before we start home for the afternoon theatre program.

In the autumn the countryside is abundant with wild grapes, chokecherries, and elderberries. The Fellowship turns out for several days at this season to harvest bushel baskets full of these native fruits. Then for several more days everyone is busy washing and squeezing them for wine. Mrs. Wright takes capable leadership of this enterprise and throughout the year we enjoy its flavor at our Sunday Evening Suppers and at all important gatherings.

During the Spring and Summer a voluntary group of apprentices undertake to farm the land and supply fresh vegetables for the summer, and root vegetables for the winter. All through April and May the noisy tractor plowing interrupts the quiet of early morning. Planting begins and goes on. Soon—shoots are up and before long worms and bugs put in their appearance to destroy the young plants. But we fight them and save at least a portion of the crop. Intense heat and drought have their fling at our tender young and if we are not careful early frosts take their toll. We live well in the summer from our garden in spite of the many hindrances and early fall finds us busy hauling squash, pumpkins, rutabagas, potatoes, and turnips into the cool, dark root cellar where they remain quietly undisturbed by growing pains throughout the winter months.

Fall and winter finds the group busy chopping trees and hauling wood. Fires have to be built and maintained in the three boilers and eighteen fireplaces. And all year 'round the roads must be kept in condition. In almost any season a passerby might see Mr. Wright holding the wheel of the road grader, being dragged along behind the tractor. In the summer he would be wearing a white shirt open at the collar and in the winter he would be bundled into his great red and black mackinaw with a distinctive beret set jauntily on his shaggy gray hair.

In the Spring the dam is apt to break from the volume of melted snow that comes rushing against it. And it usually does break and then days and weeks of reconstruction work begins. New ideas for frustrating the next flood are suggested and under the supervision of Mr. Wright one or a combination is tried. Everywhere all the time experiments are being made at Taliesin.

Mr. Wright is constantly designing; creating; and there is always a great deal of drafting to be done. All creative work in the studio is supervised and criticized by Mr. Wright who by way of his vivid imagination is able to broaden the more limited conceptions of his apprentices.

The work varies at Taliesin, there are periods of weeks at a time that activity is confined to the studios and workshops. There models of proposed buildings are made or disintegrating ones are repaired. Sometimes a whole season is spent, as was last winter, model building. The interest usually extends beyond the meticulous procedure of fitting delicate pieces together. In the experience of building the Broadacre City model we were seeing ideas take form as a great pattern that we could never have understood another way. We did not make a realistic model, instead we tried to get the feel of the landscape with abstract pattern. We succeeded, too, and spectators in New York caught the feel of it after they learned the legend. It would have been hopelessly uncorrelated if we had tried to make each tree a perfect miniature, each fence an exact replica, for it was life as a pattern that we were interested in showing, not a conglomeration of perfect details.

This same point applies significantly to the life lived within the Fellowship. One going there and expecting to become a great architect in a few months, or a year, or in several years finds himself indignant at the many apparent indignities put in his way. He wonders what cooking, cleaning, dish-washing, plumbing, farming, harvesting, driving, chapel attendance, and other work has to do with architecture. Regarded as details and hindrances, these things have nothing to do with it, but if he sticks, these things cease to be mere annoying details and become integral parts of a logical pattern that constitutes a full and organic life.

I don't think I can stress the fact sufficiently that the Taliesin Fellowship is not an architectural school; it is a life entered into by voluntary apprenticeship. It is a slow but deep way of learning, a process of absorption that goes on slowly and relentlessly for as long as the individual is not poisoned by details that necessarily compose it. Life there has a bigger time-unit than most life lived elsewhere. It is deliberate with a repose that contains all inclusive conflict. A year is not made up of examinations, semesters, and broken by a vacation, work goes on all year 'round with its accents and contrasts to be sure but without interruption. In fact, I might add that there is a feeling of suspense in the air, something always seems to be about to happen and it usually does. "Something always happens in the country," is one of our proven mottos.

Without an understanding of the constituent phases of an organic life, there can be no organic architecture. For the two are bound up together. It has been so always—all the great architectures of the past have been a reflection, a history of the life lived then.

The Fellowship is simple though composed of many interests. Music has an important accent among these. For in great music principle is at work constructing and building in much the same way that architecture is created. At Taliesin we try to see principle functioning beneath the surface of whatever we are doing or observing. Sometimes, often, we don't see it until a long while later. Many times we rely on intuition that convinces us it is there.

In what I have said you may gather that Taliesin is idealistic, abstract, and that it concerns itself too little with reality. But there never can be reality until there is an ideal and ideals are built of principles that are at work deep in life. One must live simply to perceive them, unconfused by false standards, until he may some day understand these principles and feel them at work in him creating.

When visitors criticize the workmanship about the place as they sometimes do, we explain that our efforts have gone into carrying out ideas to determine their effect and that attention has not always been given to details that would be attended in a finished job. Taliesin would lose its usefulness to its apprentices were it to be regarded as complete in every detail. The essence of its existence demands experimentation and activity. Apprentices are there to see ideas grow into structures of another sort. This spontaneous process would not be possible in an institution housed in already completed buildings and governed by fixed rules. As soon as an endeavor ignores the process of becoming and becomes, the life of that experiment necessarily dies. For when anything ceases to become, to grow, the life soon goes out of it and it degenerates because the rules that it had established are not applicable or related to inactivity.

The Taliesin Fellowship is based on the relationship of apprentice to a master; the type of association that Mr. Wright found so invaluable to him as a youth. The apprentices are among themselves a fellowship, working cooperatively together for a common ideal inspired by a great master. The tremendous tug of that ideal straightens out all friction with the group. Frank Lloyd Wright has made his principles articulate just as he has made the Taliesin Fellowship possible. It is suffused with his spirit. All activity there has direction and purpose under his leadership. Without his inspiration there would be no apprenticeship or no fellowship.

This evening I have given you my interpretation of the Taliesin Fellowship. You must realize that there are as many other interpretations as there are apprentices. And even in what I have said I regret that I have only been able to skim the surface of an ideal beneath which the essential spirit must speak for itself.[64]

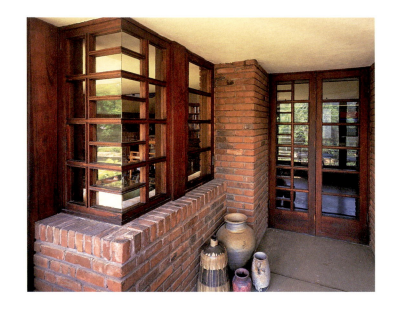

Chapter 2   The Making of the Architect, 1935–1946

It was not easy for an apprentice to leave Taliesin. To make the decision to leave, and then do so without alienating the Wrights, was something not all could manage. Bernoudy was able to remain on good terms with the Wrights, but it took some adroit self-effacement.

The extended account about Taliesin, modern architecture, and an accompanying organic way of life that Bernoudy delivered to the architecture students at Washington University in 1936 was a message he was always ready to deliver with charming seriousness. One who heard him, Laura P. Carpenter, wrote to Wright on April 3, 1936:

> Mr. Bernoudy has become a very pleasant and interesting acquaintance of ours this past winter and I have talked with him at some length about his work with you. We would like to know whether or not you think he has had enough training to undertake putting up a small house in the country. He tells me he does not consider that he has completed his course and is hoping to return to Taliesin. We like his plans but we do not feel certain about his ability as to construction.
>
> We have made no mention of our plans to him and would appreciate your candid opinion.[1]

Wright assumed the worst about Bernoudy's motives in this case. He replied on April 14, explaining in some detail a strict rule at Taliesin that an apprentice might bring architectural work to the fellowship where all would participate in it, and Wright would give criticism and suggestions. The apprentice who brought in the commission might follow up as superintendent during construction. But the apprentice was not to take architectural commissions independently. He did not explain to Mrs. Carpenter the financial implication—that all architectural fees would go to Taliesin. He continued, "This has not been followed by Billy, so it seems in your case, for some reason best known to himself." Wright added, "He has had little or no experience in building and from our standpoint is really unqualified to build a building acceptable to his Fellowship at this time." Wright sent a longer letter to Bernoudy the same day and enclosed a copy of his letter to Mrs. Carpenter. He wrote that she had asked "for my opinion of your ability to satisfactorily build a house for her. Now of course you have never asked me for my opinion in the matter and it might not be worth much to you anyway. Boys stay here for a while and

seem to decide for themselves when they are 'fit' or maybe they become the helpless pawn of untoward circumstances. . . . We would be glad to help you with a commission should you get one and in the regular way already established—with which, I believe, you are familiar."[2]

Bernoudy replied promptly, writing that he was bewildered and disillusioned and that Wright's insinuations were altogether unjustified. He had never suggested to the Carpenters that he design a house for them, but had only shown Mrs. Carpenter some of his drawings at her request, without knowing that they contemplated building. He continued that he was obliged to leave Taliesin for financial reasons and had made a point not to use Wright's name to secure employment. "I . . . have in fact avoided accepting employment from architects here who have offered me work solely because of my association with you. I have found work in disinterested fields for necessary money so that my architectural heritage would remain untainted. And in my spare time I have taught myself to draw and have done some designing in strict accordance with the ideals of the Taliesin Fellowship as I understand them." He closed, "Feeling as I do, absolutely guileless, I am deeply hurt. Sincerely and loyally, Billy Bernoudy."[3]

Wright's prompt reply began, "Dear Billy don't be silly." He didn't give an inch in a letter whose tone most people would consider patronizing, but which Wright probably meant to be conciliatory. He enclosed Mrs. Carpenter's original letter and asked what other reply he might have made. He closed by questioning Bernoudy's reasons for leaving Taliesin. "I don't believe the exodus from the Fellowship was really as much a financial matter as it so seemed to you at the time. But there was nothing to be done about that, was there?" He did sign off, "Affectionately, F. L. L. W."[4] The matter was set to rest and cordial relations were reestablished with Bernoudy's reply on April 30:

> Your statements concerning my ability as an architect were admittedly correct and to those I took no offense. My only contention was with those remarks which I felt reflected on my personal motives. I was concerned by what I felt to be a withdrawal of your personal interest and support. I am sorry if I misinterpreted your meaning, I did so reluctantly for I am not anxious to ever embitter the very grateful attachment I have for you or the Fellowship.[5]

At this time, Bernoudy was still working in the interior decorating and furnishing section of the Scruggs-Vandervoort-Barney department store. When he wrote to Wright that he had avoided employment with the architects in St. Louis who had offered him work solely because of his association with Wright, he was probably telling the truth. He had, however, tried unsuccessfully to get a federal architectural job with the Small Homes Division of the Resettlement Administration through a letter of endorsement from his senator, Bennett Champ Clark.[6] And in the midst of these letters to and from Wright, he was preparing a lecture entitled "The Relation of the Garden to the Modern Home," which he delivered to the Garden Club of Kirkwood on April 20, 1936.

Bernoudy wrote to the Beals in Lawrence, Kansas, on the day of the lecture saying that he was very nervous, but he would have a sympathetic and intelligent audience. He asked them not to let Wright know, because he "would have nothing but contempt for my feeble efforts. I had a very unpleasant letter from him last week which proved very disappointing to me to think that he could be so small in some situations."[7] Bernoudy introduced the lecture with recollections of fond childhood memories of Kirkwood. He went on to stress to his listeners the importance of clubs like theirs whose great cause is beauty. That, above all, is what the world needs, he said.

The lecture opened ambitiously with a brief survey of the history of gardening in the Western world, beginning with the Garden of Eden. With a paragraph or two for each, he reviewed the gardening accomplishments of the Babylonians and the Persians, the Romans, and the Italians, French, and English beginning in the Renaissance. He noted with approval the English development of more naturalistic gardens. He observed that Americans were becoming more interested in gardens, "and it is to be hoped that gardeners will recognize the unlimited and unexplored potentialities of their art before they make the mistake of reproducing traditional garden styles in America." He found the modern movement's invariable argument against stylistic revival and eclecticism relevant in the context of gardens, too. And more strictly in the Wright tradition, he noted that "our gardens might well be, and should be as variable as the countryside and consequently as natural." The main body of the lecture concerned the modern movement in architecture.

Bernoudy gave a spirited and eloquent argument in support of modern architecture—not all modern architecture, by any means, but the kind espoused by Wright and absorbed by Bernoudy at Taliesin.

In America, architecture in general has borne no closer relation to its environment than a tombstone bears to a graveyard. And while the effect of the latter may frequently be very picturesque the impression normally remains quite objective. Cemeteries are the same the world over, oblivious to climate and topography, but it appears a bit depressing that we should pass our lives in houses that are likewise conceived so indiscriminately.

Architecture, or I should say, the abuse of it, is usually conceived as sculpture, that is with regard to its outward appearance. It is carved and molded and finally punctured to admit light and air to the interior. Then this bit of pre-conceived sculpture is neatly super-imposed on the ground ruthlessly unaware of topography or climate and a garden is built around it to further set it off.

In a measure this procedure was pardonable in the past. Materials available there restricted construction to certain narrow limitations which could not be transcended by human imagination beyond these boundaries. Today the possibilities are virtually unlimited. With such materials as steel, glass, and re-enforced concrete almost any desired effect can be soundly wrought, completely unhampered by traditional styles or methods.

Yet perhaps the most inconsistent argument against modern architecture is the one offered in defense of tradition. A moment's reflection will disclose that tradition lives only because its outward manifestations were a natural and beautiful fulfillment of past needs. But to copy the manifestation and ignore the cause is to overlook the significance of tradition. We can be faithful to tradition and love it best by remembering what it stood for. To simulate it is to betray all that it represents and to invalidate its form. In order that tradition may live today it must as always be the logical outgrowth of present needs and desires. The form will necessarily differ if it is to honestly suit our modern and very different lives and facilities though the motivating principles remain unchanged. Consequently, if there is to be a living architectural tradition we must produce an architecture that is in every sense modern which may carry with it into the future a heritage that posterity will cherish as we have cherished what was the modern architecture of our forebears. And it is sage to assume that the architecture of antiquity would have taken quite another form if the artists who created it had had available to them the materials that we have today.

Yet it is with great reluctance that moderns subscribe to modern architecture. And feeling as I do about it, it has been hard for me to understand this hesitancy. I think I understand it better now and should in many instances join ranks with those in opposition, not to what I refer to as modern architecture, but against the so-called Modernistic and International Styles. These two styles are characterized by pipe railings, metal pipe columns, and a white cardboard look. There is about the International Style a clean straightforward appearance that does make it particularly adaptable to certain limited uses. It has been likened to a machine in its functionalism and in that definition it serves admirably for factories, offices, and other purely scientific buildings. It will, and in fact has, invaded the domestic field and we see more and more houses built by the same formula. In many instances this formula is no more than a negation of the surface forms which constituted traditional architecture. Modernistics have stripped the old styles bare of the details that gave to them what charm they possessed and have set up the same framework as a new style. The International Style has more worthy motives than this but there is something in its appearance that is similarly cold and impassive, as impassive, indeed, as the very machine it so resembles. Exponents of this school describe their house as a "machine for living" and let it go at that. While their creations may work, all presence of warmth, graciousness, and subtlety has been ignored in their mad pursuit for functionalism. Their houses are as incomplete as life without religion. They may have a fascination for man for a little while but in time he will turn away from the shiny new toy to satisfy his aesthetic hunger in a home that is touched with the breath of life.

Modern architecture is not a style and therefore should not be confused with either the Modernistic or the International Styles. Modern architecture is based on certain organic principles of growth, the interpretation of which varies according to environment, materials, and function. A style, quite obviously, could not result from such an organic concept, though by the same rule all resultant architecture would invariably have style. When we speak of styles it is with reference to appearances or surfaces. A style, therefore, is an affectation, detached from principle; an arrangement that may be copied, juggled with, and repeated thoughtlessly anywhere, regardless of materials, environment, and function.

And in this consideration modern architecture again differs widely from the International Style which by its very name suggests that it can be constructed anywhere without cognizance of local conditions. In fact one sees as many examples in Buenos Aires as in the tropics or in France, Germany, or America, all of them bearing the same complacent forms in one place as another. A shining example of "graveyard architecture."

Modern architecture is concerned with establishing a more informal and sympathetic relation between the garden and the house than has been customary. Hitherto the house has been designed according to traditional styles and quite irrelevantly set up tombstone-manner and landscaped. In modern architecture the conception is reversed. The location is studied first with regard to contours, natural plant life, climatic conditions, native building materials, and function. Then with these limitations in mind the house is planned to become a harmonious part of its environment.

Glass and steel are the mediums by which this new harmony between the garden and the house may be wrought. With steel it is now possible to span great widths, simply from overhead, eliminating supporting piers that formerly obstructed the view. An entire wall may be swept aside to admit the garden into the room. Windows are no longer rectangular or square holes cut in the wall; they may be thought of as light screens taking the place of walls. Glass may be imagined as crystallized sheets of air in air to keep air in or out as the case may be. A new sense of space prevails extending the house until it includes the garden. A house is no longer a box divided into countless other boxes. Interior walls are conceived as screens providing privacy as well as suggesting spaciousness and continuity without severing relations with the rest of the house. No one room is an entity within itself: each suggests that it is a harmonious part of a greater whole.

In the Spring the garden tumbles from earth containing features of the house and literally weds it to the soil and the garden by way of the garden itself. The dividing walls of glass may be brushed back out of sight for the summer months to be substituted by light copper cobwebs of screen. The grass becomes a continuation of the terrace which in turn is an extension of the floor of the room. Overhead, the ceiling may soar and fall gently, catching the soffit of the sheltering eaves as they sweep from the inside of the room out beyond the supporting walls.

The sheltering eaves and breeze swept floors of the house offer umbrageous coolness from the midday summer sun. All direct light is caught and reflected as the sunlight is reflected and diffused in a forest. The elimination of unnecessary interior walls facilitates a free circulation of air that rises as it warms and is drawn out through integral ventilators. The whole house breathes and lives as naturally as any organism that is the result of organic growth.

With the coming of Fall and Winter and the passing of luxuriant green foliage, the modern home instead of rearing itself stark and detached on top of the earth's bare surface, remains as in summer a harmonious part of its surroundings; its line following earth lines and its repose meeting that of nature's. The walls of glass may be drawn weather tight into position beneath the sheltering protection of broad eaves. The interior remains as spacious in winter as in summer and as visibly conscious of the outdoors. From behind great air tight windows all the sparkling brilliance of winter may be enjoyed from the prismatic icicles suspended jewel-like from the eaves to the linear patterns of winter trees against the snow. Inside, roaring fires burn cheerfully in ample fireplaces set deep in broad-rising chimneys. Warm humidified air circulates freely throughout the house maintaining a constant temperature. All day the winter sun, low in the sky, seeks the interior of the house through violet-ray windows, carrying healthful radiance with it. And at night the glow of concealed lighting illuminates the house with all the subtlety and charm of candlelight.

And as Abraham Lincoln once said of his philosophy we can say of modern architecture, that there are no accidents, each effect must have its cause. Architecture and the art of gardening have been intimately associated with the history of man and as we look back we observe that the greatest gardens like the greatest buildings are most truly satisfying when they are most completely natural.[8]

On the theoretical side, Bernoudy was well prepared for a career in architecture. The case for the brilliant work of Bernoudy-Mutrux and Bernoudy-Mutrux-Bauer is well argued in this lecture to the Kirkwood Garden Club. Only for his late work with Bernoudy Associates would one need to search out further theoretical justification. The ideas in the lecture were not original to Bernoudy, of course, eloquently as they may have been expressed. He certainly heard them many times when he was at Taliesin, and in large part he could have had them at hand in published form as he prepared the Kirkwood Garden Club lecture by turning to Wright's Princeton lectures of 1930 or the long series of articles Wright prepared for the *Architectural Record* in 1927 and 1928.[9]

But for designing and the more practical side of construction and administration, Bernoudy would seem not yet to have been prepared. This was Wright's point with Mrs. Carpenter. Bernoudy agreed and even pointed out in his letter to Wright that he was just now teaching himself drafting, which presumably he had little opportunity to learn at Taliesin. He finally got up the nerve to reestablish contact with Wright on August 28, writing a four-page letter about architecture. After ten months of observing at close range the new buildings in St. Louis, which had left him discouraged and confused, he had gone back to study closely Wright's published projects. "In looking through your works today my bewilderment diminished and I was thrilled by your interpretation of architecture which impressed me, as never before, with its force, direct-

ness, and unequivocal nature . . . though it is not possible for me to be [at Taliesin] I remain spiritually very close. Sincerely and affectionately, Billy Bernoudy."[10]

Wright's entire reply was: "My dear Billy: Your letter amused me, as it pleased me. Amused me that you should see now what I thought you were seeing all the time. Taliesin seems to be getting a chance now. Too bad you are outside looking in and not inside looking out."[11] Shortly after receiving Wright's letter, Bernoudy confided in the Beals:

> I received a letter from the Master last week—it was very upsetting. It was in answer to a very enthusiastic one I wrote him concerning some of his work that I had rediscovered and had been thrilled by. His reply was to the effect that he was amused to think that it had taken me so long to see the light and wasn't it too bad that now I was on the outside looking in rather than on the inside looking out. Aside from being very much hurt I thought that his attitude at best was certainly very smug. It continues to hurt too because I can't help seeing how great an architect he is no matter how insulting he becomes.[12]

Encouraged by the favorable response to his two lectures, Bernoudy proposed an article to *House and Garden* magazine.[13] He wanted especially to distinguish between Wright's Organic Modern architecture and others kinds of modern—or as he called it, the Modernistic. He offered to illustrate the article with a plan and perspective of a small house. A few of his drawings survive from this period, showing a maturing ability both to draw and to design according to the principles learned at Taliesin (Fig. 2–1).

Bernoudy was somewhat unusual among modern architects in being able to express his ideas clearly and at length, as he did in the two lectures. More often modern architects have been given to aphorisms, although Bernoudy could compose and adapt these, too. For example: "THE virility of art and life lies in its possibilities for growth." "MAN discovered Art when he discovered the subtle use of the useless." "GREAT Art is so contrived that the spectator becomes participant by mentally completing the incomplete." "Since it is in the becoming and not the end where the creative spirit is alive, the symmetrical lacks vitality for it stands for completeness and, worse still, repetition." "One can not learn to create beauty, one must first become the kind of person who

2–1. Drawing. Bernoudy Trust Archive.

can and does create beauty."[14] Unfortunately, *House and Garden* did not take Bernoudy up on his offer. He did receive an invitation in the fall of 1936 to participate in a series of lectures on "interior decorating" at the Jewish Center of Saint Louis.[15] He felt concerned to present a broad view of aesthetic values, by which, of course, he meant Wright's philosophy of an organic architecture.

Apart from Bernoudy's trials with Wright, 1936 was a happy year in the Bernoudy household with many social activities surrounding the engagement and forthcoming marriage of Jerome. Mr. Bernoudy's diary records that Saturday, October 17, was a perfectly beautiful fall morning, and Jerome and Mary Louise Chamberlain were married at noon. After a two-week wedding trip, the couple returned to the Bernoudy household, where they lived for two and a half months until they could move into their own house on Dougherty Ferry Road in west St. Louis County. The diary also notes that for two weeks before Christmas, Bernoudy stayed home sick, recovering slowly. His Christmas letter to the Wrights made reference to his pneumonia by way of an excuse for not having written sooner.

> Stimulated considerably by fever I dreamed a great deal both when I was awake and asleep and one of the most vivid recollections recalled that Christmas I spent at Taliesin when Mr. Wright and Abe and Bill Fyfe and I went out in a snow storm and cut down and dragged in the Christmas tree. That night, Christmas Eve, we had eggnog in the living room and Mrs. Wright wore a silver gown with silver tinsel in her hair and Iovanna wore a new white dress trimmed in tinsel and Svetlana, home for a visit, danced in a flame colored dress before the fireplace. Mr. Wright was very gay and his spirit permeated the whole party and the glow of it kept Bill Fyfe and me warm as we trudged to Hillside that brilliantly clear night through the deep blue snow and bitter cold.
>
> As various and as vivid as my memories of Taliesin are, I suspect that if I came back now I would find myself pretty much of a stranger—progress and change are so constant there. However, I want very much to return someday and am extremely impatient for the time when circumstances will enable me to see all of you again at Taliesin. You have always my best wishes and loyalty.[16]

Bernoudy did not know until he received a very friendly five-page handwritten reply from Mrs. Wright that, by unhappy coincidence, Wright was even more desperately ill with pneumonia at the same time.[17] She wrote that Wright was recovering, sitting in his bedroom by the fireplace, designing a house. This was an important new commission from Herbert Johnson for a large residence near Racine that would become known as Wingspread. Johnson, for whom Wright had previously designed the Johnson Wax Building in Racine, had given Wright a Capehart radio and record player for Christmas, "so we have music all the time," Mrs. Wright wrote. After pleasant gossip about Svetlana and Wes Peters, she returned to an earlier theme: "when are you coming back?" She concluded with a short essay on false pride, which she saw as the obstacle preventing his return to Taliesin: "it may lead you into more ambush than any other apparently insignificant meanness of your nature (we all have them, you know)—and I know you pretty well."[18]

Bernoudy kept in touch with several of the apprentices he had met at Taliesin, particularly Beye Fyfe and Phil Holliday. Holliday had gone to Taliesin to study painting, and both he and Fyfe had stayed for just two years, leaving a year before Bernoudy. Fyfe wrote in the summer of 1936 with thanks for a gift of the famous beaten biscuits. He was working on his family's farm in Woodstock, Illinois, and wrote, "Often while out in the fields working—or in the barn milking, I think of two things you've said sometime past—about only being understood by older people, and wishing for yourself that eventually you may have someplace to welcome your friends graciously and pleasantly." He asked for details about Bernoudy's job, something Bernoudy probably kept vague out of embarrassment, and added the news that Holliday was in Washington, D.C., "a junior architect to Uncle Sam."[19]

Fyfe wrote again from Oak Park on March 1, 1937, apologizing for not having sent greetings for Bernoudy's birthday on December 4, or for Christmas or New Year's, but finally offering greetings with an invitation to come for a visit.[20] Holliday sent a letter on March 23 from Washington, with thanks for a recent gift, news that a freighter trip to Mexico would cost only thirty dollars, a caricature of James Drought, who was another of the original apprentices, and the observation "that Jim D. can be damned tiresome."[21] Drought, from Milwaukee, had gone to Taliesin to study landscape architecture and had left at the same time Fyfe and Holliday did. A letter from Drought, also sent from Washington, where Drought was working as a landscape architect for the government, reached Bernoudy soon after the letter from Holliday. Drought and Holliday were "going riding Sunday—weather permitting."[22] Fyfe and

Holliday visited Bernoudy in St. Louis later that year, in October, and they "talked a great deal and laughed a great deal."[23] But by then Bernoudy's life had changed significantly.

In April 1937, Bernoudy received a letter from yet another former apprentice, Harold Wescott. Wescott was from Milwaukee, a painter and a teacher at the State Teachers' College, who had spent the summer of 1935 at Taliesin. He, too, asked further about Bernoudy's job, but then went on to write at length about the Katherine and Herbert Jacobs house in Madison, Wisconsin. This key example of what Wright called the Usonian house must have been of great interest to Bernoudy. The first house that he would build with his new partner, Edouard Mutrux, in 1938–1939 would grow directly out of the Usonian concept. The idea for it was well developed in two earlier unbuilt projects by Wright that followed the Willey house in Minneapolis, which Bernoudy would have known from his stay at Taliesin. Both the Hoult project of 1935 for a house in Wichita, Kansas, and the Lusk project of 1935–1936 for a house in Huron, South Dakota, were early drafts for the Jacobs house, designed in 1936. Wescott wrote in some detail about the house's design and with great concern for its radical innovations: the thin batten walls, the concrete floor slab of this one-story house set on grade without a basement, the radiant heating built into the concrete floor slab, the extensive windows, the flat roof, and the carport in place of an enclosed garage. Wescott and a partner were to do furniture for the house and did not look forward to negotiating with Wright—never one to compromise—about the design of it.[24] Wescott did not comment on the radical Usonian plan, Wright's new solution for providing a low-cost house for the middle-class American family living without servants, which had a kitchen at the center generously open to the dining area and large living room, a living room with an entire wall of French doors opening directly to the yard, and the bedrooms lined up compactly in a quiet separate wing.

Bernoudy's job at the department store obviously left much to be desired, but it did provide an income—enough of an income that on June 5, 1937, he bought a nearly new 1936 Ford Deluxe Cabriolet for $653.50 from the MacCarthy Motor Company, a very classy convertible with a rumble seat.[25] He put down $167.50 and signed a note for eighteen payments of $27.00 each. Although Bernoudy could not afford the tuition at Taliesin, he could afford a car. There were new and different priorities in his life.

Bernoudy finally left his job at Scruggs-Vandervoort-Barney and headed for California on July 11, 1937, with a friend who offered him a free ride. He explained to the Beals, "I came West on an adventure. I felt I would become a pathological case if I didn't get away on my own for a little while and make a few decisions for myself."[26] He went first to Los Angeles, where he was very well taken care of, "in the luxurious lap of an aunt in Pasadena," Flora Gearhart. She provided him "with a lavish room in her attractive apartment and with her chauffeur." They visited fashionable resorts, including Lake Arrowhead and Mission Inn, and also some of the Wright buildings that the fellowship had seen on the excursion from La Hacienda in March 1935. Bernoudy was distressed at the condition of the Barnsdall house and of the Millard house, which was filled with "mouldering old Italian things which obscure most of the features that Mr. Wright intended." He was concerned that "it gives most casual observers a very bad impression of Mr. Wright's work."[27]

On August 3 he left for San Francisco, where in stark contrast he found himself on the streets penniless and without a job. He intended to try himself "against the world," he told the Beals in the heroic language of Taliesin. To his amazement, he found an interesting job the first day he looked with G. F. Marsh and Company, the most reputable and fashionable Oriental art importers in San Francisco. He did not explain to the Beals that his aunt had connections with the firm. He was "installed as designer—made drawings of old Chinese shrines and little tables and vases, etc." This had to have been a stimulating environment for someone from Taliesin where the Oriental influence, particularly the Japanese influence, was so strong. Bernoudy had written about Japanese prints for an "At Taliesin" article. A page on Marsh and Company letterhead survives among Bernoudy's papers with a rather ironic quotation from Lao Tzu, "A man may know the world without leaving the shelter of his roof; through his own windows he may see the Supreme Tao. The further afield he goes, the less likely he is to find it. The Sage, then, knows things without traveling, names things without having seen them, and performs everything without action."[28]

Bernoudy worked for G. F. Marsh and Company for six weeks before being "lured back to St. Louis by bright and glittering promises from my former employer," Scruggs-Vandervoort-Barney. He arrived in St. Louis on September 19, 1937, only to learn that his department at the store had been discontinued in the meantime. Serendipitously, the alumni office of

Washington University, where he was registered as looking for employment, called Bernoudy with news of an available position with a local landscape architect. He interviewed with Mortimer Burroughs at Cobble Stone Gardens on October 1 and went to work for the firm immediately. He particularly enjoyed the fact that the office was in the country but only one and a half miles from his home so that he could walk there if he felt so inclined.[29]

Cobble Stone Gardens was a happy place for Bernoudy to find employment given his Taliesin values about the importance of landscape and nature. His work there not only provided him with the opportunity to do a good deal of drawing but also gave him experience at landscape design and the selection and establishment of plant materials, even if the landscape design philosophies of Taliesin and Cobble Stone Gardens were not in complete agreement. He also spent a great deal of time in the field supervising construction and gardening work.

Mortimer Burroughs was the son of William S. Burroughs, a partner in the American Arithmometer Company, founded in St. Louis in 1886.[30] The company moved to Detroit in 1904 and was incorporated there in 1905 as the Burroughs Adding Machine Company. Around 1912, having sold most of his interest in the company, Mortimer Burroughs moved back to St. Louis. He bought a plate glass company, which he renamed the Burroughs Glass Company. In the later 1920s, he became increasingly prominent in gardening circles and frequently was mentioned as an officer of different garden clubs and as a lecturer and writer on gardening. Around 1926, he and Edith S. Mason formed Cobble Stone Gardens.

Edith Mason was a student of landscape design at the Missouri Botanical Garden in 1922–1923 and took night courses in the School of Architecture at Washington University at the same time. She continued her studies at the Cambridge School of Architecture and Landscape Architecture for Women in Cambridge, Massachusetts. At the turn of the century, progressive-minded people considered landscape architecture a particularly apt profession for women. The Cambridge School of Architecture and Landscape Architecture for Women, founded in 1916, was one of a few institutions created to further this idea, and it was influential and highly regarded.[31] Mason worked in Boston for a landscape architect before returning to St. Louis. There she became associated with John Noyes, who is noted for his work in developing the Missouri Botanical Garden, before she teamed up with Burroughs. In a brochure published by Cobble Stone Gardens, Burroughs is identified as a "garden architect" and Mason as a "landscape architect."

Cobble Stone Gardens provided complete landscaping services, from design to construction to the selection of plants to the final planting, and it welcomed large or small projects. It represented Wayside Gardens—the prominent horticultural supply firm of Mentor, Ohio—in St. Louis, and it was developing its own grounds to show as many as possible of the varieties of small trees, shrubs, perennials, and bulbs that could be grown successfully in the St. Louis region. In addition to extensive display beds, there were two geometrical gardens and a walled patio, certainly too traditional and rigidly geometrical as measured by the ideals Bernoudy expressed in his lecture to the Kirkwood Garden Club. Even more traditional was the Colonial Revival office building, which, although comfortably arranged with a reception room and library for use by prospective customers, had a rigidly axial relationship to the adjoining gardens. The geometry of the landscape plan did not yield an inch to the meandering line of a stream along one side of the property. Bernoudy worked at Cobble Stone Gardens for two and a half years as a draftsman and a designer of landscape projects, none of which exceeded five thousand dollars.[32]

James Drought, Bernoudy's fellowship friend in landscape architecture, now back living in Milwaukee, visited St. Louis in early May 1938. Like Bernoudy and other apprentices, he had met the landscape architect Jens Jensen and visited his log home and nature school on Ellison Bay on the Door County peninsula of Wisconsin. Jensen was admired by Wright for his regional, naturalistic approach to landscape design. In a thank-you note to Bernoudy, Drought reflected that approach in commenting on a visit to Cobble Stone Gardens, which he described as "much too busy and jumbled, lacks repose."[33]

Mortimer Burroughs was married to Laura Lee, the daughter of a prominent minister in St. Louis. Their son William, who was three years younger than Bernoudy, would become well known as a novelist. He was drifting around doing a variety of things in the years following his 1936 graduation from Harvard, and even before that had begun experimenting with drugs. The two Billys, Burroughs and Bernoudy, knew each other well enough to take a week's holiday together in Galveston in the summer of 1939.

Other more important friendships were being forged in these years, too. Edouard Jules Mutrux and William Adair Bernoudy must have met

around 1937, perhaps introduced by Mutrux's brother Robert.[34] Their meeting marked the beginning of a professional association that would last for nearly thirty years. Bernoudy's partnership with Mutrux was as essential for his architectural career as was his participation in the Taliesin Fellowship. The Mutrux brothers, both architects, came from an extraordinary family. Their father, Louis Eugene Mutrux, attended Washington University's School of Fine Arts in 1892. He went on to a very successful career as a designer and developer of apartment buildings and as the president of a realty company that managed the buildings he designed. Edouard, born in 1907, was the first of twelve children. They lived on ten acres off Dielman Road at 6 Sumac Lane, then in the country, in a large house the father had designed, which has only recently been demolished. The Mutruxs were Swiss by background, and French was the language they spoke at home. The children were all given names that could be either French or English. Edouard, or Ed as his friends mainly called him, did not learn English until he started school. His father was successful enough that in 1925 he could afford to take the entire family on a fifteen-month trip to Europe, where the children attended school in Switzerland. The cultural life within the family led many of them to careers in the arts, especially in architecture.

Edouard and Robert were the first to follow their father to Washington University, where they both received B.S. degrees in architecture in 1930.[35] Edouard received a Master of Architecture degree in 1931; his thesis was a design for an "Open Air Theatre," a project in the Beaux Arts tradition. He received Washington University's Frederick Widman Prize in 1930 and continued his studies in France in 1931 and 1932. He spent the first year at the American School in Fontainebleau and then moved to Paris, where he studied mural painting with Jean Despujols, a painter, designer, writer on art, and winner of the Prix de Rome in 1914.[36] Mutrux's future wife, Elsa Krull, also attended Washington University, where she received an A.B. in 1935. Among several other members of the Mutrux family who studied at Washington University was a brother, Jean Louis Mutrux, who received a degree in architectural engineering in 1932. He went on to a distinguished career as a furniture designer and maker, often working on projects with the Bernoudy-Mutrux architectural firm.

Edouard Mutrux was in Paris at an exciting time in the development of modern architecture. The great pioneer there was Le Corbusier, and some of his most influential buildings, such as the Villa Savoye in Poissy, just outside Paris, or the Hostel for Swiss Students at the Cité Universitaire in Paris, were new. It was the moment when the modern movement in European architecture first crystallized, and it was that architecture that was at the heart of the first architectural exhibition held at the Museum of Modern Art in New York, in 1932. The exhibition was organized by Henry-Russell Hitchcock, an architectural historian and critic, and Philip Johnson, a curator of architecture at the museum. At the suggestion of Alfred Barr, the director of the museum, they gave this architecture the name *International Style*.[37] In what was an unhappy experience all around, Wright's work had a prominent place in the exhibition, but, as Hitchcock made explicit in a new foreword for the 1966 republication of the exhibition catalog, it was there to serve as a contrast to the truly modern architecture. Mutrux was attracted to this International Style architecture, but not Bernoudy. This was the style Bernoudy usually called modernistic, the kind of modern architecture he so denigrated in his lecture to the Kirkwood Garden Club.

Back in St. Louis, Mutrux began practicing architecture in the mid-1930s. In 1938 he designed a combination residence and office for Dr. Samuel A. Bassett, which was built at 1200 South Big Bend Boulevard in Richmond Heights. The two functions were effectively integrated yet kept independent in a design on three levels that made effective use of the site. This very early work of Mutrux's attracted national attention and was published at length in the *Architectural Record* in 1939.[38] Under the editorship of James Marston Fitch, the *Architectural Record,* which had earlier given a great deal of space to Wright, was still championing the cause of modern architecture. With its flat roofs, curved corners, corner windows, and glass blocks, the Bassett house and office was a pioneering example of the International Style in St. Louis.

When Mutrux and Bernoudy teamed up, they persuaded Mutrux's sister Suzette and her husband, Dr. C. Hudson Talbot, to let them design their new house. Discussions and design work must have begun sometime in 1938, as the Bassett office and residence project was going up. The Talbot house project marks the beginning of the Mutrux-Bernoudy partnership and the beginning of Bernoudy's architectural career. A field trip was included among the preliminaries. Suzette Talbot, Mutrux, and Bernoudy spent two weeks in July 1938 going first to Chicago—where they visited Fyfe and Holliday and certainly toured Wright's work in the

area—and then traveling on to Taliesin. Mutrux remembers being quite overwhelmed at meeting Wright, "a genius," and that it was on this visit that he "got religion" about modern architecture. It is not surprising that the house designed for the Talbots was not in the International Style of Mutrux's Bassett project but rather a Usonian house reflecting very directly Wright's current work.

Bernoudy may have brought architectural religion to the partnership, but Mutrux brought professional training—he knew about construction, contract drawings, specifications, and the technical details that were necessary if he and Bernoudy were to function as a viable architectural firm. The firm identified itself as Mutrux-Bernoudy at this stage (Fig. 2–2). The partners were not busy, with just two commissions carried through construction before they both went off to war in 1942, and Bernoudy continued to hold additional employment during this period. But the Talbot house was a wonderful challenge and a propitious beginning for the firm.

2–2. Edouard Mutrux and William Bernoudy, ca. 1937. Bernoudy Trust Archive.

Bernoudy had kept in touch with Taliesin through letters and visits with other apprentices, but the trip with Mutrux and Suzette Talbot was his first visit there since his departure almost three years earlier. The three must have talked with people there about the Talbot project, but whether or not the Talbot house design was far enough along for any close review is hard to say. The project was closely studied by the two young architects before it was built, and eventually a model was prepared, as well as drawings. Wright may have learned about the Talbot project during the July visit, but he certainly learned of it in January 1939 when he visited St. Louis.

One subject that did come up in July, quite predictably, was the question of when Bernoudy would return to Taliesin. He wrote the Wrights more than a month after his return to St. Louis saying he still was no closer to raising the funds that would enable him to do so.[39] He went on at some length about the sense of "belonging" that he experienced once again at Taliesin and about his hope that, when and if he could afford to return, they would find a place for him. Wright made a counteroffer: if Bernoudy could contribute $500 a year—not the set $1,100 tuition—for the next year or two, they could then put him on a senior basis where he would pay nothing and have a small stipend for personal expenses, and "eventually something more if we prosper as we expect."[40] Other apprentices had done this, including Bernoudy's friend Edgar Tafel, who by this date held a position of significant responsibility in Wright's office, if not one of significant remuneration.[41] Bernoudy did not take up the offer. The Wrights did not seem to take offense and wired an invitation to the customary Halloween masquerade.

Wright came to St. Louis during the second week of January 1939 and on the evening of Sunday, January 8, lectured to about a thousand people.[42] The lecture was vintage Wright and, to anyone familiar with the lectures he was giving all around the country at the time, would have been very familiar. The Bernoudys were his hosts, and his lecture was sponsored by the Liberal Forum of the Young Men's and Young Women's Hebrew Association of St. Louis, which brought in a series of distinguished speakers, often representing controversial positions. Among the long list of notable speakers was Lewis Mumford, Wright's good friend and effective champion.

Wright arrived in the afternoon by train and was met by Bernoudy and a group of newspaper reporters and photographers. He noted that he liked Theodore Link's Union Station, which he described as "full of vital-

2–3. From the left: Gilbert Harris, secretary of the Young Men's Hebrew Association, William Bernoudy, Frank Lloyd Wright, and Benedict Farrar, president of the St. Louis chapter of the AIA, at Union Station, St. Louis, January 8, 1939. *St. Louis Globe-Democrat* photograph in the Bernoudy Trust Archive; courtesy St. Louis Mercantile Library, University of Missouri–St. Louis.

ity and dignity." Wright would have alit from his train under the train shed and proceeded into the lower level of the head house and up the stairs to the Great Hall, a richly decorated space very much like the work of Louis Sullivan, Wright's *lieber Meister*.[43] After he had posed for photographs and shown off to advantage his distinctive costume, the group began an architectural tour of downtown St. Louis (Fig. 2–3). While waiting in front of the station for Bernoudy to bring up the car, Wright noticed Klipstein and Rathmann's Civil Courts Building to the east, built in 1930. This remarkable building, dressed up in Greek Revival details, carries a Greek temple, based on an archaeological reconstruction of a mausoleum at Halikarnassos, at the top of its ten stories. This mausoleum was a model for many buildings in this period, including Masonic temples, and Wright's first question of the reporters was, "What is that, the Scottish Rite Temple?" When asked if he liked it, he replied, "I neither like it, nor dislike it. I deplore it"—a comment he had rehearsed in front of quite a few other buildings in other cities.

The Wainwright Building at Seventh and Chestnut was the destination of their automobile tour. Along the way they looked at other buildings from the car that, like the Civil Courts building, were part of a major Civic Center beautification project of the 1930s, all done in similar classical revival styles. The Post Office, Federal Court House, Soldiers Memorial, and Municipal Auditorium all came in for sarcastic treatment, with Wright insulting quite a number of the leading architects of the city. The midpoint on the tour was the Wainwright Building. Wright had worked for Adler and Sullivan when it was designed and had written about the great moment of creation when Sullivan conceived it, an event he had witnessed. He lectured the others in the car briefly about the historical significance of the Wainwright. "A real moment in American architecture," he said. "Its noble assertion of simplicity, when once achieved, is forever." Turning east on Market Street and returning on Chestnut Street, the tour concluded at Aloe Plaza and *The Meeting of the Waters* fountain by Carl Milles, then under construction. "St. Louis should be congratulated for obtaining the services of such a fine sculptor," Wright said.

Wright's lecture was entitled "Organic Architecture" and opened with a dire critique of American culture and drastic suggestions for dealing with the situation—shut down the universities, close the museums, decentralize the cities, get back to honest hard work on the land, learn by doing. Wright was a lively, entertaining lecturer, and sarcastic references to the new buildings seen on the afternoon tour punctuated his talk. Almost nothing was sacred. The Parthenon, Michelangelo, and Christopher Wren were held up to scorn and ridicule. A true American architecture would rise, he argued, only when Americans quit borrowing from other cultures and concentrated on creating one of their own. An organic architecture, on the model of his work, would lead the way in the creation of an authentic American culture. The lecture ended with a discussion period, following which a small reception for admirers lasted until midnight at the Bernoudy house.

Wright left the next day, but the newspapers managed to keep up the controversy for three more days. Benedict Farrar, the president of the St. Louis chapter of the American Institute of Architects (AIA), spoke for most local architects in refusing to take Wright seriously: "Mr. Wright always talks just this way . . . the show was fine." He wondered how anyone

could accept the argument that only Wright of the 10,000 architects at work in the country could be right while the other 9,999 were wrong. The architects of the new buildings in the Civic Center, which Wright had held up for ridicule, also had their chance to dismiss his comments as little more than amusing. At a meeting of the St. Louis AIA chapter on Tuesday evening, many anticipated a heated discussion of Wright's remarks, but none developed. Lawrence Hill, head of the School of Architecture at Washington University, said simply in regard to Wright's criticisms of architectural education, "He's wrong." Bernoudy rose to the

2–4. Talbot house, rendering. Bernoudy Archive, West Campus Library Annex, Washington University, St. Louis.

2–5. LEFT. Talbot house, living room. Photograph 1939 by Piaget, Bernoudy Trust Archive.

2–6. BELOW. Talbot house, plan.

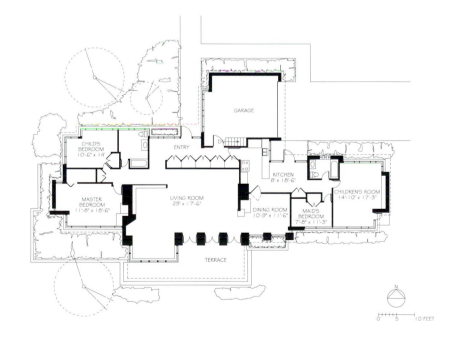

occasion: "It is regrettable and keenly disappointing that the presence and public address of such a man as Wright should provoke no more worthy responses from his own profession here in St. Louis than the deprecatory and altogether irrelevant comments appearing in yesterday's" newspapers. One report did observe that an unusual number of pedestrians were seen looking closely at the buildings in the Civic Center following Wright's critical comments.

Bernoudy collected the newspaper accounts and sent them to Wright along with a warm letter of thanks for the visit. He commented especially on how grateful those who had gathered at the Bernoudy house after the lecture had been for that opportunity and on his parents' pleasure in having Wright as their guest. By the time of Wright's visit, work had started on the Talbot house. Bernoudy confessed to the Beals in a letter written just before the visit, "I don't know whether to tell him of the house or not—he's so unpredictable." But afterward he wrote that he did "show it to Mr. W. and he commented favorably on it and suggested only one change which I am incorporating" (Figs. 2–4, 2–5, 2–6).[44]

2–7. Talbot house, north side. Photograph 1939, Bernoudy Trust Archive.

Bernoudy was still working for Cobble Stone Gardens, dividing his evenings between architectural drawing and practicing on his new Chickering grand piano. The Talbot house was to have hot water radiant heating in a concrete slab on grade of the kind Wright was now advocating and had used in the Jacobs house in Madison. In January the small basement for the mechanical equipment was in place and Bernoudy and Mutrux were preparing for the laying of the heating pipes and the pouring of the slab. The heating man "is interested, but will guarantee nothing," Bernoudy wrote to the Beals. "Naturally the work on the house has taken most of my spare time but fortunately my partner, who is a young architect here, has been able to give most of his days to drawing."[45] Construction of the house started after May 1. Bernoudy wrote a description of it at the time:

> The Talbot house lies long and low, slightly below the level of the road, on a shelf of land rising gently from a rolling hillside. The low uninterrupted

eave line to the North, which is the elevation facing the road, provides generous protection for the long bands of narrow windows which admit light and air to the less important rooms to the north, and because of their height from the ground, give a feeling of complete privacy [Fig. 2–7].

In contrast to the restrained window treatment on the north, the entire southern exposure is thrown open to the light, air and view. Walls in the traditional sense are non-existent. The low eave line, interrupted by the bulwark of the two massive chimneys is resumed again by the line of the cantilevered canopy which projects out over the living room terrace. The sunlight and air which ordinarily would have been shut out of the living room by the canopy, floods into the room by way of clerestory windows set in an uninterrupted band above the canopy roof. In the living room, as in many of the rooms throughout the house, the ceiling follows the exterior roof line and becomes a reflecting surface for lights concealed in built-in lighting shelves [Fig. 2–8].

In the living room the brick walls of the chimneys are exposed and their surface is relieved by decorative brick ventilating grills which in summer provide an outlet for the hot air collected at the ceiling [Fig. 2–9]. The French doors opening out on the terrace permit the slightest breeze to enter the room and the wide canopy and overhanging eaves of the clerestory screen the room from the intense heat of the summer sun.

In winter the low lying sun enters freely into the house and the general atmosphere of warmth and cheerfulness is augmented by the three fireplaces set deep in the broad rising chimneys.

The house was planned to conform quietly to its location and to provide the maximum of privacy and view to the most important rooms. The master bedroom and child's bedroom have direct access to the entrance hall and so may be reached without passage through the living room. The large room in the extreme east wing of the house was planned to serve as a school room for a small nursery school operated by Mrs. Talbot. Entrance to it may be gained either through the spacious service entrance or by its own outside door. Located as it is away from the main section of the house none of the activities carried on there need intrude on the routine of ordinary living. Proximity to the kitchen makes the serving of morning milk to the children a simple matter and during those seasons of the year when the school is not in session the room becomes an ideal party and recreation room.[46]

Bernoudy wrote about the architecture but did not mention the radically innovative mechanical equipment in the form of the radiant heating system. The *St. Louis Post-Dispatch*, however, featured it in a detailed, technical article on May 26, 1940. By this date, the system had been in

2–8. LEFT. Talbot house, view of the living room looking toward the dining room. Photograph 1939 by Piaget, Bernoudy Trust Archive.

2–9. BELOW. Talbot house, ventilating grille.

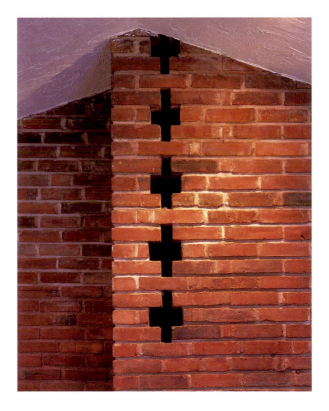

2–10. Talbot house, window.

use for one heating season, and the architects and owners had carefully monitored its performance. Other than the mechanical room, which measured nine feet by twelve feet, the house was built with no basement. A coil of one-and-one-fourth-inch copper pipes was laid on a nine-inch-deep bed of gravel beneath the concrete floor slab. The gravel bed was designed to act as insulation so that heat would not be lost into the ground. The pipes were spaced nine inches apart from center to center and covered practically the entire floor area. Careful measurements taken the first winter showed that all interior wall, ceiling, and floor surfaces had higher temperatures than the enclosed air in the house, and that the air temperatures at all levels in the house varied by little more than one degree. One of the arguments used in favor of radiant heating systems is that when the floors are kept warm, the ambient air temperatures can be lower. In this case, the newspaper article noted that just 64 degrees of air temperature created a feeling of comfort. Bernoudy and Mutrux designed a few more radiant heating systems after World War II, but even though radiant heating remained an article of faith in the Usonian doctrine, Bernoudy and Mutrux soon abandoned it for perimeter forced-air heating systems.

Bernoudy wrote to the Beals in December 1939, just as the roofing on the house neared completion.[47] He was optimistic about the heating system because the pipe grid provided better coverage than the system Wright had used in the Jacobs house. He explained that although the Talbots had little money to put into the house, he and Mutrux had used the best materials and design they could. He singled out the use of old brick, something that appealed to him not only for its warm and variegated color and texture but also for its connection with the traditional architecture of St. Louis. The specifications called for laying the bricks up with deeply raked-out horizontal mortar joints and flush vertical joints, a subtle detail Wright had used since early in his career to emphasize the horizontality of the overall design and create a small-scale pattern of horizontal shadow lines across the brick surfaces.

Bernoudy also mentioned that the window sash had arrived and were "really exciting looking" (Fig. 2–10). The patterns in the window mullions start with a rectangular shape that is halved once and halved again

to create a simple geometrical harmony. In Wright's nineteenth-century Transcendentalist thought, geometry lies at the heart of nature, giving deeper meaning to geometrical harmonies, such as those found in these windows.[48] Bernoudy was also familiar with theories about proportion in ancient art, especially ones that were current at the time under the name *dynamic symmetry*.[49] The glass in the windows is mitered at the corners so that no vertical mullion marks the corner joint, one of the details Wright created in the quest for the destruction of the box in architectural space, a theme Bernoudy had espoused in his lecture to the Kirkwood Garden Club.[50] The window frames are made of milled boards with simple rectangular cross sections, free of any curving molded profiles, and with a stained finish. Wright had advocated this treatment in his series of articles in the *Architectural Record,* saying that flat, smooth surfaces reveal the natural beauty of the wood grain, whereas carving or molding of the wood distracts from its beauty, while painting obscures it entirely.[51]

2–11. Talbot house, dining room with built-in furniture and light fixture. Photograph 1939, courtesy Mr. and Mrs. Michael Smith.

As with Wright's buildings, the plan is governed by a module, or what Wright called the "unit system," to establish a further geometrical harmony. In this case the modules measured four feet by four feet.[52] Geometrical themes were further developed in exposed light fixtures along the brick piers of the living room. Although they do not survive, similar lights were originally used above the dining room table in a long fixture on the ceiling that folded and came down the wall against which the table abutted, as is indicated by an early photograph (Fig. 2–11). Bernoudy described how the spatial qualities of the house unfolded as one moved through it, with interior spaces opening to the outside as any sense of the box was destroyed through the banks of windows and the shifting wall planes, so that the space of the interior was not sharply separated from the exterior. A continuity in exterior and interior materials, brick especially, serves a similar purpose. In contrast, a strong sense of enclosure and shelter is created by the different planes of the ceilings and the great hearths of the three fireplaces. The dialogue between prospect and seclusion, resolved with a mood of repose, is at the heart of the experience of this first Mutrux-Bernoudy house.

There were a few other examples of modern houses in the St. Louis area at this time—Mutrux's Bassett residence and office and the early works of Charles Eames and Harris Armstrong—but the Talbot house was unique as a mature example of Wright's organic architecture. The *St. Louis Post-Dispatch* published a second article on the Talbot house on June 9, 1940, inaugurating a series on houses in the region with novel or interesting architectural features. The second article was more general in nature than the earlier one about the heating system, with a brief text and five photographs by Clint Murphy, a staff photographer.

As early as March 21, 1937, when most of the public media were either ignoring Wright or persecuting him, the *Post-Dispatch* ran an article in its Sunday magazine about his recent work with a perceptive and very positive text by Max Putzel of the magazine's staff. The article focused on the house Wright had designed for the Kaufmanns at Mill Run, Pennsylvania, which was not yet finished and had not yet been given its familiar name, Fallingwater.[53] This must have been one of the earliest articles on this famous building and probably the first to publish Wright's celebrated perspective drawing of it that would appear on the cover of *Time* magazine the following January. Joseph Pulitzer Jr., whose father was the publisher

2–12. Doris house. Photograph ca. 1940, Bernoudy Trust Archive.

of the *Post-Dispatch* at this time, and William Bernoudy were close friends over many years, and one can not help but feel that they knew each other at least as early as this 1937 article. Pulitzer did not become editor and publisher of the *Post-Dispatch* until 1955, but he was a member of the staff in 1937. Public attention such as that paid to the Talbot house is, of course, important to the success of an architectural firm, especially one specializing in residential work. Mutrux and Bernoudy were off to a good start. Years later, Mutrux recalled the project for Nancy Smith, the current owner of the house: "This was the beginning of a dream, and it didn't get any better than this."[54]

The house has evolved over the years. By 1951, Mutrux's parents were living in it. The original garage had been converted to additional living quarters, with a new garage added to the north and an additional living room added to the east. Part of the area under the dramatically cantilevered roof to the south of the living room had been enclosed as a screened porch.

In the midst of the excitement of building the Talbot house, Bernoudy received the customary invitation from the Wrights for Halloween 1939. The celebration would mark the seventh anniversary of the fellowship, and it was going to be held in the Hillside school buildings, which were finally ready for use. Mrs. Wright added by hand to the typed letter, "could you leave 'the rut' long enough to be with us on Halloween?" A few weeks later she wrote again, wondering why he was "missing one of the greatest experiences in your life—working at the side of one of the greatest men of our era."[55] Bernoudy finally did return to Taliesin in June 1940. He wrote asking if he could come with two old friends for a weekend, and he was warmly received. With the letter, he enclosed photographs of the Talbot house and a copy of the June 9 *Post-Dispatch* article, noting that this was the house that "Ed and I have just finished building. I am both eager and hesitant for you to see it." He added that he hoped it was evident that he had tried his best to follow Wright's principles and that he looked forward to going over the project with him.[56] There is no record of how that discussion went.

A second project came to Mutrux-Bernoudy in 1940, a house for Charles Lee Doris on Maret Drive in Kirkwood (Fig. 2–12). The drawings were completed in August. On a site similar to that of the Talbot house, the Doris house also opens up to a falling grade on the south side. This time the firm designed a two-story version of the Usonian house. Brick on the lower level and frame above, the house is built into the falling site. The long horizontal lines of the flat roof with its deep eaves are echoed in the broad clapboards of the sheathing of the upper level and the ribbons of windows that wrap around the corners. The house was enlarged for the original owner in 1957.

A third project that was not built but was carried through preliminary designs was a house for Dr. and Mrs. Robert Elman in 1941 (Fig. 2–13). This nicely planned and proportioned house looks back to Wright's earlier Prairie buildings—especially in its elevations—with a continuous sill line on the second floor windows, banding them together in long dark ribbons that leave the low-pitched hip roof hovering above the house. The house was designed for a narrow urban lot, possibly where the Elmans were living at 4456 Maryland Avenue or a similar city location. The L-shaped plan of the ground floor is closer to the contemporary Usonian houses. The plan allowed a maximum of outdoor private space behind the house, away from the street, and focused on a pool. This allowed the characteristic opening of the interior space—the living room and dining room in this case—to the outdoors.

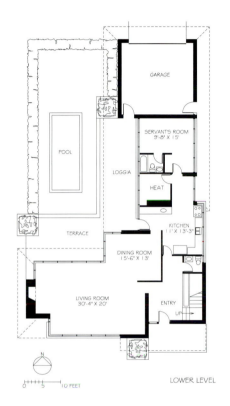

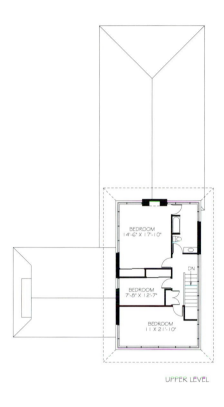

2–13. Elman house, plan.

By the end of the 1930s, Bernoudy had established himself as an architect in the St. Louis community. When reporting events such as Wright's
visit in January 1939, the newspapers sought him out as a spokesman for
at least one point of view about modern architecture. The Mutrux-
Bernoudy partnership did not yet provide full-time work, but Bernoudy
was finding other work as an architect. He was still working for Cobble
Stone Gardens early in 1939 but probably left there sometime in the
course of the year. In his application for registration as an architect just
after World War II, Bernoudy indicated that he had worked for Harris
Armstrong for nine months in 1938–1939, doing perspective layouts and
working drawings for houses. This is an interesting connection, since
Armstrong and Bernoudy have often been regarded as the two most
influential pioneers of modern architecture in St. Louis, Armstrong
representing the International Style and Bernoudy representing a very
different kind of modernism.

Armstrong, born in 1899 in Edwardsville, Illinois, was eleven years older
than Bernoudy. Neither had been successful academically, Armstrong even
less so than Bernoudy. He went to high school in Webster Groves but did
not go on to college. He began exploring modern architecture in his
work in the late 1920s. For six months in 1929 he was employed by the
pioneer architect of modern skyscrapers, Raymond Hood, working on
Rockefeller Center in New York. He got this job through Hugh Ferriss,
an architect and America's foremost architectural delineator, who maintained connections with St. Louis, where he had been raised and trained,
after moving to New York in 1913. By the time Bernoudy worked for
him, Armstrong had completed such important projects as the Shanley
Building in Clayton of 1935.[57] Late in 1941 Bernoudy was working with
Forrest T. Campbell of the Adult Study Center on organizing a course to
be offered through the center, presumably on modern architecture. On
December 8, the day after the bombing of Pearl Harbor, Bernoudy wrote
Campbell saying that the recent events precluded his assuming any responsibilities at the center, but that Harris Armstrong might be interested.

At the end of 1939, following the period during which he worked for
Armstrong, Bernoudy traveled to New York for a two-week holiday, the
first record of any trip to the East Coast.[58] Snapshots of Wright's Fallingwater in Pennsylvania survive among his things from the period, suggesting that he visited Fallingwater on the trip. Sometime later in 1940
Bernoudy worked as an architect with the Historic American Buildings
Survey (HABS), an unlikely alliance. The U.S. National Park Service had
organized HABS in partnership with the AIA and the Library of Congress as a depression-era project to give work to unemployed architects.
The project sent architects and photographers around the country to
make detailed measured drawings of historic buildings and professional-
quality photographs, an archival project modeled on similar, well-estab-
lished ones in Europe. The National Park Service administered the project, the AIA identified available architects and recommended sites to be
recorded, and the Library of Congress received the records and set them
up for use. The project produced such valuable results right from the beginning that it was continued and, in fact, remains in operation today. It
has now produced one of the largest archives of its kind in the world and
is the most frequently consulted collection in the Division of Prints and
Photographs in the Library of Congress.

In 1940 a mobile HABS unit was established as part of the St. Louis
office of the National Park Service to go into areas that had been beyond the reach of earlier HABS teams. As a member of the architectural
drawing team, Bernoudy traveled to Illinois, Kentucky, Mississippi, and
Louisiana. He was a junior architect, one of seven under the direction of
F. Ray Leimkuehler, considered to be one of the finest draftsmen in St.
Louis. Charles E. Peterson, whose memorandum to Secretary of the Interior Harold Ickes in 1933 led to the creation of HABS, was stationed
in St. Louis with the Park Service when the mobile unit was created. He
recalls that the architects and photographer were provided with a station
wagon and money for travel expenses. An exhibition of some of their
drawings and photographs, with the theme "Ante Bellum Houses of the
Mississippi Valley," was shown in the Fine Arts Room of the St. Louis
Public Library in October 1940.[59] Wright had little if any appreciation
for early American architecture and its preservation, and from early in
Bernoudy's career, this was a clear point of difference between him and
Wright. The HABS work fitted with Bernoudy's reputation at Taliesin
for representing an older, more gracious southern way of life. In 1934,
when home on a holiday from Taliesin, Bernoudy had written to the
Beals about going to a dinner party in "a very old and beautiful Colonial house way out in the country," not a description one would expect
to hear from Wright or one of his followers.[60] The selection of used
brick for the Talbot house had also been a reflection of Bernoudy's historical taste.

In 1941, with the United States preparing for war, Bernoudy sought military construction projects that could use his architectural abilities. In April he went to Fort Leonard Wood, Missouri, where he worked on drawings and specifications for troop housing and recreational facilities. Much of this work involved large-scale planning of the buildings in relation to the site and to each other. In June he returned to St. Louis to work for the St. Louis architectural firm of Mauran, Russell, Crowell, and Mulgardt, which had a large government commission for a U.S. ordnance plant in St. Louis to manufacture small arms. Bernoudy worked for the firm as an architectural draftsman, preparing architectural and construction details for the project. He and Mutrux were still trying to carry on some private work, too—for example the Elman project. But this became more difficult as the war approached. In the middle of October he wrote a long and engaging letter of apology to a friend for whom he was to have designed a bookcase and fireplace for a living room, saying he did not know if he would be able to undertake the project. He was spending more and more evenings each week working overtime on the ordnance-plant project, often not getting home until midnight.

With the outbreak of the war, Bernoudy immediately began inquiring about possible military assignments for which he might volunteer. He hoped to be able to make use of his architectural qualifications and avoid being drafted and assigned to some other kind of duty. Through his contacts in St. Louis and Washington, D.C., he soon was directed to the navy. Seeking a commission, he needed a letter of recommendation from Wright about his time in the Taliesin Fellowship. Wright obligingly provided exactly the kind of letter Bernoudy needed,[61] in spite of his own well-publicized opposition to the war and his efforts to help a number of apprentices at Taliesin obtain conscientious objector status. Although Wright's outspoken opposition to the war was later investigated by the FBI, Bernoudy's acceptance into the navy proceeded without delay. He received his commission as a lieutenant, junior grade, on March 12, 1942, effective from March 1 (Fig. 2–14).

Bernoudy served in Washington, D.C., throughout the war as an architectural liaison officer with the Bureau of Medicine and Surgery. He was not a member of the architecturally more elite Construction and Engineering Corps of the navy, but he was given major architectural responsibilities. He had sole responsibility for the preliminary drawings for a project that included a research laboratory, an all-weather building,

2–14. William Bernoudy in uniform during World War II. Photograph by Bachrach, Bernoudy Trust Archive.

and a temperature-controlled animal house. This $1.5 million project was executed by the Bureau of Yards and Docks with Bernoudy as liaison officer.

The Society of Architectural Historians was founded in Cambridge, Massachusetts, in 1940. It would grow to become the principal professional organization in the world for architectural historians, architects with an interest in historic buildings, and historic preservationists. Six people, including Bernoudy, were present at the founding of the Washington, D.C., chapter on March 30, 1943; four of them were St. Louisans in Washington because of the war.[62] In these early days of the society, members not only gathered in local chapters to read papers on architectural history—many of which were subsequently published in the society's journal—but also organized study tours to visit interesting examples of historic architecture in their regions. Joining the society was a logical continuation of Bernoudy's association with HABS—in fact, a number of the founders of the society had worked for HABS—but it was not

2–15. Wedding photograph of Euretta deCosson and Perry T. Rathbone; William Bernoudy is at the far right with Curt Valentin next to him. Bernoudy Trust Archive.

something that would have been of interest to Wright. Bernoudy also joined a local Washington preservation group, named for William Thornton, a physician and architect best remembered for winning the competition for the design of the U.S. capitol building in 1792. Thornton was also the architect of the Octagon, built in 1798–1800, one of the great houses in Washington of that period. Today it has been preserved by the AIA, but its future was uncertain in the 1940s when the Thornton Society was founded to work for its preservation.

One of Bernoudy's longest and closest friendships was with Perry Rathbone, who moved to St. Louis in 1940 to serve as director of the City Art Museum. Rathbone, too, had joined the navy during the war; after duty in the Far East he was transferred back to Washington, where he and Euretta deCosson were married in 1945 (Fig. 2–15). It was an elegant event with most of the men in navy uniforms, including Bernoudy. One person present but not in uniform was the New York art dealer Curt Valentin, a recent refugee from Nazi Germany.[63] Valentin shared an interest in German Expressionist art with Rathbone and was a dealer with whom Bernoudy's friend Joseph Pulitzer Jr. worked in the early years of building his art collection. Gertrude Turnovská Lenart, who would marry Bernoudy in 1955, was associated with Valentin in his New York gallery, but almost certainly not until later in the 1940s.

Bernoudy was released from active duty in 1946 with the rank of lieutenant commander, U.S. Naval Reserve. He returned to St. Louis to resume his career as an architect.

By the summer of 1946, Bernoudy was back in St. Louis, working as an architectural draftsman for the Veterans Administration. From their office in the Old Post Office and Custom House, the VA architects were responsible for preliminary and working drawings for the remodeling of existing hospitals in Missouri, Oklahoma, and Kansas.

On September 12, 1946, Bernoudy completed his application for registration with the State of Missouri as a licensed architect. At that time, it was possible to become a licensed architect on the basis of experience, and Bernoudy was amply qualified in that respect. In his application, he indicated that he had graduated from University City High School in 1929 but made no mention of his one disastrous year at Washington University. On the other hand, his years at the Taliesin Fellowship with Frank Lloyd Wright were included. For his experience, he listed two and a half years as a draftsman and designer with Cobble Stone Gardens, nine months as a draftsman for Harris Armstrong, one year as a draftsman with Mauran, Russell, Crowell, and Mulgardt, and four years as an architectural liaison officer with the navy with sole responsibility for the preliminary drawings of a very large research laboratory in Washington, D.C. He also indicated that he had been a partner in the Mutrux-Bernoudy firm, with responsibility for all aspects of design and construction for the Talbot and Doris houses in 1939–1941. The application indicated, too, that Mutrux and Bernoudy were back in business at 225 North Meramec Avenue in Clayton. When Bernoudy's registration was accepted, the order of their names was soon reversed, and for a decade the firm practiced under the name Bernoudy-Mutrux.

On September 14, 1946, two days after preparing his application for registration, Bernoudy agreed to rent a basement room on Forsythe Walk in a building owned and occupied by Mary Potter Love, Inc., a prominent residential real estate firm, at the rate of $40 per month. The agreement was contingent on Bernoudy being able to fit his drawing table into the basement. At first he used the same address as Mary Potter Love, 2 Forsythe Walk, but later the address changed to 7 Forsythe Walk. The space was unpromising, not only because it was in an unfinished basement but also because, as the letter of agreement noted, in severe weather the heating system was inadequate and in heavy rain there was a certain amount of seepage. But the move proved to be a wise one.

The office was in an attractive business section of Clayton, under development since the 1930s by Sidney M. Studt. Studt and his architect,

Beverley T. Nelson, had done a particularly effective job of reviving the English Renaissance architecture of Colonial Williamsburg, with its distinctive brick construction and detailing. Ever since 1926, when John D. Rockefeller Jr. was persuaded to undertake the restoration of Colonial Williamsburg, the impact of that project on educated architectural taste in America had been growing. The Colonial or Georgian Revival had been a strong movement in American architecture since the 1890s, but the extraordinary team of historians and restoration architects that was assembled for the Williamsburg restoration, the vast scale of the project, and the tremendous amount of publicity that resulted gave strong new focus to the Revival. Clayton, zoned for buildings not more than three stories high, provided a welcome ground for the style. Forsythe Walk, a special place within this Williamsburg landscape of Clayton, with small shops and art galleries, lasted from 1937 until 1973 and is fondly remembered by those who knew Clayton at that time.

One can imagine what Frank Lloyd Wright would have said about neo-Georgian Clayton. It embodied many of what he saw as the worst aspects of American architecture. He had little interest in or appreciation for American Colonial and Georgian architecture. The idea of reviving any historical architecture was inexcusable. To Wright, eclecticism represented a cultural bankruptcy to be avoided at all costs. Yet Clayton was where Bernoudy chose to go.

Bernoudy, with his well-developed taste for the historical architecture of America and the associated decorative arts, must have felt confident that he could bring these traditions together with the Organic Modern tradition of Wright. Bernoudy frequently spoke of the tradition of building in brick of St. Louis architecture, and he specified old brick for his projects when he could. His tactile appreciation for the patina of weathered old brick in soft variegated colors is quite in contrast to Wright's preference for hard new brick with crisp edges in strong, even colors. With his redesign of 7 Forsythe Walk, Bernoudy showed how right he was in believing that Organic Modern architecture could live happily in a Williamsburg Revival setting.

By March 1947, the newsletter of the Junior League noted that a "charming patio is being built in what was formerly the garden next to the small building which is the office of Mary Potter Love." The article went on to say that "the patio is being designed by William Bernoudy, architect, who studied a number of years under Frank Lloyd Wright," and added, "Mr. Bernoudy's office will be approached through the patio." With the patio project, Bernoudy completely transformed the basement office (Fig. 3–1). The patio lay midway between grade and the basement floor level. After Bernoudy's design was in place, one approached the basement office by walking down a brick sidewalk under a pergola and turning to go down a set of seven winding steps to the broad patio, also paved in brick in a basket-weave pattern. A low brick terrace on the far wall created an area for a profusion of informally arranged plants. To reach the office one crossed the patio, turned, and went down six more steps to enter a newly built glass-enclosed conservatory, added across the garden side of the basement. The timber framing of the conservatory echoed the forms of the pergola a story above. A broad door and two broad windows opened between the conservatory and the basement office, flooding the little basement room with light and extending the perceived space of the basement to include the patio and garden.

The basement room was paneled in wood, and it and the patio were furnished with simple, mass-produced, functional modern furniture of the period, almost like a showroom. Modern planters, including one designed by Bernoudy, brought the outdoors inside. Pieces of sculpture, positioned carefully on focal points both outside and inside, organized vistas within this limited space. The basic rule of modern architecture, the integration of interior and exterior, was amply demonstrated.

When the weather allowed, conferences with clients moved to the patio. These conferences were often beguiling experiences for clients, opening their eyes to the creative possibilities of even the most modest settings and the smallest budgets. The message fitted well with the egalitarian, democratic conviction held by many modern architects in the years after World War II that even the humblest building project deserved the services of an architect, that even small houses of the kind that FHA and VA mortgages were making ubiquitous should be designed with the same creativity as larger, more costly projects. For a decade, in fact, just such projects came out of the Bernoudy-Mutrux office.

House Beautiful published an illustrated article about 7 Forsythe Walk in May 1953 entitled "Add a New Room to Your Old House." The article described how the basement room had been opened to the sun and the garden outside and offered it as a model to homeowners. The general theme of the issue was that modern architecture was entering a "New Age of Enrichment." The Bernoudy-Mutrux office, with its richly articu-

3–1. Bernoudy (center) with clients at the Bernoudy–Mutrux office on Forsythe Walk in 1949. Photograph by Hedrich-Blessing; CHS neg. #HB-12216-A, courtesy Chicago Historical Society.

3–2. Pulitzer pool and pavilion. Photograph by André Kertész, courtesy *House and Garden,* copyright 1953 by Condé Nast Publications.

lated conservatory echoing the pergola above, its warm texture of brick all around, and its informal integration of plant materials, fitted well with the general theme.

Among the first projects Bernoudy brought to the new firm, one unlike anything he had done previously, was a pool and pavilion for his friends Louise and Joseph Pulitzer Jr. (Fig. 3–2). The conception and design of this spectacular combination of art, landscape, swimming pool, and pavilion owe as much to the patrons as to the architects. Preliminary design began as early as 1946, although the revised working drawings and the specifications are dated 1948. The pool and pavilion were so successful that the Pulitzers soon realized that the pavilion could be used as a place of permanent residence during the hot summer months. To enable it to function more conveniently in this manner, a wing was added to the north in 1951 with a child's room and a nurse's room that opened out to a play yard. The project received national attention when it was featured in *House and Garden* in 1953.[1] Half a century later the pool has never looked better. The landscaping is fully matured and carefully nurtured, the building has been conscientiously preserved as an important work of architecture, and the collection of sculptures and paintings displayed by the Pulitzers has grown and evolved with the passing of time.

The idea was to have a pleasantly cool, airy retreat for the summer from the Pulitzers' town house in the city of St. Louis (Figs. 3–3, 3–4). Land was available on the family farm in Ladue. In 1960, the architects described the project for *Progressive Architecture:*

> The ten-acre site was a sloping meadow dropping off to the south, completely framed by deep and undisturbed woods. The approaching drive winds upward through the woods emerging in the open at the high extremity of the meadow. We excavated at this point and created a shelf or plateau rather formal in shape. The pavilion and pool were then laid out on this created setting. Formal but not symmetrical planting became a part of the plan—the pavilion overlooking the pool and manicured-grass-area surrounding it. Beyond this artificial mesa, the meadow remains untouched. To begin with, the building site was treeless—in a way, a fortunate circumstance, as we felt free to install large trees where they would provide necessary shade and framing for the compound.[2]

The pavilion is simple, almost classical in its serenity (Figs. 3–5, 3–6). Flat roofs hover at three levels—the ceilings are twelve feet high over the main living area, nine feet high over secondary areas and the bedroom or dressing room wing, and seven feet high over the entranceway and corridor—almost invisibly supported by a slender steel framework. A clerestory window between the two upper roof levels adds to the floating quality (Fig. 3–7). The plan is unified by a four-foot module. The walls are of cypress in the horizontal board-and-batten detail, twelve inches on center, that Wright introduced in the Jacobs house, originally rubbed with white paint to give them a silvery color. The wooden trim, of the same standard milled wood that was used in the Talbot house, continues the use of flat, stepped surfaces. Solid walls and high windows close off the pavilion on the uphill, north side, but it opens on the south to the terrace and pool and lawn beyond through large screened doors. In bad weather canvas curtains can be buckled across the screen doors, but otherwise the pavilion is wide open to every breeze from outside, and ceiling fans encourage the movement of air. This very direct relationship of interior and exterior space is pleasant in hot weather but not comfortable in cold weather, even though the large fireplace works well (Figs. 3–8, 3–9). The character of the original informal, practical furnishings—with their outdoor textures—survives, as do a few original pieces, in particular the Pierre Jeanneret webbed chairs sold through Knoll Associates, for whom Bernoudy had become the St. Louis dealer.

The pool and the pavilion with its terrace are about the same size, placed close together in an easy relationship. The living area is raised just enough above the level of the pool to create wonderful vistas across the surface of the water to the landscape beyond. A flight of concrete stairs leads in four steps from the terrace to the water and then continues uninterrupted into the water—something one critic questioned on punctilious safety grounds. A second, smaller, higher pool, to one side, feeds into a broad waterfall that adds an audible aspect to the view of the water.

During the summer season, modern works of painting from the Pulitzer collection have always been hung in the pavilion. Over the years, additional works of sculpture have been added to the grounds, their positioning something Joseph Pulitzer Jr. himself determined with great sensitivity to the lighting and the arrangement of other works and landscape features. The house is entered from the east, down a landscaped walk with increasingly engaging views of sculpture among garden features, past the long blank wall of the bedroom and dressing room, to the entrance to the terrace and the pavilion. In 1973 Pulitzer and his second wife, Emily

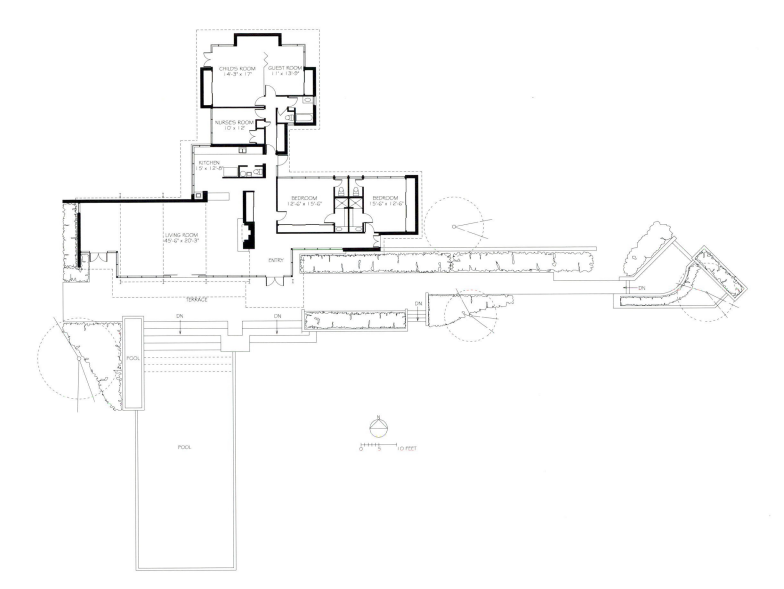

CHILD'S ROOM
14'-3" x 17'

GUEST ROOM
11' x 13'-9"

NURSE'S ROOM
10' x 12'

KITCHEN
15' x 12'-8"

BEDROOM
12'-6" x 15'-6"

BEDROOM
15'-6" x 12'-6"

LIVING ROOM
45'-6" x 20'-3"

ENTRY

TERRACE

DN

DN

DN

DN

POOL

POOL

N

0   5   10 FEET

3–3. LEFT. Pulitzer pool and pavilion, view from the terrace.

3–4. ABOVE. Pulitzer pool and pavilion, plan.

3–5. LEFT. Pulitzer pool and pavilion, ca. 1948. Photograph by Clarence John Laughlin, Historic New Orleans Collection.

3–6. RIGHT. Pulitzer pool and pavilion. The dogwood tree seen here fully mature is the same one shown in Figure 3–5, shortly after Bernoudy selected it for this location half a century earlier.

3–7. LEFT. **Pulitzer pool and pavilion, living room.**

3–8. ABOVE. **Pulitzer pool and pavilion, view from the dining area.**

3–9. RIGHT. **Pulitzer pool and pavilion, fireplace.**

3–10. Pulitzer pool and pavilion, entrance walk, with the illuminated sculptural piece commissioned from Dan Flavin in 1973 at the right.

Rauh Pulitzer, commissioned Dan Flavin to design an illuminated sculptural piece that is attached to the long blank wall (Fig. 3–10). Bernoudy's appreciation for later modern sculpture did not keep up with that of the Pulitzers, and he did not like the Flavin addition to his design.

Even before the new office on Forsythe Walk was ready, other work was coming to the firm. On October 24, 1946, Bernoudy signed a contract to design and supervise the construction of a private home for Wayne Leeman in Webster Groves, a project that never got beyond a few preliminary drawings. In November and December, Bernoudy was negotiating with Landon Martin for another residential project in Webster Groves. The proposed contract identified William Bernoudy and Edouard Mutrux together as the architects, but there is no record of the contract having been signed or any work having been done. From the point of view of professional practice, the proposed fee structure was unusual. Under both contracts, the architects would be paid a flat fee of $400 for preliminary drawings, working drawings, and specifications, plus 4 percent of the gross cost of the house for supervision and administration of the construction. The firm undertook a few other small landscaping and remodeling projects in 1946 and 1947, not all of which were built.

One of Bernoudy's friends from Taliesin, Edgar Kaufmann Jr., the son of the builders of Fallingwater, had met John McAndrew, the curator of architecture and industrial art at New York's Museum of Modern Art, in the fall of 1937 during a visit to Fallingwater. McAndrew later invited Kaufmann to join the staff at the museum, where he remained until 1955.[3] In 1946 Kaufmann invited Bernoudy to design a garden for his Manhattan town house, in a slightly irregular rectangular space about forty-five feet wide and twenty feet deep. By March 1947, Bernoudy had offered two interesting preliminary designs.[4] Both called for two different paved levels with pools, trees, simple ground covers, and plantings to create settings for sculpture. Again the project was not carried out, but it did provide Bernoudy with an opportunity to visit New York, where Kaufmann introduced him to suppliers of interesting furniture. Bernoudy's friend Perry Rathbone, the director of the City Art Museum of St. Louis, was in New York at the same time, and he and the art dealer Curt Valentin joined Bernoudy for a party at Kaufmann's house.

Kaufmann was working on a booklet for the Museum of Modern Art to be entitled *What Is Modern Design,* intended as a companion to two other successful publications, *What Is Modern Architecture?* and *What Is Modern Painting?*[5] Kaufmann sent a draft of the introduction to Bernoudy in June 1947 asking for his comments and reactions. Bernoudy replied promptly in detail, not hesitating to criticize when he felt that the example of creative genius in the face of prevalent conditions and ideologies—drawing, of course, on his experience with Wright—was not stressed sufficiently. He also thought the text too brief, even glib, and basically asked for a book, not a booklet. Kaufmann politely wrote back that the comments were the most useful of all that he had received.

Another opportunity to put the name of the Bernoudy-Mutrux firm before the public came on July 28, 1947, when Bernoudy was featured on the City Art Museum's radio program, *Art in St. Louis,* on KFUO, interviewed by Mary Galt of the educational department of the museum.[6] Bernoudy made the most of this chance. Once again he distinguished between good and bad modern architecture, contrasting the burning desire to explore new materials and new machine processes with the ill-considered exploitation of streamlining, corner windows, and what he called "that cardboard look." Modern architecture is not a style, he claimed, but a good modern building has style.

Bernoudy identified three basic principles that provide that style. Because of the new planning freedom made possible by modern structural systems, space—that is, the area under the roof—rather than mass had become primary. Because the walls no longer needed to carry the overhead sheltering structure, intangible elements such as space and light and the interrelationship of each room or area to the whole could become fundamental concerns of the architect. A second principle, with which Bernoudy was very familiar from his intimate knowledge of Wright's architecture, is that the grounds and the space outdoors are extensions of the house. A third principle, one held by Bernoudy but not necessarily by Wright, is that the planning process must allow ample opportunity for the clients to add their own personality to the design.

Bernoudy spoke as well to regional issues. Missouri's climate of extreme heat and cold suggests the use of sloping roofs and deep eaves. Brick is a traditional material in St. Louis, the heart of the brick industry. It is attractive and both warm in winter and cool in summer. The hot summers of the region call for windows to the floor, generous terraces, and a smooth transition from interior to exterior, both visually and physically, which in turn emphasizes the gardens. Bernoudy noted that with the use of indigenous plant materials, of which Missouri offers an unusual number and variety, gardens need not be much work. Hospitality and love of entertaining he identified as a part of Missouri's southern heritage.

Bernoudy continued by saying that modern architecture opens a limitless field for the imagination and for design, hence living in a modern house offers an infinite number of variations from a fixed pattern of life. Therefore, he admonished his listeners, choose your architect carefully and let him know about your philosophy of life, your way of living, and the things that are important to you. Then, when the house is turned over to you, it will be yours, not the architect's.

Henry H. Bauer grew up in Alton, Illinois, and came to St. Louis to study architecture at Washington University. Even before graduating in 1948, Bauer was working for Bernoudy, and while at Washington University he studied with Mutrux, who was an assistant professor in the School of Architecture, where he taught design. Bauer's wife, Ann, who was also from Illinois, studied art at Washington University at the same time. Soon after graduating, they began building a house that he had designed, very much in Wright's Organic Modern tradition, and that in large part he built himself. Bauer quickly became an integral part of the firm that eventually would carry his name. Bernoudy, Mutrux, and Bauer shared the work of the firm in an extraordinarily effective way that made for a successful partnership. Although there was no clear separation of responsibilities and expectations, in general Bernoudy brought in the clients and developed the preliminary designs with them, at which point Mutrux began to play a larger role with design development, after which Bauer would follow through with construction documents and project administration.[7] Unlike Wright, whose partners—including Wesley Peters, Edgar Tafel, and Curtis Besinger, among Bernoudy's Taliesin friends, and others too from the beginning of his career—remained very much in the shadow of the master, Bernoudy was happy to associate with Mutrux and Bauer as equal partners.

Bernoudy incorporated a separate interior design firm in 1948, called Bernoudy Associates, with Henry Bauer, John Luten, Paul Tuttle, and Pearl Vickroy as partners. In addition to providing professional design services, the firm served as the St. Louis representative for more than a dozen lines of modern furniture and furnishings. It had the only display room in the region for Knoll Associates, about the most exciting of the new lines of modern furniture of the period, challenged only by Herman Miller, whose products it also handled. The long list of Knoll designers included such well-known names as Harry Bertoia, Ludwig Mies van der Rohe, Isamu Noguchi, and Eero Saarinen.[8] The firm put into production two designs by Bernoudy. One, which was marketed nationally, was a rectangular metal urn of cast aluminum with sloping sides on a low, open, angular base, for plants and flowers. A number survive in the St. Louis area (see Fig. 5–63). The other was a tall candle stand for outdoor use. It was made of black metal with two circular shelves eighteen inches in diameter and three slender legs, the tallest rising to five feet in height, carrying glass chimneys to shield the candles. Bernoudy's interest in offering interior design services and his wide knowledge of modern furniture further distinguish him from his master, Wright. The design firm quickly evolved as some members moved away, and eventually it was folded into the architectural partnership. Luten continued in the business first in California and then in New York. He wrote from there in 1957 suggesting that the aluminum urn be put back in production.[9] Tuttle went on to a become a Taliesin fellow—just one of several whom Bernoudy recommended to Wright—and had a distinguished career as an architect and furniture designer in California.[10]

Richard Carney was another young aspiring architect Bernoudy recommended to Wright. Carney, a World War II veteran, was a rather disinterested student of architecture at Washington University when he met Bernoudy, quite by accident, in the spring of 1948.[11] Following an event at the art museum, Bernoudy and the Rathbones stopped at a night spot in Clayton. Carney happened to be seated near enough to overhear their conversation. When the Rathbones left, he and Bernoudy began talking. An acquaintance developed that soon led Bernoudy to urge Carney to apply to Taliesin. Bernoudy even coached him on how to do so. Both Carney and Tuttle were at Taliesin by January 1949. Carney remained, and in the years following Wright's death in 1959 he played a major role in the reorganization of that complex enterprise.[12] Eventually three separate entities evolved. The architectural practice became the professional firm of Taliesin Associated Architects. The Taliesin Fellowship became the Frank Lloyd Wright School of Architecture. The immense cultural obligation of maintaining the two Taliesins fell to the Frank Lloyd Wright Foundation. Taliesin West, originally conceived as a winter camp, evolved into a permanent base along with Taliesin in Wisconsin. Carney became CEO of

3–11. LEFT. Butler house, photographed when owned and occupied by Jennifer Ross.

3–12. BELOW. Butler house, plan.

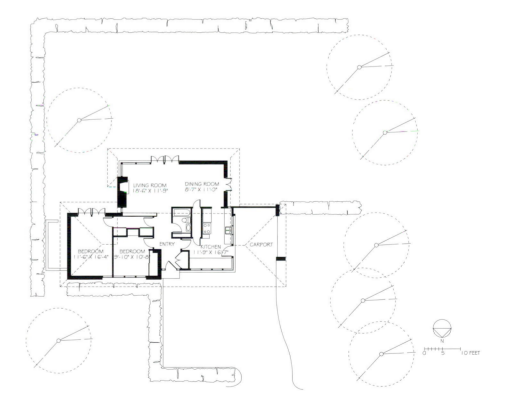

the foundation that through imaginative management of its resources has secured the preservation of these two national treasures, Taliesin in Wisconsin and Taliesin West. Carney also became dean of the school of architecture, which achieved national accreditation in 1996. He was named chairman of the board of trustees of the foundation on his retirement in 1996 and died at Taliesin in 1998.[13]

Business for the Bernoudy-Mutrux firm began to pick up in 1948 with commissions for three houses, and like much of their work, all three were in the developing suburbs of St. Louis. The small houses built for Mrs. Lucille W. Butler on North McKnight Road in Ladue and for Mr. and Mrs. Julius Klyman on Dielman Road in Olivette are typical of the commissions that would come to the firm for several years. The third house, for Mr. and Mrs. Donald Grant, although planned together with the neighboring Klyman house, was altered extensively over the years and is discussed later in connection with a Bernoudy addition to it. Through 1955 the firm would average about five projects a year, mostly residences, in addition to a few remodeling and landscape commissions.

The Butler house and the Klyman house both are of one story with a low-pitched roof and an open interior plan, built on a concrete floor slab without a basement. They are spacious in spite of their small size, reflecting Wright's Usonian ideas and Bernoudy's experience with the Broadacre City project. Both, like the earlier work of Bernoudy-Mutrux, turn a relatively closed face to the entrance front on the north and open generously to the more private garden space on the south. The young firm managed to have both projects published in national magazines, the Butler house in *Better Homes and Gardens* in April 1953 and the Klyman house in *Good Housekeeping* in February 1953.

A letter of agreement between Bernoudy and Butler, dated July 2, 1948, indicates that the firm was now charging the standard AIA fee of 10 percent of the actual cost of construction, with one-fourth to be paid upon acceptance of the preliminary designs, half upon completion of the working drawings and specifications, and the final fourth for supervision of the construction of the project. The plans and specifications for the Butler house were complete by September 9, and in a letter of September 29, the Kuni-Jacobsmeyer Construction Company offered to build the house for $18,488. The acceptance of this offer marked the beginning of a long association between Bernoudy's architectural firms and Kuni-Jacobsmeyer.

Again old brick was used for the walls, with the horizontal mortar joints deeply raked out to form continuous horizontal shadow lines and the vertical joints filled flush with the face of the brick. The brick walls continue from the outside into the entry hall, the dining room, and the fireplace. The floor-to-ceiling glass walls on the south are sheltered under a four-foot overhang of the roof. The character of the interior space is set by the ceilings. The low ceiling of the entryway, at the height of the doorways, six feet ten inches, flows into the living-dining area. There it gives way to the ceiling of the living area, which follows the roofline to a height of twelve feet eight inches. At the high point, a window, tucked in alongside the chimney mass, illuminates the high ceiling, in contrast to the darker low ceilings, and providing a glimpse of the sky (Figs. 3–11, 3–12). This is a detail Bernoudy would have known from the work underway while he was at Taliesin on Wright's Willey house in Minneapolis.

There were the usual number of troublesome details in completing the project. Stuart Butler, the owner's son, wrote a concerned letter to Bernoudy not just listing them but complaining about them. Bernoudy replied in detail, concluding: "Basically, I believe, when a client lives closely with his growing house he is inclined to see it only in terms of details and headaches, and fails to enjoy it as a whole until all the loose ends are finally tucked away and the thing becomes a unit. . . . My only advice is to stand off and give your house a chance to prove itself. A house can be successful only if 1) the client has unlimited money to

3–13. Klyman house, exterior. Photograph ca. 1948, Bernoudy Trust Archive.

spend, or 2) the client uses his own imagination and vision to make it more than an assemblage of concrete, stone, and wood. In every respect, the latter way is the one by which a client can derive the greatest satisfaction. With your cooperation, I know we can iron out all the irritating details."

Bernoudy was right. As with many other Bernoudy projects, the original owners remained in the house for many years. It was thirty-two years before Mrs. Butler was ready to sell her house. It was bought by someone with connections through family and friends to Bernoudy and his architecture, Jennifer Ross. And fifteen years later, when she wanted to sell, Tom Kahn, who had grown up in a Bernoudy house his parents built, became the new owner.

The Klyman house, in its original form, was very similar to the Butler house (Figs. 3–13, 3–14, 3–15). In plan the two houses are almost mirror images, but in the Klyman house all the rooms are slightly larger. Similar materials and ceiling designs also were used. Again a lower ceiling defines the dining area, but with recessed lights in a geometrical field. A chimney breast of plaster edged in copper against the brick wall of the fireplace was a new variation. The Klyman house, like the Butler house, was built on a concrete slab on grade, but both lack the radiant heating system embedded in the slab used to such fanfare in the Talbot house. Instead, the houses are heated by a perimeter hot-air system with ductwork under the floor slab, a system that became standard in later projects. There is no record of why Bernoudy abandoned the use of radiant heating, but the difficulty of maintaining such systems if leaks should develop in the piping—not an infrequent occurrence—is sufficient reason.

The Klyman house has been enlarged significantly over the years in a sympathetic fashion. In 1987, the living room was extended to the south and down two steps from the original living room and a studio was added at the southwest. Both of these additions were done by the architect Alvin Cullman, who had worked with Bernoudy on several of his late projects and who asked Bernoudy to review the design for this project. To the east, a utility room and breakfast room also have been added.

Bernoudy was prompted to reestablish contact with the Wrights in the fall of 1946 when he learned of the tragic death in a car accident of Olgivanna Wright's older daughter, Svetlana. Her husband, Wesley Peters, another of the original apprentices, had stayed at Taliesin and become a key member of Wright's architectural team. After expressing his sympathy,

3–14. ABOVE. Klyman house, view from dining area.

3–15. BELOW. Klyman house, plan.

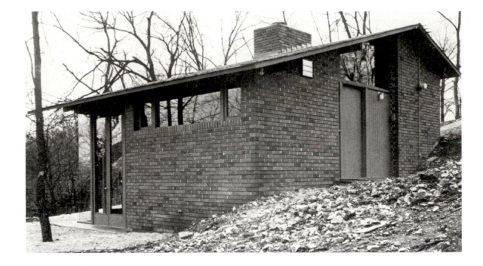

3–16. ABOVE. **Coleman house. Photograph ca. 1951 by Nowell Ward and Associates for** *Living For Young Homemakers,* **courtesy Street and Smith Publications.**

3–17. BELOW. **Coleman house, plan.**

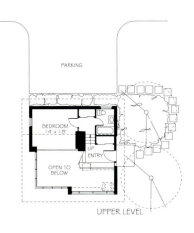

Bernoudy continued that he hoped he would be welcome to visit.[14] He did for a week the following August. While Wright was still living, Bernoudy found these visits a true recreation, but he only infrequently managed to find time for them.

Bernoudy wrote to Wright again in January 1948, saying, "I have been closely associated with a number of the faculty members of the Architectural School of Washington University." On behalf of the school, he invited Wright to come to St. Louis and lecture.[15] The faculty member Bernoudy was most closely associated with, of course, was Edouard Mutrux, who continued to teach architecture at Washington University until 1952. He is still warmly remembered by his students and received a Distinguished Alumnus Award from the School of Architecture in May 1998. Mutrux developed his own connections with Wright and with his secretary, Eugene Masselink, taking his students on field trips to Taliesin and recommending aspiring apprentices for study there.[16]

Wright was pleased to accept the invitation to lecture at Washington University, but because of scheduling conflicts he was unable to do so until November 23, 1948. This lecture did not achieve the notoriety of the one in 1939, but it was reported in the newspapers and attended by some six hundred people.[17] The lecture was given in conjunction with the general convention of the Scarab architectural fraternity, whose Washington University chapter Bernoudy had addressed about the Taliesin Fellowship in 1936. Again Wright lashed out at the failure of American architecture, which he described as imitative of every other architecture the world has seen but not true to itself. His hope was that America would develop culturally to the point where its architecture would have its own authentic rhyme and reason, rather than being just a grab bag of decorative gadgets. It was a familiar theme for Wright, and one that was given its most famous public delivery the following spring in Houston when the AIA presented him with its gold medal.

In 1950, Bernoudy began a series of projects in Columbia, Missouri, that came to him through his friendship with Thomas Putnam, an interior designer and at that time the chairman of the Interior Design Department at Stephens College. A new area on the east side of Columbia was being developed on a high cliff overlooking Hinkson Creek. Several members of the Stephens staff were among the original buyers of lots in the development, and through Putnam they engaged the Bernoudy-

Mutrux firm. The first was Mary Coleman, for whom the firm designed the smallest house of its entire oeuvre, but one of the most ingeniously spacious in spite of its small size (Figs. 3–16, 3–17). The original house, much enlarged later, was only twenty-four feet square and one-and-a-half stories high. From a split-level entry one went up half a flight of stairs to the right to a bedroom and bath, straight down half a flight to a beckoning dining-living room. An efficient kitchen opened to the left. Under a pitched roof the ceiling rose a full two stories at the center, while the wall ahead and to the left dissolved in floor-to-ceiling windows at the edge of the cliff, opening to a view that extended for miles. The bedroom was a balcony open to the floor below, providing a low ceiling over the living room area and creating a secluded inglenook of space by the fireplace. The full Wrightian theme of prospect and seclusion was expressed in this little house, which has to have been one of the most wonderfully spacious expositions of this theme ever achieved within the limited compass of 864 square feet.

Bernoudy and Coleman had met in the fall of 1948 at the home of Tom and Jane Putnam. The following April, Coleman wrote to Bernoudy that she had purchased a lot on what would soon be named Cliff Drive and was ready to build a modest house. The architect and client signed a contract in February 1950, and a contract with D. L. Johnson Jr. to build the house for $10,942.50 was signed in June. After the usual delays, Coleman moved in early in 1951, although problems with leaks around the large windows plagued her and her architects for another three years. The Coleman house was published in the widely circulated magazine *Living for Young Homemakers* in June 1951.[18] In response to a letter from a reader in Connecticut who asked about buying the plans, Coleman replied, "It certainly is a very compact and easy-to-keep house and I am most pleased with its features."[19] By 1954 Coleman had left Stephens and was a partner in the Red Paisley, a decorative arts and gift shop. By 1962 she was in a financial position to more than double the size of the house, and she again contacted Bernoudy-Mutrux. This project fell to Mutrux, and construction began in 1963, all but obliterating the original little house.

Dorothy Pollock and Janice Janes, also at Stephens, met Bernoudy in the fall of 1948 as well. In November of that year they signed the usual letter of agreement stipulating a 10 percent architectural fee. For the next year and a half they enjoyed themselves thoroughly, corresponding with Bernoudy and Mutrux as the design for their house developed and sharing their experiences with their friends who also were building in this new development. A contract with W. E. Bailey Construction Company to build the house for $23,500 was signed on April 8, 1950. As Wright did with some of his projects, such as Fallingwater, the house was given a proper name on the drawings, Hillside House, in keeping with its placement at a spot where the hill began to fall away. Two early schemes, one L-shaped and the other more open with two wings positioned at a 45-degree angle to each other, placed the carport and bedrooms on the uphill, entrance side and stepped down inside in half flights of stairs following the slope of the hill. The final scheme was a simpler rectangular plan with the entry and principal rooms on the upper level and the bedrooms on a lower level on the downhill side, at grade. The living-dining space opens out through long ribbons of windows on the entrance side at grade and in the downhill direction is at the level of the treetops (Fig. 3–18). The interior woodwork is cypress, also a favorite material with Wright, and among the Wrightian details are mitered glass corner windows (Fig. 3–19).

Robert Detchemendy, later a history professor but head of the Personal Appearance Department at Stephens at this time, built a third Bernoudy-Mutrux house near the other two on Cliff Drive (Figs. 3–20, 3–21). This time the house was placed on a nearly level site, just before the hillside drops away. The open-angled scheme that was not used for the Pollock-Janes house was used here and more successfully developed. The two wings intersect—rather than simply meeting—placing walls at 45 degrees and 135 degrees to each other as well as at 90 degrees. This scheme, which had a precedent in designs by Wright,[20] imparts a flowing, spatial quality to the living-dining area of this relatively small house. A light shelf that continues the soffit of the deep eaves on the interior and plays off against the higher ceilings that follow the pitch of the low hipped roof also helps to define this flowing, dynamic space, which is anchored by a large brick chimney at a center point. Twelve-inch vertical redwood sheathing with a V joint was used on the exterior. The floor surface is cork tile—a favorite material of the period that was also used by Wright at Fallingwater. The house, named Arrowhead, was completed in January 1951, only a year after planning started, and was built by the J. E. Hathman Construction Company for $12,116.

3–18. LEFT. Pollock-Janes house.

3–19. RIGHT. Pollock-Janes house, dining area with mitered corner windows.

3–20. LEFT. First Detchemendy house.

3–21. RIGHT. First Detchemendy house, interior view. Photograph ca. 1951 by Nowell Ward and Associates for *Living For Young Homemakers*, courtesy Street and Smith Publications.

The Detchemendy house was featured along with the Coleman house in the article in *Living for Young Homemakers*. Thomas Putnam had persuaded both Coleman and Detchemendy to let the furnishing and decorating of their houses be projects for his students. A special challenge for the students had been to work with both Mary Coleman's antique family furniture and the classic modern furniture that Robert Detchemendy had been collecting, including a George Nelson low table, Charles Eames molded plywood chairs, and an Isamu Noguchi coffee table with a free-form wood tripod base and a thick plate-glass top. The project worked well and made great copy for *Living* magazine, and *Perfect Home* magazine ran a similar story soon afterward.[21] The national publicity given to the firm brought regular requests from all over the country to buy plans. If they had chosen to do so, Bernoudy and Mutrux could have turned such requests into a steady business, as did some other architects, but to do so did not strike them as ethical. Their standard reply mentioned their concerns, saying that an architect served a particular client with unique needs building on a specific site, and that they were happy to offer such personal service at their usual fee.

In the midst of these Columbia projects, Bernoudy did manage to get away for another vacation at Taliesin. For a week in August 1949, he and the Beals took up the lives and work of apprentices again.[22]

In 1956 Robert Detchemendy was ready to build again, in the same neighborhood but on a much more precipitous site (Fig. 3–22). The low-set house was built into the hillside with its entrance on the uphill side and a full three stories on the downhill side. The plan was based on a triangular module generating 60-degree and 120-degree angles, with the roof rising to a high prow over the three-story side. The walls, of thin slices of limestone on the interior as well as on the exterior, give way to expanses of glass under the high prow. The triangular module has precedents in Wright's work. The firm had used such a module occasionally since 1950, especially in projects most likely designed by Mutrux, as is the case with this house. The area of the house was just 1,079 square feet, and the architect's accurate estimate for its cost was based on a figure of $15 a square foot.

3–22. Second Detchemendy house.

In 1950 Bernoudy and Mutrux both built new houses in Ladue for themselves, Bernoudy on Litzsinger Road and Mutrux on Sumac Lane off Dielman near the Talbot house and the house built by his parents. Technically, the new house on Litzsinger belonged to Elizabeth Bernoudy. After returning to St. Louis, Bernoudy had continued to live with his parents at the house they had bought in 1917 at 7033 Lindell Avenue. After his father died in 1948, his mother's sale of the house on Lindell in 1950 made it financially possible to build the new house, and the Bernoudy-Mutrux drawings identify the project as her house.

The half-acre site is on the south side of Litzsinger Road, sloping down to the south. The house turns it back to the road but is situated close to it to maximize the private yard on the south, and the view is extended by vistas into the adjoining property, the "borrowed landscape," a Japanese idea (Figs. 3–23, 3–24, 3–25). The elongated hexagonal roof, inspired by primitive tentlike dwellings, shelters the walls of glass and brick. In an interesting geometrical counterpoint, the walls of the orthogonal plan step in and out at right angles, always sheltered by the hexagonal roof but not following its hexagonally angled eave line. A broad chimney sits at the center of the plan, at the point where the six planes of the roof converge. The long roof cantilevers twelve feet at both ends, to form a carport on the east and to shelter a terrace on the west (Fig. 3–26). The familiar brick extends from the garden walls, pool, and terraces to the exterior and interior walls of the house. The deep low eave lines, at the height of the doorways, continue inside as light shelves around the perimeter of the house, their low elevation in contrast to the higher ceilings that follow the pitch of the roof to a high point against the fireplace chimney (Figs. 3–27, 3–28). In a small detail that was used frequently, the brick walls do not rise directly out of the ground but rest on a low brick foundation about four inches wider that indicates on the exterior the level of the floors inside.

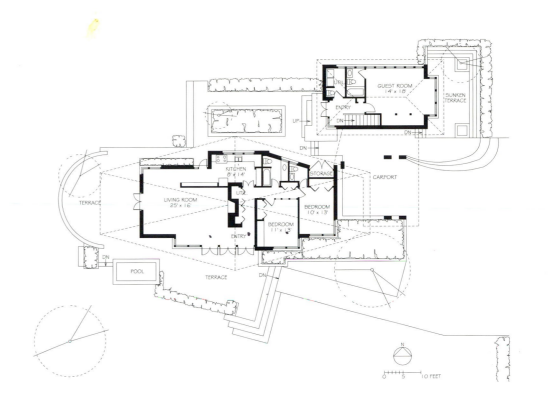

3–24. Bernoudy house, plan.

3–23. Bernoudy house, entrance approach.

3–25. LEFT. Bernoudy house, aerial view.

3–26. RIGHT. Bernoudy house, west terrace sheltered by the deep cantilever of the roof.

3–27. LEFT. Bernoudy house, entry looking toward living room.

3–28. BELOW. Bernoudy house, view from dining area.

Most of the furnishings were relatively inexpensive, of the functional modern kind for which Bernoudy was a dealer. His Chickering grand piano sat at the far end of the living room. In the manner of Taliesin, built-in bookcases formed a prominent feature of the living room, and their shelves provided room to display small decorative objects. Most prominent was a Tang period Chinese horse that Bernoudy bought in New York when the house was new, his first major art acquisition and the beginning of a growing collection.[23] Specifically Oriental details appear in the design for the house and garden, such as the shoji, traditional Japanese paper screens, in the entry hall (Figs. 3–29, 3–30). In addition to the modern furniture, Bernoudy also acquired a nineteenth-century Biedermeier dining room table and chairs. They were well built and well designed, and he felt that they fitted appropriately into the house both in scale and in style; as the house quickly became a place to interview prospective clients, they also made the point that antique furniture would go well in a Bernoudy-designed house.

On July 29, 1951, the *Post-Dispatch* devoted the entire first page of its Pictures section to the new house, providing six color photographs and a plan in addition to a brief text by Paul Berg. The house was published

3–29. ABOVE. **Bernoudy house, passageway from the entry to the kitchen.**

3–30. RIGHT. **Bernoudy house, small bedroom.**

3-31. LEFT. Aerial view of Sumac Lane, showing the Talbot house (4 Sumac Lane) at the far right, the Edouard and Elsa Mutrux house (2 Sumac Lane) at the lower left; the Simms house (3 Sumac Lane) above that; and the Geneva Mutrux house (5 Sumac Lane) at the upper right.

3-32. BELOW. Edouard and Elsa Mutrux house.

many times later, at least five times in nationally distributed magazines and books. Mother and son lived together in this house until 1955, the year Bernoudy married.

Three projects from this period, at 2, 3, and 5 Sumac Lane, the street off Dielman Road that was developed from the Mutrux family property (Fig. 3–31), probably were designed primarily by Mutrux with little involvement from Bernoudy, but they are interesting in the context of the work of the firm. They are the first Bernoudy-Mutrux designs to use hexagons and equilateral triangles as plan modules—something that had appeared earlier in Wright's work, for example in the Honeycomb House for Jean and Paul Hanna in Palo Alto, California, of 1936 and in the Wall house in Michigan of 1941.[24]

The house built at 2 Sumac for Edouard and Elsa Mutrux had exterior walls of Cemesto panels (Fig. 3–32). This fire-resistant insulation board, introduced by Celotex in 1937, could be surfaced on one or both sides with an asbestos cement, and Bernoudy-Mutrux used it in a few other projects as well. Here the panels, simply painted as finished wall surfaces both on the exterior and on the interior, were set in contrasting wood frames, providing a vertical expression of the modularity of the plan. Cork tile was used again for the flooring (Fig. 3–33).[25]

For the Simms house at 3 Sumac (Figs. 3–34, 3–35, 3–36), prices were obtained for having the cork tile specially cut to fit with the module, in parallelograms measuring sixteen inches on a side, with opposite angles of 60 degrees and 120 degrees, the form generated by two equilateral triangles placed back to back. It nearly doubled the cost. A harmonious addition to the rear was designed by Theodore C. Christner.

3–33. Edouard and Elsa Mutrux house, central fireplace open to living area, dining area, and kitchen.

3–34. LEFT. Simms house.

3–35. ABOVE. Simms house, interior showing the sixty-degree and one-hundred-and-twenty-degree angles generated by the module.

3–36. RIGHT. Simms house, horizontal wood paneling showing a detail also used in other projects.

3–37. LEFT. Pinkney house.

3–38. BELOW. Pinkney house, plan.

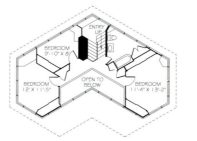

UPPER LEVEL

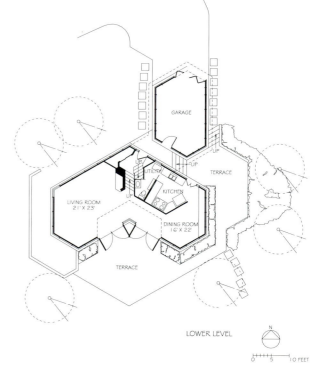

LOWER LEVEL

Two particularly interesting houses based on triangular modules were designed by Bernoudy-Mutrux for the Pinkneys in Columbia and the Schweisses in St. Louis. By the time Helen and David Pinkney bought their lot on Cliff Drive, the lots on the precipitous hillside were taken, and theirs was a relatively level lot on the inside of the street, away from the cliff. In 1944 Wright had designed a second house for Katherine and Herbert Jacobs in Wisconsin, a solar hemicycle in which the inner curve, all glass and two stories high, faces south. The bedrooms are on an upper level off a balcony set back from the glass wall and overlooking a large open space for living, dining, and cooking.[26] Bernoudy and Mutrux must have had this house in mind when they used the same general arrangement for the Pinkney house, but with the perimeter of the building following the facets of triangles rather than the arcs of circles (Figs. 3–37, 3–38).

Again the architects could take advantage of a lot sloping gently to the south, with a split-level entry on the closed north side of the house. The house is ingeniously compact, almost shiplike, in the way the many components of the interior fitted together (Figs. 3–39, 3–40, 3–41). The steel beams that carry the balcony are cased in wood and are partially supported by steel rods from the roof. In addition to the familiar palette of brick, wood, glass, and concrete, two-inch-thick Cemesto panels—like those used for the Mutrux house and which Wright had considered for the second Jacobs house[27]—were used for the outer walls, exposed on both the exterior and the interior. The triangular motif occurs throughout the design, even on the small scale of the strikingly effective built-in

3–39. Pinkney house, stairway.

3-40. LEFT. Pinkney house, balcony.

3-41. BELOW. Pinkney house, living room.

wood light fixtures (Fig. 3–42). With David Pinkney painting the house himself, including the Cemesto panels, which originally they had hoped could be left in their asbestos color, the project was kept to its $16,000 budget. Because ordinary furniture does not fit into these angled rooms, several pieces were designed by Bernoudy-Mutrux as the Pinkneys could afford them over the next ten years. A dining table was built by Jean Mutrux, and a sharp angled, hand-tufted living room carpet by V'Soske was made in Puerto Rico.

Kate Rogers, the present owner, acquired the house when the Pinkneys moved to the West Coast three decades ago. She added a wing for a guest room on the north side, parallel to the garage and harmoniously designed by Pon Chinn, a Columbia architect. She also had an end table especially built to fit the angled space by the fireplace. Rogers, the retired chair of the Department of Housing and Interior Design at the University of Missouri, has preserved the original house meticulously while she has enjoyed living in it.

3–42. Pinkney house, integral light fixture.

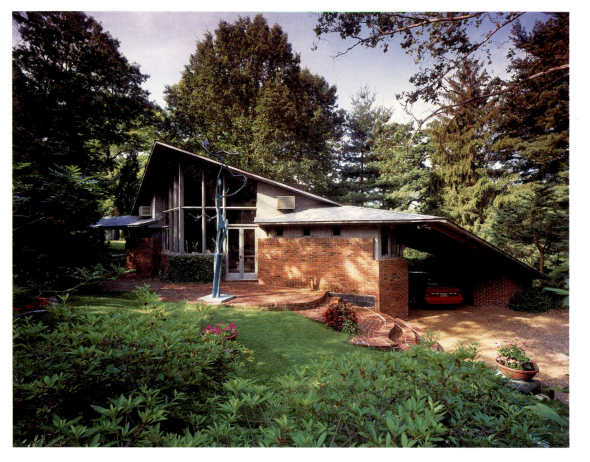

3–43. LEFT. Schweiss house.

3–44. BELOW. Schweiss house, plan.

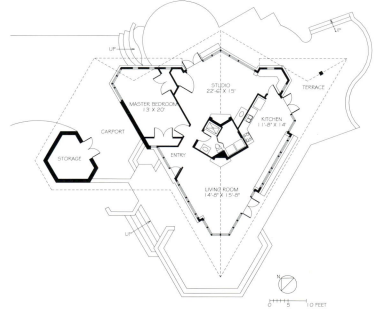

Ruth Schweiss had trained as a sculptor at Washington University and at Cranbrook, where she met Wright. Her desire to have a house in the Wright tradition led her and her husband, Frank, to Bernoudy in 1951, when they were ready to build in Ladue. Their small house is very open around a central brick tower containing a utility room, a bathroom, and two fireplaces, the whole laid out using parallelogram modules with 60-degree and 120-degree angles (Figs. 3–43, 3–44, 3–45). The parallelogram modules are outlined with brass dividing strips in the green concrete floor, which is kept waxed and polished. The composition sweeps up under broad roof planes, from the carport, which is seven steps below the level of the house, to the high prow at the back of the house that provides the requisite high ceiling for the sculpture studio (Figs. 3–46, 3–47). As in the Talbot house, small vents high in the center brick chimney lead to their own flue, to encourage the flow of air when the French windows on all sides of the house are opened during hot weather. Frank Schweiss remembers that Mutrux also played a role in the design of the house. Even though Schweiss was a senior officer in a major industrial firm, the banks would not lend money for this daring design. The Schweisses hired an electrician, a plumber, and a carpenter but did most of the construction work on the house themselves over the next three and a half years, paying as they went.

Five houses from this period of the early 1950s follow the rectilinear schemes of earlier projects. The Hudak house across the Mississippi River from St. Louis in Collinsville, Illinois, for which planning began in late 1949, seems to have been the last for which a radiant heating system was specified (Figs. 3–48, 3–49). The original portion of the house was built on a tight budget of $10,000 with the clients supervising the construction themselves. It consisted of a notched square section under a forty-foot-square gable-on-hip roof with an adjoining rectangular bedroom wing and carport under a hipped roof. The design was unusual in having a dominant fireplace mass set diagonally in the larger square portion. The gable-on-hip roof provided gable zones high up near the chimney for dramatically placed small windows. The original plan had just one bed-

3–45. Schweiss house, living room.

3–46. LEFT. Schweiss house.

3–47. BELOW. Schweiss house, looking into the studio.

William Adair Bernoudy, Architect

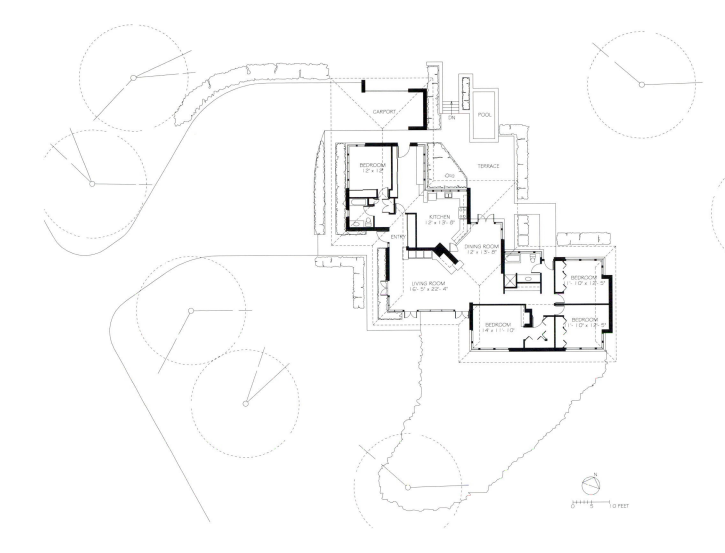

room; a 1982 addition on the east added three more and blended perfectly with the original. The dining area opens to a brick terrace on the north behind the house, with a plunge pool—a pool large enough to plunge into for a cooling dip but not large enough for swimming—made of brick and much like the one Bernoudy had built for his own house. The Hudak house stayed with the original owner until early 1997, by which time it had acquired some unsightly additions, especially a prominent solar collector on the roof. The house needed considerable sympathetic maintenance; happily, a retired architect, Archibald Hosier, and his wife, Barbara, have taken this challenge in hand.

3–50. Czufin house.

The house built by the Kuni-Jacobsmeyer Construction Company on Dielman Road for Rudolph Czufin, beginning in the fall of 1950, had the largest budget of any Bernoudy-Mutrux project to this time, $35,043 (Figs. 3–50, 3–51, 3–52). The two-story house, built into the hillside, has a brick exterior with horizontal sheathing on the upper floors, as did the prewar Doris house. But unlike the Doris house with its flat roofs, the Czufin house has hipped and sloped roofs that mount up to a gable-on-hip roof from which emerges a broad chimney. The larger budget allowed the architects to design a more spacious interior. Lower ceilings at doorway height play off against higher ceilings in the familiar way but take on new elaborations with framed cutout patterns. The treatment of the horizontally sheathed upper walls on the exterior, in which the sheathing steps out as it rises, carries over to the inside and is typical of Bernoudy-Mutrux work during this period. The same treatment was used for the balcony front in the Pinkney house and for the second Detchemendy house in Columbia.

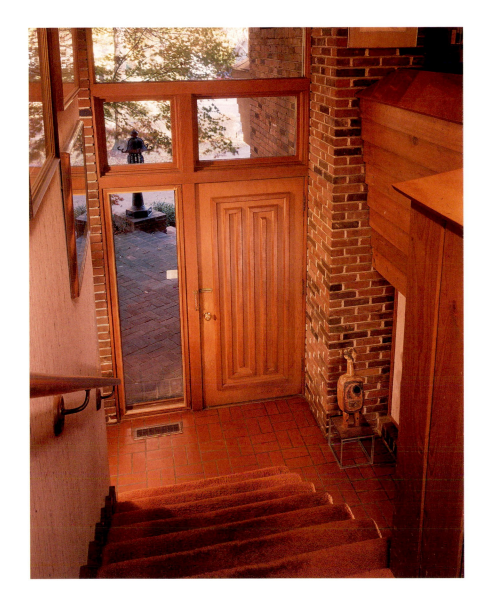

3–51. LEFT. Czufin house, interior of the entry.

3–52. BELOW. Czufin house, living room.

3–53. Moscowitz house.

Shortly after construction began on the Czufin house, construction began as well on a house commissioned by Morris and Marilyn Moscowitz with an even larger budget of $45,000 (Figs. 3–53, 3–54, 3–55, 3–56). Built on a level lot, the house has a larger, one-floor plan that opens out in more than one direction from many points of the interior, augmenting the continuity between interior and exterior. The extended eaves have flat roofs separated from the low-pitched roofs over the main parts of the house. Mr. and Mrs. Moscowitz continued as patrons of Bernoudy for later additions and alterations to their house. In 1969 they commissioned an art-glass panel from Bernoudy, something he began designing about that time. This brightly colored panel, dominated by three large circles with smaller vertical and horizontal bands, spells out in emblematically disguised fashion the name Moscowitz. Eventually, the panel ended up in Bernoudy's own bedroom (see Figs. 3–30, 5–57).

Two other houses of this period, for George Eichelsbach in Hillsboro, Missouri, and for George Lueders in St. Louis, are one-story examples of the rectangular schemes on relatively level lots. The Lueders house was built in 1952, on budget, for $17,500. Eichelsbach, a vice president with Magic Chef, initially specified a budget of $36,000 in the contract he and Bernoudy signed in the spring of 1952. The bidding the following July called for a base bid and two optional additions. The low base bid, from Mike Roehm, came in at just under $35,000, but the owners chose both additions and the house was built for just under $43,000. The project went smoothly and was completed by June 1953. The owners were pleased with the work of the contractor, Roehm, who was also a successful bidder on other Bernoudy-Mutrux projects.

3–54. Moscowitz house, bedroom wing.

3–55. LEFT. Moscowitz house, dining area.

3–56. BELOW. Moscowitz house, studio.

The Bernoudy-Mutrux firm was known for its residential designs, but occasionally commercial work came its way too. Joseph Pulitzer Jr. twice commissioned Bernoudy to design interiors for his offices at the *Post-Dispatch*. A simple 1948 scheme was not built. A design of 1954 was built, but does not survive. It had custom designed, built-in furniture and storage cabinets and a light cove that followed the perimeter of the room. Additional furnishings were acquired from Widdicomb, McCobb, Knoll, Dunbar, and Finland House.

A modest interior project for the American Stove Company is interesting for a surviving sketch of a wall elevation with "controlling lines" used to adjust the proportions, evidence that Bernoudy used the systems of dynamic symmetry and ancient geometrical proportioning that had remained current since the 1920s. A Bernoudy-Mutrux design for the Occupational Therapy Workshop of St. Louis, a Community Chest agency, was published in the *St. Louis Star Times* on July 19, 1949. The Wrightian design called for a two-story building with flat roofs and cubistic brick massing. A balcony and broad expanses of windows opened to an enclosed garden. The project would have cost $100,000, if built. In 1950 Morris Moscowitz commissioned an office addition to his commercial laundry on Brentwood Boulevard, an extraordinarily effective design that adapted all the familiar features of Usonian architecture to a commercial function.

One institutional project does survive, the gymnasium of the Thomas Jefferson School in Kirkwood (Fig. 3–57). The architectural program called for a regulation-size basketball court with seating for two hundred spectators. The structure was kept low in height to be in scale with the domestic character of the school's other buildings. This was accomplished by using a barrel-vaulted roof structure to span the seventy-foot-by-eighty-six-foot floor area and by sinking the gymnasium floor four feet below the entrance level, with broad concrete steps on the excavated slope to serve as seats for spectators. The long vault of the roof is supported by a lamella truss system that was furnished and installed for $7,691 by Roof Structures, Inc., a Webster Groves, Missouri, company that also handled systems such as laminated arches for churches. For lighting, skylights were placed within some of the diamonds formed by the framing members of the lamella roof. Once again, Cemesto panels were

3-57. Thomas Jefferson School gymnasium. Photograph by Paul Piaget. Reprinted with permission from *Architecture*, December 1956, ©1956 BPI Communications Inc.

used for the walls. Joseph Schiermeier was the general contractor. The project was published and attracted some attention, but it did not lead to further school commissions.[28]

In 1952 Bernoudy designed a concert pavilion on the Washington University campus in memory of L. Benoist Tompkins for the Little Symphony Association, whose president was Bernoudy's friend Perry Rathbone. The promotional letter announcing the summer season of six concerts extolled the pavilion for the beauty of its design and for its acoustics.[29] The original building must have been considered temporary, because it had wood planks laid directly on the ground and guy wires attached directly to surrounding trees, a feature that had already caused problems by the next spring from the swaying of the trees. Also in 1952, Bernoudy was consulted about a studio project at Washington University for an educational television station, which would have been a pioneering project at this early date if it had gone forward. Bernoudy-Mutrux

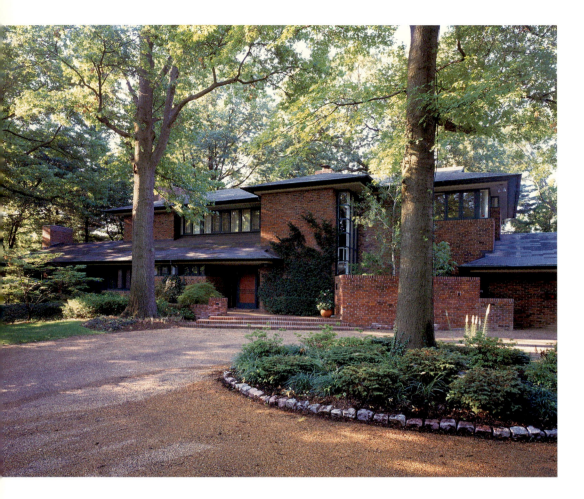

3–58. LEFT. Catlin house, view from entrance drive.

3–59. BELOW. Catlin house, garden facade.

also undertook renovations for Straub's market on Brentwood Boulevard in Clayton beginning in 1954. The most interesting of these commercial projects was a new restaurant for Straub's that opened in May 1955 but no longer survives.

The standard AIA architect-client contract that Bernoudy-Mutrux signed with Mr. and Mrs. Theron Catlin for a residence on Brentmoor Park in Clayton specified a budget of $60,000. When the project was completed in the summer of 1955, with Joseph Schiermeier as the contractor, it had cost $135,322. This became more and more of a pattern with the firm, not because its partners could not estimate costs accurately, but because some clients who could afford it could not resist the beautiful things that Bernoudy-Mutrux could give them with larger budgets.

The Catlin site rises slightly at the center where the house is located, and the entrance is up three steps past a high brick wall, set at an angle from the house, that shelters a small private garden (Fig. 3–58). The house is two stories high with low-pitched roofs with deep eaves at several levels. Major features such as the long bands of windows under the eaves and the large-scale, cubistic handling of the brick masses hark back as much to Wright's work early in the century as to his more recent work (Fig. 3–59). With the larger budget, new care could be given to many details, such as the stepped soffits under the eaves marked by an oversize dentil molding, or the fine oak floors of the interior laid in patterns, the most surprising of which is the very traditional French pattern of the parquet flooring in the entry hall (Fig. 3–60). The usual light shelves around the perimeters of the rooms are absent. Raised center panels with tapered sides set up in the ceilings replace them in the living room and dining room.

3–60. Catlin house, entry hall.

3–61. Tenenbaum house, ca. 1958. Photograph by Clarence John Laughlin, Historic New Orleans Collection, #12159.

Mr. and Mrs. J. Arthur Baer II, the second owners of the house, added a pool and adjoining pool room to the west in 1964; a young Taliesin apprentice working for the firm at the time, Thomas H. Saunders, was primarily responsible for the project. In 1972, after the Bernoudy-Mutrux-Bauer partnership had been dissolved, the Baers added to the house on the east, enlarging and enclosing a porch. The house continues to be maintained in an excellent and sympathetic manner by its third owners, Larry and Noveen Marcus, who acquired it in 1993.

House Beautiful, "The Magazine Dedicated to the Business of Better Living"—as it described itself on the title page—was a strong advocate for organic architecture under the editorship of Elizabeth Gordon and frequently published work by Taliesin fellows as well as by Wright. A succession of Taliesin fellows served on its staff as architectural editors, including John DeKoven Hill, Curtis Besinger, James De Long, and Kenneth Lockhart.[30] The association began when Wright sent Gordon a letter of congratulations for publishing a scathing attack on Mies van der Rohe's house for Elizabeth Farnsworth—a pristine, minimalist white box of glass and steel delicately poised in a picturesque landscape. The temper of the magazine began to change toward the end of the 1950s with a growing tolerance for traditionalism.[31] An indication of this change was its publication in 1959 of a Bernoudy-Mutrux pool-house conversion project of 1953–1954 for Mr. and Mrs. Harry Tenenbaum in Ladue (Figs. 3–61, 3–62).[32] The original poolside structure, part of a larger estate that was being subdivided as a result of development of the St. Louis suburbs, consisted of a large screened pavilion with an enclosed brick wing at either end, each wing containing a guest room and dressing facilities. Bernoudy-Mutrux converted this summertime pavilion into a permanent residence for the Tenenbaums. The screened pavilion was enclosed with glass on the side facing the pool and extended on the opposite side to create a large living room with a fireplace. The extension continued with a kitchen, dining room, and entry loggia. The original pavilion had a French Provincial look with each of its three units under a steeply pitched slate hip roof with flared eaves. This appearance was retained, and a similar roof was raised over the new extension. *House Beautiful* commented approvingly, "To an imaginative mind the problem of preserving the best quality of the old and giving it a fresh vitality and significance can be a stimulating challenge. It need not mean the over-

3–62. Tenenbaum house, ca. 1958. Photograph by Clarence John Laughlin, Historic New Orleans Collection, #12167.

3–63. Close house.

sentimental preservation of the past or its heartless destruction in favor of the new." When the house was demolished in December 1996, a number of the custom-built cabinets that had been designed by Bernoudy-Mutrux and built by Huttig Sash and Door Company were preserved by Larry Giles of St. Louis Architectural Antiques.

The contract with Henry and Mary Florence Guhleman for their new house in Jefferson City, Missouri, dated November 12, 1953, is one of the few signed for the firm by Mutrux rather than by Bernoudy. The house centers around a living-dining room at the center of two main wings set at 120 degrees to each other. The angled motif, generating 30-degree and 60-degree wall intersections as well, echoes throughout the house and is most thoroughly developed in the entry hall, around the centrally located mechanical room and fireplace chimney, and into the living-dining room. The plan went through several stages of development from January to April 1954. The Guhlemans remember that Mutrux took the lead for the firm at this stage, and the project file supports their recollection. Although the documentary record is not entirely clear on the question, it would seem that designs not based on square or rectangular modular systems were a special contribution of Mutrux to the work of the firm. The house for the Guhlemans was completed in May 1955.

The house designed for Mr. and Mrs. Robert M. Close in Ladue in 1953, however, points up the difficulty of drawing generalizations about attributions to one member of the firm or another. Again the contract was signed by Mutrux, as was most of the project correspondence. But this time the design, a fine example of the Bernoudy-Mutrux firm's interpretation of the Organic Modern style, is entirely rectangular and takes good advantage of a rolling site (Figs. 3–63, 3–64, 3–65). The contract

3–64. Close house. The addition to the west appears on the left.

3–65. Close house, interior showing characteristic complex spatial relationships.

with the Kuni-Jacobsmeyer Construction Company for $40,473 was close to the budget of $36,000 specified in the architect-client contract. The current owners, who have lived in the house for nearly twenty years, had Bernoudy add a dressing room on the west, modify the fenestration, and add a balcony to the living room. In 1996–1997 a large and compatible addition to the east was built, designed by Thomas Saunders, who had been an associate of Bernoudy's.

The house built for Lawrence and Jane Kahn in Ladue in 1953–1954 went through a complex evolution in design, beginning with several variations on the same theme used for the Guhleman house, with wings projecting at 120 degrees. In the most geometrically developed versions, hexagons or equilateral triangles appear in the plan, echoing Wright's Honeycomb House of 1936 for Jean and Paul Hanna.[33] As finally built, however, the Kahn house—similar to the Close house in its siting and size—is entirely rectangular. It is an outstanding example of the work of the Bernoudy-Mutrux firm at this time (Figs. 3–66, 3–67, 3–68, 3–69). Only a large angled window above the light shelf suggests the direction their work would take in the future. In 1982, when Bernoudy was elected to the College of Fellows of the AIA, Kahn sent him a note of congratulations: "We continue to derive great joy and contentment as we and 8 Robin Hill grow older together. It has been and continues to be all we expected."[34] The Kahn family owned the property for almost thirty years until it was sold to Mr. and Mrs. William Upthegrove.

3–66. Kahn house, garden view at twilight.

　William Adair Bernoudy, Architect

3–67. LEFT. Kahn house, entrance viewed from living room.

3–68. ABOVE. Kahn house, interior from dining area.

3–69. RIGHT. Kahn house, a variation on the integral wood light fixture.

3–70. First Wolfson house.

William Adair Bernoudy, Architect

3–71. First Wolfson house, plan.

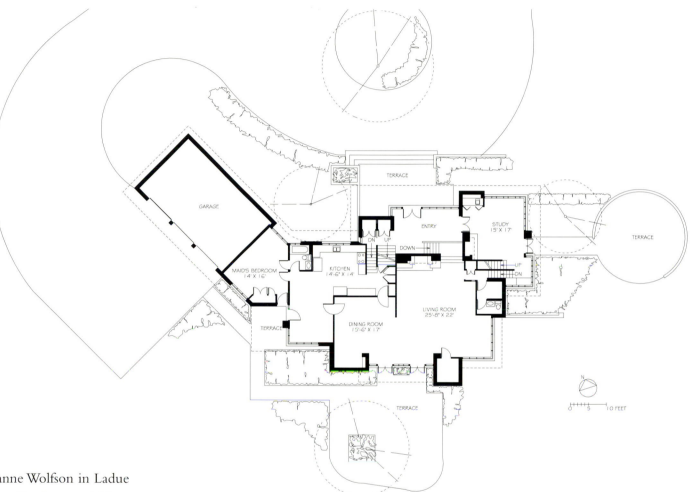

GARAGE

TERRACE

MAID'S BEDROOM
14' X 16'

ENTRY

STUDY
15' X 17'

TERRACE

KITCHEN
14'-6" X 14'

DOWN

UP
DN

DINING ROOM
15'-6" X 17'

LIVING ROOM
25'-8" X 22'

TERRACE

TERRACE

N

0   5   10 FEET

TERRACE

A two-story house built for Robert and Suzanne Wolfson in Ladue in 1953–1955 was acquired by Mr. and Mrs. Solon Gershman within a decade and has been beautifully maintained over the years by them. It is much like the Kahn and Close houses, although larger, and it is also set in a rolling landscape (Figs. 3–70, 3–71, 3–72). The entry and a large study sit a half level below the bedrooms and a half level above the principal rooms, which open out to the rear at grade. The Wolfsons hoped to spend $70,000 to $80,000 for their new house, but in the end it cost them $100,000. These three houses—in their siting, use of materials, and spatial development—represent handsomely the mature style of the Bernoudy-Mutrux firm at a moment when the nature of their practice was about to change.

3–72. First Wolfson house, entry.

4–1. Gertrude Bernoudy, Prague, 1939. Bernoudy Trust Archive, Missouri Historical Society, St. Louis.

In 1955, Bernoudy's life changed significantly with his marriage to Gertrude Lenart. The new Mrs. Bernoudy was born Gertrude Turnovská in Prague, Czechoslovakia, on November 20, 1914 (Fig. 4–1).[1] Her father, Richard Turnovský, was a banker and in the jewelry business. Her mother, Irma Turnovská, and her father were divorced following a scandalous affair involving the mother when Gertrude and her older sister, Ilsa, were young. The girls lived with their father in a turn-of-the-century apartment building at 9 Kozí Street in the Jewish Quarter of the Old Town of Prague and were cared for by a nanny, Žofie Rosenbergová. The elegance of the apartment building suggests that life was comfortable for them (Fig. 4–2). Nevertheless, in that era before antibiotics, Ilsa died of pneumonia in 1932. In 1936 Gertrude passed a comprehensive examination in Italian—language and literature—administered by the historic Charles University in Prague with the highest scores. Family members recall that she had numerous escorts but remember especially Francesco, an Italian race-car driver.

The late 1930s were turbulent years in Czechoslovakia, with Hitler putting increasing pressure on the divided country. A photograph dated March 3, 1939, which Gertrude must have saved and may have taken, survives among the Bernoudy papers (Fig. 4–3). It shows the triumphal German army marching into the heart of Prague down Na Príkopě, the traditional parade route of conquering forces. Gertrude only narrowly escaped; her family did not. As a Jew, she was stripped of her citizenship by the Germans when they occupied the country and was stranded as a stateless person. She and Harry Schenker, a businessman from New York City fourteen years her senior, had been married in Prague on February 2, 1939. On April 27, the American Consulate in Prague issued her an Affidavit in Lieu of Passport and a Nonquota Immigration Visa, as the wife of a U.S. citizen. The Germans honored these documents and on May 25 issued Gertrude Schenker a one-way transit visa to cross Germany, valid through June 24. She cleared immigration in Bremerhaven, a German port on the North Sea, on June 1 and with her husband sailed tourist class on June 4 on the German steamship *Columbus*.[2] In New York later in June, the Schenkers changed their name to Lenart and settled into a small, modern apartment at 30 Beekman Place. Gertrude was naturalized as a U.S. citizen on November 8, 1943, under the name Gertrude Charlotte Lenart.

During her first years in New York, Gertrude Lenart learned to fly small airplanes (Fig. 4–4), enjoyed skiing in Quebec (Fig. 4–5), and worked for a time as a research assistant for a medical scientist. The Lenarts were divorced in 1947, but they remained friends, and he provided generously for her support for the rest of her life.[3] She stayed in the Beekman Place apartment, and he moved out.[4] The wit, grace, and charm for which she is remembered in St. Louis clearly served Gertrude well during her New York years, and she made many friends among celebrities in the arts. In 1948 she turned up on the set during the filming of *The Treasure of the Sierra Madre* (Fig. 4–6).

4–4. LEFT. Gertrude Lenart, third from the left, with her flying class. Bernoudy Trust Archive.

4–5. ABOVE. Skiing in Quebec. Photograph by N. C. Cowan, Ste. Agathe des Monts, Quebec. Bernoudy Trust Archive.

4–6. RIGHT. Gertrude Lenart on location with Humphrey Bogart during the filming of John Huston's *Treasure of the Sierra Madre*. Photograph by Mac Julian, Warner Bros., *The Treasure of the Sierra Madre* © 1948, Turner Entertainment Co. Bernoudy Trust Archive.

At some point, Gertrude Lenart became a friend and assistant to the art dealer Curt Valentin, who was unusual among New York art dealers of the time. Valentin was a German who had worked in Berlin, first for the leading dealer in advanced modern art, Alfred Flechtheim, and from 1934 for the Berlin art dealer and bookseller Karl Buchholz. In 1937 he opened a gallery in New York under the Buchholz name. In 1951 he changed the name to the Curt Valentin Gallery.[5] A brilliant dealer, Valentin vastly extended the appreciation for modern art in the United States. He was also the most successful dealer in the sometimes dangerous business of acquiring works that the Nazis had deaccessioned from German museums under Hitler's orders.[6] The Nazis had undertaken to cleanse the German museums of what they called "degenerate art," by which they meant works from almost all of the progressive modern movements of twentieth-century art. A large auction of this purged art took place in Lucerne, Switzerland, on June 30, 1939, at which Valentin was a major purchaser. He persuaded his friend and client Joseph Pulitzer Jr., in Europe on his wedding trip, to attend as well. Another important St. Louis friend and client was Perry Rathbone, who as the director of the St. Louis City Art Museum shared Valentin's interest in German Expressionist art. Bernoudy knew Valentin not only through these two friends but also through Edgar Kaufmann Jr., his friend from Taliesin days. But somehow these connections never led to a meeting between Bill and Gertrude.

Through her association with the Curt Valentin Gallery, Gertrude Lenart built a significant collection of modern art for which she became known in New York, resulting in an article in *House and Garden* in 1954 about her apartment and collection (Fig. 4–7).[7] Gertrude also came to know many of the artists who were represented by Valentin and were his friends, as well as some of his more important clients around the country.

Valentin died on August 19, 1954, at the home of the Italian artist Marino Marini. He was in Italy on a typically exhausting tour, visiting museums, galleries, and artists' studios. Following his death, Gertrude Lenart was one of a group that kept the gallery going—organizing the previously planned shows and a special memorial exhibition for which twenty-five museums lent works—until the executor of Valentin's estate closed the gallery following the 1954–1955 season. One of many who commented on Gertrude Lenart's abilities as an art dealer and connoisseur was the St. Louis collector Morton D. May, who was an important

4–7. Gertrude Lenart's apartment at 30 Beekman Place in New York. Photograph by André Kertész, courtesy *House and Garden*. Copyright 1954 Condé Nast Publications.

client of Valentin's. May wrote to her at the Valentin Gallery on January 21, 1955: "I enjoyed working with you at the gallery very much and the highest compliment I can pay you is that I felt that I was really dealing with Curt. You have his same enthusiasm, understanding and appreciation for beautiful things."[8] Euretta Rathbone remembers that Gertrude Lenart "went around like a widow" following Valentin's death.[9]

4–8. William and Gertrude Bernoudy. Photograph by Benny Greenberg, Bernoudy Trust Archive.

There are many variations on the story of how William Bernoudy and Gertrude Lenart finally met. In her own version, Gertrude had decided to build a house and had gone to Los Angeles to interview the architect Richard Neutra in the fall of 1954. The interview did not go well, he being Austrian and she Czech. Reading a magazine on her return flight to New York, she saw an article about a Bernoudy house. She said the article was in *Town and Country,* but that magazine never published such an article; what she probably saw was an article about Bernoudy's own house in the June 1954 issue of *House and Garden.*[10] She called someone in St. Louis to ask about him—there would have been several possibilities from her Valentin Gallery connections—and was invited to come to St. Louis for Christmas and a round of parties. It was at one of the parties that they met. The visit was a great success. In her telling, she fell in love first with Bernoudy's architecture and then with him. Many years later a friend remembered flying to New York in March 1955 on the same plane with Bernoudy, who was on his way to propose. The friend reported that "he was one of the happiest people I've ever seen."[11] In April, Gertrude returned to St. Louis for the Bal Masque du Printemps at the City Art Museum, staying at the Park Plaza Hotel. Another friend remembered sharing an elevator in the hotel with Bernoudy and described how he raised his eyes to the ceiling and said in a wistful sigh, "Oh! I am sooo in love."[12] The couple soon flew off to spend two weeks in Bermuda, where they were married by the registrar general, William T. Angelo-Thomson, on June 17, 1955 (Fig. 4–8).[13]

With the marriage and Gertrude's move to St. Louis, the house on Litzsinger became a home not only for her but also for her spectacular and large collection of modern paintings, drawings, and sculpture. Because the house was not large enough for three people, Elizabeth Bernoudy moved to an apartment at 7747 Kingsbury Boulevard. She later moved to the Gatesworth Manor, where she lived until her death in 1963. Plans began almost immediately after Gertrude's arrival to build a guest house with a large bedroom and bath on the main floor and a new studio on a lower level looking out to a sunken terrace. The work on this addition was completed in 1956 (Figs. 4–9, 4–10, 4–11). What earlier drawings had identified as the kitchen garden on the north side of the house was transformed into a Japanese garden of great simplicity. The austere aesthetics of Japanese architecture and landscape design stemming from the influence of Zen Buddhism were powerfully attractive to European and

4–9. ABOVE. Bernoudy house, guest house addition and Japanese garden. Photograph ca. 1960 by Maynard Parker for *House Beautiful*, reprinted by permission from *House Beautiful*, copyright © February 1961 by the Hearst Corporation, all rights reserved.

4–10. RIGHT. Bernoudy house, guest house addition with sunken garden and new carport.

4-11. Bernoudy house, guest house entry.

William Adair Bernoudy, Architect

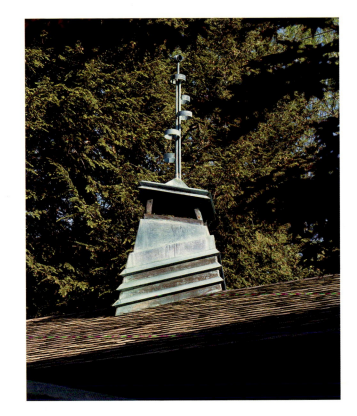

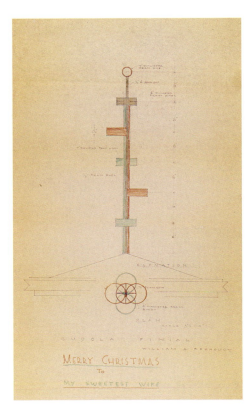

4–12. Bernoudy guest house cupola and drawing.

American modern architects at this time, and the redevelopment of this space at the Bernoudy house is a good example of how the influence affected Bernoudy's work.[14] The guest house is crowned by a cupola in a distinctively Wrightian design that functions both as a chimney and as a signature piece. Gertrude received a colored rendering of the elevation drawing of the cupola inscribed to her with Christmas wishes from Bill (Fig. 4–12).

The few decorative objects that Bernoudy had acquired, such as the Tang period Chinese horse, were utterly eclipsed by the stunning collection of dozens of pieces of early modern art that Gertrude brought with her. The collection continued to evolve over the years, but much of its base was there at the time of her marriage, including three spectacular Paul Klee paintings, a landscape by Ernst Ludwig Kirchner, and works by German, Italian, British, and eastern European artists that were outside the range of interest and appreciation of most American collectors of the pe-

riod. The collection very much reflected the pioneering role played by the Valentin Gallery. Visitors now came to see not just the house but also an important collection of modern art (Fig. 4–13). The Bernoudys were generously hospitable to all kinds of people—large groups from out of town on art tours, sophisticated collectors, celebrities, old friends, students and young friends, and, of course, potential clients of the architectural firm.[15]

None of the art was of a kind that would draw the slightest attention from Frank Lloyd Wright, yet it all found an attractive, natural setting in the Bernoudy house. In the best tradition of Organic architecture, the house and the collection together reflected the rich life of the occupants. Wright, at the age of eighty-nine, paid his last visit to St. Louis in November 1956, just two and a half years before his death,[16] and came to the Bernoudys' house for dinner. Bernoudy confessed that he seriously considered taking down the paintings, but he did not. Wright came and enjoyed a leisurely look through the entire house; finally he commented

simply, "Well Billy, this has the Spirit! I can see you have gone to the Source." Bernoudy understood that this was a major compliment, as much as any former apprentice might hope for from the master, and enjoyed recounting the story later. Henry Herold, a friend of the Bernoudys from St. Louis, was an apprentice at Taliesin at this time. He recalls discussing different apprentices with Wright, who commented, "You know Bill Bernoudy—that's the kind of person we want to come here." Wright added with a tone of parental pride, "Bill's on his own now and he is doing well. I'm pleased."[17]

It was, of course, obligatory that Bernoudy should take Gertrude to Taliesin to meet the Wrights, which he did in the fall of 1955. There were striking similarities between Olgivanna Wright and Gertrude Bernoudy, including their eastern European origins, their heavily accented English, their extensive experience with the arts, their captivating physical beauty, and, above all, their absolute dedication to the artistic careers of their husbands. But Gertrude Bernoudy found the ambience of Taliesin—the obsequiousness of the apprentices and the heavy Gurdjieff air that Olgivanna Wright gave to the place—repellent. "Witchcraft!" is how she described it later with a shudder to a St. Louis friend who had been an apprentice at Taliesin.[18]

With his marriage to Gertrude, Bernoudy became a world traveler. No longer were weekends at Taliesin and jaunts around the country to visit Wright buildings enough to satisfy his wanderlust. The first major trip came in the spring of 1956, with a honeymoon visit to east Asia and Japan in particular. The Bernoudys sent the Wrights a picture postcard of Wright's Imperial Hotel in Tokyo with the message that they were "surrounded by your presence." A certain amount of inventory for the interior design practice of the firm was also acquired and shipped back to St. Louis. Gertrude, of course, was widely acquainted with Europe from having grown up there. She had returned on visits during the time she lived in New York and had many friends and relatives in various places. She proved an excellent guide for Bernoudy when they made a grand tour in the fall of 1961, his first visit to Europe.[19]

The changed circumstances in Bernoudy's personal life were reflected in changes in his practice. As he and Gertrude became more active in the cultural life of St. Louis, the firm was able to attract more wealthy clients, and the projects undertaken during the years 1955–1965 were far less modest than those of the previous decade. Henry Bauer, who had been a key member of the firm since joining it in 1948, was made a full partner in 1959, when the firm became officially known as Bernoudy-Mutrux-Bauer. It was an ideal partnership. In general, the pattern remained that Bernoudy brought in the clients and worked with them through preliminary design. Gradually Mutrux got more involved with design development, and as a project moved into contract documents and construction, Bauer became the key player.[20] The firm gave up its attractive office at 7 Forsythe Walk and moved to a former residence at 281 North Lindbergh Boulevard. The move was meant to be temporary, but Bernoudy's office remained there until his retirement in 1986.

The large, elegant house built in 1955–1956 for Mr. and Mrs. Cecil M. Guthrie is a prime example of the projects undertaken by the firm during this period. Located on eight and a half acres in Huntleigh, a St. Louis suburb, it is beautifully maintained by its third owners, Fred and June Kummer (Figs. 4–14, 4–15). The house sits at the west end of the property, with the land falling away to the east in gently rolling contours. It fits naturally into its setting and is especially attractive when viewed from the southeast, where descending brick terraces and stairways lead to the swimming pool, continuing the color and texture of the brick of the house far out into its landscaped setting. Hallmarks of the Organic Modern style characterize the one-story design: low-pitched hip roofs with deep eaves and solid masses of brick walls giving way to planes of glass that continue around corners. In this case, the lower edge of the eaves is enriched with a dentil course, one sign of a generous budget (Fig. 4–16).

4–13. Bernoudy house, living room.

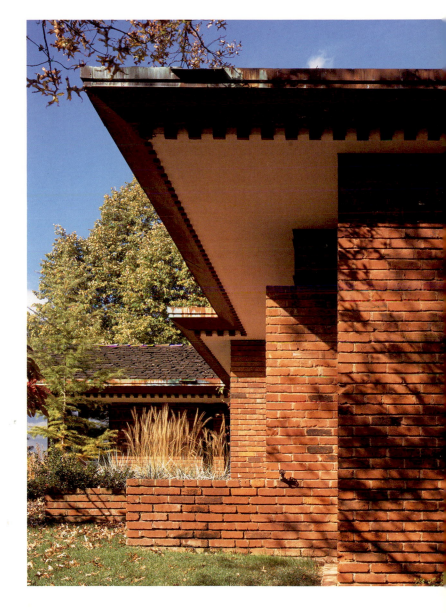

4–14. LEFT. Guthrie house, from the southeast.

4–15. ABOVE. Guthrie house, aerial view from the northeast.

4–16. RIGHT. Guthrie house.

4-17. LEFT. Guthrie house, loggia detail.

4-18. BELOW. Guthrie house, the entrance garden patio.

The influence of Japanese themes can be seen in the lattice screens placed across some of the high windows, the enclosed entrance garden or patio, and the use of shoji and built-in lights that continue the shoji motif (Figs. 4–17, 4–18, 4–19). The scale is large, and the wood for the millwork—mahogany, spruce, and cypress—adds to the sense of finish and quality. The familiar contrast between low ceilings and high ceilings that follow the sloping faces of roof planes is given a dramatic expression in the large living room, whose enclosing shape is formed by a dramatically rising ceiling faced with richly finished cypress (Fig. 4–20).

The plan of the Guthrie house with its large principal rooms shows a new formality of arrangement (Fig. 4–21). There is a strong symmetrical axis in the living room on which the fireplace is centered. This axis continues beyond the windows of the room to be completed to the east by the broad hemicycle of the brick terrace. To the west it continues as the center line of the enclosed entrance garden. The symmetrically placed broad entrances from the living room to the dining room on the north and the garden room on the south define a cross axis. The expression differs distinctly from the inglenook effect created by placing the fireplace at an inner corner and using built-in furniture to form the secluded L-shape that was characteristic of earlier buildings, such as the Butler house or Bernoudy's own house. Bernoudy's earlier designs had avoided the symmetry of axial schemes, following one of his own mottoes quoted above from his post-Taliesin days, "Since it is in the becoming and not the end where the creative spirit is alive, the symmetrical lacks vitality for it stands for completeness and, worse still, repetition." There were ample precedents for this axial symmetry in Wright's early work, but it was not used in his work at the time Bernoudy met him and in his later residential designs. Bernoudy's move toward a more traditional formality marks another departure from the Wright tradition he knew and followed so closely at first.

4–19. Guthrie house, garden room and passage to the master bedroom.

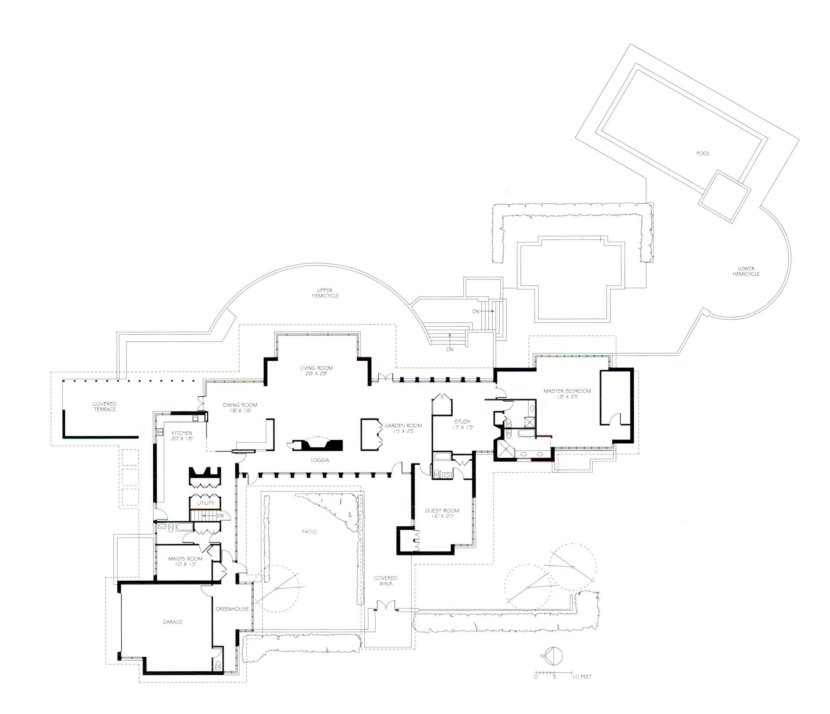

POOL

LOWER
HEMICYCLE

UPPER
HEMICYCLE

DN

DN

LIVING ROOM
28' X 29'

MASTER BEDROOM
18' X 25'

COVERED
TERRACE

DINING ROOM
18' X 18'

GARDEN ROOM
15' X 25'

STUDY
17' X 19'

KITCHEN
20' X 18'

LOGGIA

UTILITY

DN

GUEST ROOM
16' X 20'

PATIO

MAID'S ROOM
10' X 15'

COVERED
WALK

GARAGE

GREENHOUSE

N

0   5   10 FEET

4–20. LEFT. Guthrie house, living room.

4–21. ABOVE. Guthrie house, plan.

4-22. Friedman house, entry.

The current owners of the Guthrie house, the Kummers, have made a number of changes. June Kummer is an architect and gardener, and under her guidance these changes have been very much in the style of the house. A two-bedroom unit was added at the north end for children, and what had originally been a covered, screened dining terrace now serves as an enclosed sitting area leading to the new bedrooms. The original plate-glass windows, mitered around the corners, had deteriorated so much that they allowed serious water damage; they were replaced by Thermopane windows with thin mullions at the corners. The original guest room is now an office that incorporates the area that had been an adjoining bathroom. Of the original shoji custom-made for the house by J. M. Hirai, a Japanese cabinet maker in San Francisco, only one survives, alongside the door leading to the master bedroom. Originally the dining room was lightly screened from the kitchen by a series of shoji; these were removed as part of a project of remodeling the kitchen.

Shoji are also prominent in a house designed for Mr. and Mrs. William S. Friedman in Ladue in 1955 and built in 1956 by the contractor W. D. Errant (Figs. 4–22, 4–23, 4–24, 4–25). Friedman had written that he would be very disappointed if the cost went over $45,000 but settled for a final cost of slightly more than $57,000. The familiar design of this one-story house includes low-pitched hip roofs or gable-on-hip roofs with broad eaves opening to the terrace behind. The house makes particularly effective use of the screening effect of shoji at the entry and around the living room.

4–23. Friedman house, patio.

4–24. LEFT. Friedman house, entry room.

4–25. BELOW. Friedman house, living room.

In the years following 1955, the firm was busy with a variety of residential commissions. It designed a large new living room, landscaping, and other changes for the residence of Mr. and Mrs. Ben Roth in Richmond Heights, a St. Louis suburb (Fig. 4–26). The living room used the familiar motif of a low-pitched roof with deep eaves, the low eaves continuing on the inside as a light shelf while the rising ceiling follows the pitch of the roof over the center of the room. Floor-to-ceiling windows provide continuity to interior and exterior spaces, and a brick fireplace forms a focal point for the room. For Alden J. Perrine the firm designed a large frame house, with vertical sheathing, in Centralia, Illinois, in 1956. It rises one and a half stories above its level site. The upper floor projects slightly beyond the lower floor, which has long ribbons of windows with sills at ground level. A more familiar treatment is found in a diagonally placed wall connecting two wings of the house that is glazed the full height of the house. More unusual were the additions designed in 1955–1956 for a structure in Sappington, a St. Louis suburb, owned by Mr. and Mrs. Leo Phelan to convert it to a house (Figs. 4–27, 4–28). These included a broad circular garden pavilion and a double-curved stairway winding down behind a fireplace. The design for the stairway made use of embellished truss forms to articulate the upper zones of the interior, a feature that would reappear occasionally in later projects.

4–26. Roth house, living room addition.

4–27. LEFT. Phelan house, stairway.

4–28. RIGHT. Phelan house, garden pavilion and house.

4–29. Bush house, winter exterior.

A new motif that resulted in quite different spatial effects was first used by Bernoudy-Mutrux-Bauer in 1956 in a house designed for Mr. and Mrs. Frank Bush in Ladue (Figs. 4–29, 4–30, 4–31). Here gable roofs replaced the familiar hip roofs, with a slightly steeper pitch than usually found with the earlier hip roofs. Again, the ceilings follow the roof pitch, but now the windows, in strategic locations and of generous size, carry right up to the highest slopes of the ceiling. Gone are the low eaves, their soffits carried into the interior as light shelves, which oriented the view to the outside in long, low horizontals. In the earlier designs, the great volume of space contained under the roof was characteristically closed to the exterior, as the ceiling came down on all sides to solid brick fireplaces or to light shelves that projected from solid walls or from ribbons of windows where the soffits could continue out as deep eaves. In the Bush house that sense of enclosure is exchanged for a more direct visual link to the treetops and sky. Light shelves are still present, but in new locations and sometimes with large windows rising above them. The Bush house is sited so that the land falls off from the living room. The large window wall of the living room, rather than opening out to a terrace on grade, opens to a large balcony, heightening the sense of being up in the trees rather than on the ground. This sense of being in the trees happened earlier, for example with the houses on Cliff Drive in Columbia, where the precipitous sites made it almost inevitable, but now it becomes a more consciously sought aesthetic goal in the work of the firm.

A summer house that William Bernoudy designed for Mr. and Mrs. Thomas Hall at Northeast Harbor, Maine, is one of his most complex and interesting works. He and Mary Taussig Hall had known each other from childhood, and the Halls and the Bernoudys were close friends. The Halls, whose primary residence was in St. Louis, had spent the summer of 1955 on Maine's Mount Desert Island. At the end of the summer they bid unsuccessfully on a house and then bought a building lot. Sensing the rich potential of the site, Mary Hall wanted a "philosopher" to design the house, and the commission went to Bernoudy. The Halls spent three weeks in Kyoto after acquiring the property, one of several trips to Asia that influenced the development of their Maine project. Planning began in 1956, and the shell of the house went up in 1957. During that time, in April and May 1957, the Bernoudys also visited Japan. It took several years to finish the interior, and a separate studio in the style of a Japanese temple was added in 1957.

4–30. Bush house, living and dining area.

4–31. Bush house, bedroom.

The Halls named their summer house and its garden Landfall (Fig. 4–32). The site is on high ground at the ocean entrance to Northeast Harbor, dropping down sharply to the shore. To the south is a glorious view to the open ocean and a passage into the harbor called the Western Way. A large four-story building, known as the Wheelwright house, had been built on the site around 1900. It had been demolished in 1930, but its sturdy foundations of finely cut local granite remained on this rocky, broken, wooded piece of ground. The Halls had considered the possibility of reusing the foundations, but Bernoudy creatively responded to the site by positioning the new house behind the old foundations and using them for garden walls. In response to his powerful sense of the place and its building traditions, Bernoudy at first planned to construct the house of local pink granite. When this proved too costly, he changed to frame construction with wood shingles left to weather to gray, a material as common as granite in the local vernacular tradition.

The entrance drive circles around a huge outcropping of granite called The Island that is heavily grown over with evergreens. The house rests on a level site under broad sloping roofs, with the guest bedrooms on the second floor opening to projecting balconies. The Japanese quality in the attention to detail and the intimate spatial relationships between the house and the adjoining gardens is immediately evident. The plan is similar to those of other Bernoudy-Mutrux-Bauer houses of the period (Figs. 4–33, 4–34). A low entry hall opens vertically to reveal an exposed stairway and invites one in to a living room that focuses, on the one hand, toward an inside corner with a large, granite fireplace and, on the other hand, past a wall of windows to the garden beyond and the view of the ocean. Mary Hall had asked for a pitched roof that would open upward to the dramatic view, but Bernoudy felt that the ocean could be too forbidding—glaringly bright or fearsomely stormy. The two-story-high living room ceiling comes down to low eaves under which the view can be seen fully, but from the security of the great enclosing space of the living room. The familiar Wrightian spatial dialectic of prospect and refuge is especially strong. A moon window high up by the fireplace chimney provides another visual release to the outside and a position for a naturally sculptural evergreen.

4–32. Hall house, from the southwest.

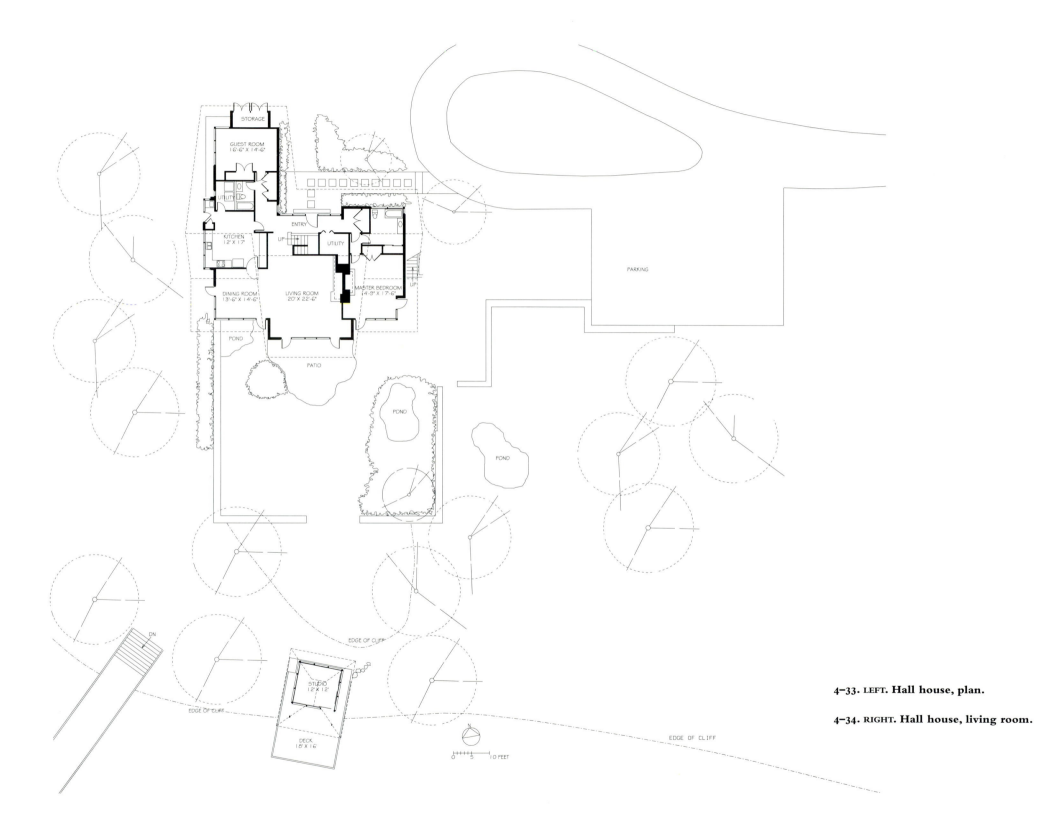

STORAGE

GUEST ROOM
16'-6" X 14'-6"

UTILITY

KITCHEN
12' X 17'

ENTRY

UP

UTILITY

DINING ROOM
13'-6" X 14'-6"

LIVING ROOM
20' X 22'-6"

MASTER BEDROOM
14'-9" X 17'-6"

UP

POND

PATIO

POND

POND

PARKING

EDGE OF CLIFF

DN

EDGE OF CLIFF

STUDIO
12' X 12'

DECK
18' X 16'

N

0   5   10 FEET

EDGE OF CLIFF

4-33. LEFT. Hall house, plan.

4-34. RIGHT. Hall house, living room.

4–35. LEFT. Hall house, dining room.

4–36. BELOW. Hall house, master bedroom and its flower garden.

Howard Kneedler Jr., a landscape architect from Philadelphia, collaborated with Bernoudy and Mary Hall in the design and development of the gardens, which run all along the south side of the house (Figs. 4–35, 4–36, 4–37). The pool set into the natural shatter rock outside the dining room, the lawn and terraced areas outside the living room, and the flower borders outside the master bedroom offer a great variety of views. Following Bernoudy's advice, the garden was conceived as a series of rooms defined by the old foundations, with natural ledges, pools, changes in elevation, and a wide variety of plant materials. Around every corner is a new surprise; from the sunny flowerbeds one path leads past a pool to a moss garden in shaded woods, a secluded, meditative place. Just over the edge of the first sharp drop to the sea is the studio built as a private retreat for Thomas Hall, near to but not visible from the house (Figs. 4–38, 4–39). The use of traditional Japanese architectural forms is very evident in this eclectic building, going well beyond Wright's way of taking inspiration from the same source.

4–37. Hall house, from the patio looking in to the dining room.

4–38. LEFT. Hall house, studio.

4–39. RIGHT. Hall house, studio interior.

4–40. Grand house. Photograph ca. 1959 by Maynard Parker for *House Beautiful.* **Reprinted by permission of** *House Beautiful.* **Copyright © May 1960 by the Hearst Corporation, all rights reserved.**

There were numerous precedents in Wright's work for flat roofs on houses, including the Jacobs house of 1937 and the Goetsch-Winkler house in Okemos, Michigan, of 1939, another early Usonian structure. The first example after the Pulitzer pool pavilion of 1948 in the work of the Bernoudy-Mutrux-Bauer firm came in 1956 in a house designed for Mr. and Mrs. Joseph Grand in Ladue (Figs. 4–40, 4–41).[21] Here the flat roofs were placed at two different levels. The roof over the central area of the living room was lifted above the level of the roofs of the surrounding rooms, and a band of clerestory windows was inserted into this space between the roofs. The principal light source for the living room is a tall, projecting bay of windows that faces toward a view. The plane of the upper roof is carried forward over this bay of windows, giving them further height. In the lower part of the living room this light source is augmented by light from the adjoining dining room and music bay and from the entry beyond. In the upper part of the room the clerestory supplies additional light to the center of the room, both direct light and reflected light from the ceiling, creating a wonderful balance. The extended plan, never more than one room deep, turns back on itself to enclose an entrance porch and opens in all directions to the court, the terrace, or the yard (Figs. 4–42, 4–43). Wright, too, had used clerestories with flat roofs in a number of his Usonian houses to achieve similar lighting effects.

4-41. LEFT. Grand house, living room. Photograph ca. 1959 by Maynard Parker for *House Beautiful*. Reprinted by permission of *House Beautiful*. Copyright © May 1960 by the Hearst Corporation, all rights reserved.

4-42. BELOW LEFT. Grand house, entrance court. Photograph ca. 1959 by Maynard Parker for *House Beautiful*. Reprinted by permission of *House Beautiful*. Copyright © May 1960 by the Hearst Corporation, all rights reserved.

4-43. BELOW RIGHT. Grand house, plan.

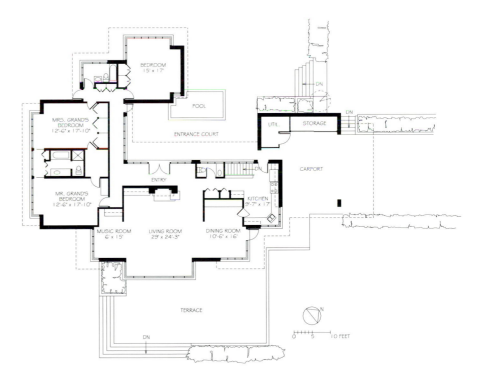

4–44. Terrace for the Singer house.

William Adair Bernoudy, Architect

In addition to the large residential projects, the Bernoudy-Mutrux-Bauer firm continued to receive a variety of small commissions, for additions, remodelings, interior designs, and landscaping. An attractive example is a brick terrace designed for James W. and Nancy Singer in Clayton in 1956, in which circular motifs play off against each other (Fig. 4–44).

For one of the projects in the St. Louis suburb of Ladue, Bernoudy-Mutrux-Bauer was engaged to design a house with a specified budget of $45,000. A small conceptual drawing of the house is dated October 17, 1956.[22] A contract with Arnold Vouga, a general contractor, to build the house for $44,688 was signed on September 10, 1957. The owners remember that their house was designed by Bernoudy and engineered by Mutrux with the construction managed by Bauer. The lot falls gradually to the south from the entrance approach, with the two-story house set into the slope (Figs. 4–45, 4–46, 4–47). The principal rooms are on the lower level, on grade at the south side of the house. At the front, steps lead down to a generous terraced entryway at the level of the main floor. From the entry one moves left to the kitchen, right to the master bedroom, up to children's bedrooms on the second floor, or directly ahead to the living-dining room. A balcony that serves as a passageway to the bedrooms on the second floor overlooks the high living room and shelters a low-ceilinged area around the fireplace.

4–45. A residence in Ladue, entrance porch.

4–46. RIGHT. A residence in Ladue, fireplace and balcony.

4–47. BELOW. A residence in Ladue, plan.

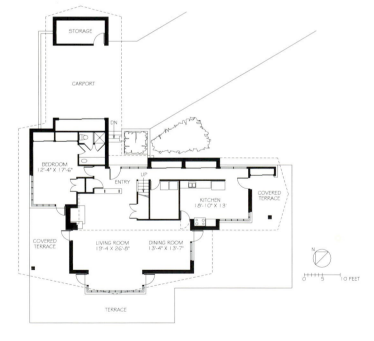

The more open treatment introduced at the Bush house, with large windows that follow the slopes of the gable roofs up to their peaks, finds a distinctive elaboration here (Figs. 4–48, 4–49, 4–50). The living room opens to the south under a broadly sloping gable roof that rises to the full height of the two-story house. A projecting bay of windows is covered by a lower, pent roof positioned within the high gable. The extension of the roof planes is designed to shade the interior from the summer sun while allowing the lower rays of the winter sun to reach deeply into the house—an effective solar design. The pitched roofs are supported by composite beams made of two two-by-eight-inch timbers flanking a two-by-ten-inch timber, resulting in a stepped profile. These beams, spaced ten feet on center, carry two-by-six-inch tongue-and-groove roof decking joined with V joints, a material that was used as well for some of the interior walls. This type of construction, with the exposed wood given a warm, natural finish, was widely used at the time. It was especially popular with those architects identified as the Pacific Northwest School who were seeking a more naturalistic alternative to the hard, machinelike forms of the International Style. The lower floors of this house designed by Bernoudy are covered with terrazzo, marked off by brass strips into rectangles measuring three feet by three feet five inches. The upper floors are covered with cork tile or are carpeted. The architecture of the main house was continued in a guest house added to the east in 1963–1964 (Fig. 4–51). Bernoudy advised on landscaping, too. The planting list included white pine, dogwood, American holly, rhododendron, azalea, Wards yew, viburnum, Washington hawthorn, and ivy. In keeping with the solar considerations used in the design of the roofs, he positioned the conifers on the north and the deciduous trees on the south, where they would provide shade in the summer and allow the sun's light to enter once they dropped their leaves in the fall.

4–48. A residence in Ladue, from the southwest.

4-49. LEFT. A residence in Ladue, living room.

4-50. BELOW. A residence in Ladue, child's bedroom.

4-51. RIGHT. A residence in Ladue, guest house.

Striking evidence of the fact that Gertrude Bernoudy and her first husband, Harry Lenart, remained on cordial terms was Lenart's effort to commission an office building from the Bernoudy-Mutrux-Bauer firm in 1957. This speculative project in Scottsdale, Arizona, was never built, and Bernoudy wrote Lenart expressing his frustration with the problems that can plague architects dedicated to high-quality design:

It would be difficult to tell you how keenly we are distressed by the turn of events in Scottsdale. On one hand by the obvious lack of vision of so called business men and on the other, their lack of faith in your judgement. As a man who has grown up with Scottsdale, familiar with every phase and direction of its growth, also familiar with the living habits and climate of Arizona it strikes me as preposterous that advisors from the outside should feel qualified to make decisions over your head, based, apparently, on some statistical rule of thumb, which even in itself is not accurate. Since cold statistics seem to be the measure, let me first contest their point of view on this basis alone. As I recall, one of your advisors from the west coast pointed out to you that $12.50 per square foot building cost should not be exceeded. Regardless of the fallacy of arbitrary figures, we can show that the building designed by us can be built for this figure or less. So much for building economics since this is only one of the economic considerations involved in a project of this nature. Architecture has always been the most faithful record of civilization—man's vision has forever bucked the accepted way, the so called secure way, by a series of thrusts forward to open up new and better ways. This is the responsibility of the architect.

It is my opinion that your advisors consider themselves practical men. They undoubtedly are according to a fixed pattern—I only wish to point out that the pattern is changing—at best, they can only wring dry a concept of real estate that is hopelessly old hat. They may make a fast buck on what they propose (I even doubt that) but they are not only destroying an opportunity to establish a progressive and stable long term investment, they are imperiling the value of one of the outstanding sites in the Phoenix area.

Why would any prospective tenant choose to occupy a dreary office in a minimum building squeezed against a building line, overlooking a dusty expanse of desert, sprouting billboards—when he could remain in the relatively pleasant surroundings of Scottsdale? It doesn't make sense. Unless you can provide something better than this, an office that men and women can take pride in—a garden they and their clients can relax in—what have you got to offer? As I see it perhaps a fast buck 'til someone comes along (as they will) and does the job right. When that time comes this cheap money making building might well be a total loss and the value of the site itself undermined.

At the risk of being repetitious I feel it pertinent to point out the development of the motel in recent years. It is my contention that as recently as five years ago had an architect proposed to the cautious developer that a motel should include swimming pools, gardens, patios, etc. he would have been considered an impractical visionary. Today it is a necessity—even the most modest motels around Phoenix now have bowed to this pattern. Similarly, I feel that any less realistic approach to an office building today is heading for disaster.

In conclusion, if your associates prefer to have a local architect of their choice do the job, there is no point of discussion. However, if their decision is an economic one, let me refer back to paragraph 2, in particular to the point that building by building our cost would be the same—any so called extravagance on our part would be the relationship of these buildings to each other and to the site and in this regard we feel this to be an immediate as well as a long term economy.

We have never accepted a commission where there was not a basis of faith between client and architect. We only feel it our responsibility to state our point of view and approach to a given problem. This long and perhaps tiresome letter is an effort to refute the implication that we were proposing an impractical and unrealistic solution.[23]

The Bernoudy-Mutrux-Bauer firm occasionally did obtain commissions for commercial projects, but primarily its work remained residential. This would become more and more a problem due to the lower profits derived from residential work. Every house done by an architect is a new design that must take into account the unique requirements of the client as well as the characteristics of the site. Houses have endless details that must be custom designed in every instance. Residential clients rarely have experience at building and development and need to be guided and encouraged along the way. All of this adds up to a prodigious amount of professional time, which is the one commodity the architect has to sell. Even the most expensive houses cost substantially less than even a medium-size commercial project, and the standard 10 percent fee never proved very remunerative.

A large, low, brick house built for Mr. and Mr. Edward J. Walsh Jr. in 1957 in St. Charles County is dramatically positioned on the bluffs of the Missouri River. It shows variations on the new theme of introducing generous expanses of window above the light shelf (Figs. 4–52, 4–53). In this case, gables rising above the hip roof have their vertical faces filled with glass. The mullions pick up the angles of the roof planes, creating strikingly contrasting—even jazzy—rhythms overhead. The house is beautifully detailed and preserves a great deal of simple, elegant cabinet-work and furniture designed by Bernoudy-Mutrux-Bauer (Figs. 4–54, 4–55). The back of the house opens up to extensive brick terracing and a pool that steps down the steep hillside.

4–53. Walsh house, living room.

4–52. Walsh house, entrance.

4-54. LEFT. Walsh house, foyer.

4-55. BELOW. Walsh house, dining area.

A house designed for Mrs. Jay C. Hormel and built in 1958 in Bel Aire, California, stands in sharp contrast to the midwestern work of Bernoudy-Mutrux-Bauer (Figs. 4–56, 4–57, 4–58). From a low chimney mass at the center, the house extended far to either side in a precisely symmetrical composition. The crisp, clear volumes with stuccoed surfaces in light colors, the ribbons of windows and the window walls of plate glass carried in metal frames, and the flat roof planes delicately carried on exposed steel pipe columns all seem closer to the International Style than the Organic Modern architecture of Wright's followers. Although pipe columns were basic structural elements in the fifties and Bernoudy-Mutrux-Bauer had used them frequently, previously they had always been encased in wood. The appearance of the house must relate to the fact that Bel Aire is a wealthy, exclusive section of greater Los Angeles. Just as Bernoudy from the beginning had responded to the old tradition for brick architecture in St. Louis by specifying used brick for most of his buildings there, or with the Hall house in Maine had turned to two possibilities drawn from local vernacular traditions, he perhaps sought a modernistic expression for the Hormel house related to the cultural and architectural context of southern California. It is impressive to see how well the firm could design in what at first seems to have been an antithetical style.

4–56. Hormel house, rear exterior view.

4–57. LEFT. Hormel house, living room with Los Angeles skyline.

4–58. BELOW. Hormel house, moon view windows.

At the same time, the Bernoudy-Mutrux-Bauer firm produced one of the finest examples in its familiar style for Dr. and Mrs. C. M. Waggoner in Columbia, Missouri, near the group of houses the firm had designed around 1950. Again the contact between the clients and the architects was Tom Putnam. The house is poised on a steep hill near the edge of a cliff that drops off on the east (Figs. 4–59, 4–60). The ground level at that side of the house is a full story and a half below the grade at the entry terrace, putting the basement at ground level on the east. A long wall of floor-to-ceiling windows projects from the east side of the house, extending from the dining room past the kitchen to the family room and looking out to the treetops. Brick terraces at the entrance and to the south off the living room are dug into the hillside or built up from it.

Unlike St. Louis, Columbia had no used brick market. When the architects suggested used brick, Dr. Waggoner arranged to buy it from a mid-nineteenth-century building in nearby Fulton that was being demolished. The Waggoners devoted many evenings to cleaning the brick of old mortar, keeping just ahead of their brick mason, Edward Sullivan. D. L. Johnson was the general contractor. Early designs were begun in the summer of 1957, construction drawings were completed by February 1958, and the owners moved into the house in 1960.

From the entry, one goes down five steps to the principal rooms or up a flight of stairs to the second-floor bedrooms. A large hallway of unusual spatial complexity rises a full two stories in height and leads directly to virtually every room in the house (Figs. 4–61, 4–62). This space is given definition and articulation by the elegantly finished woodwork in the railings, partitions, edging strips, and free-floating beams that support nothing. The high ceiling of the living room follows the pitch of the gable roof. In the style introduced in the Bush house, windows set in a broad projecting bay rise from the floor line to the ceiling plane of the roof, supported by very simple, elegant window frames, with the plate glass mitered at the corners. The unusual ladderlike trellises at the forward corners of the roof were an afterthought, designed to correct unanticipated sagging of the deeply cantilevered roof planes. Throughout the house, attention has been paid to the quality of the materials and their finish as well as to the design of the details and of the furniture custom-made for the house (Figs. 4–63, 4–64).

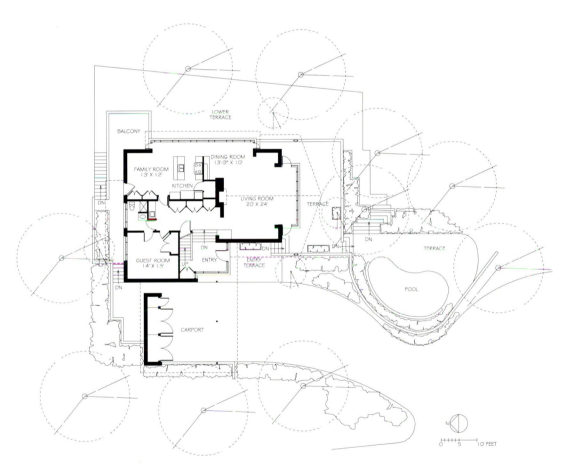

4–59. Waggoner house, plan.

4–60. LEFT. Waggoner house, from the southwest showing the living room terrace.

4–61. BELOW. Waggoner house, entry.

4–62. RIGHT. Waggoner house, looking toward the living room from the lower level of the entry.

4-63. LEFT. Waggoner house, custom-designed furniture in the living room.

4-64. BELOW. Waggoner house, a variation on the integral light fixture.

The house of 1959–1960 that Bernoudy-Mutrux-Bauer built for Mr. and Mrs. John Childress in Ladue shows another variation on the new motif of high windows following the slope of a gable roof (Fig. 4–65). In this design, flat roofs are combined with a low-rising gable roof over the living room and the dining room. Narrow slits of windows follow the sloping ceiling planes to their peak, offering a glimpse of the treetops and the sky. Equally striking by its absence is that strong separation of the ceiling form and volume from the walls and spaces below that was found in the earlier houses, a separation clearly articulated by prominent light shelves with unbroken wooden fascias. Traces of these forms appear along the edges of the lower ceilings and at the tops of cabinets and space dividers, playing a decorative role rather than the strong architectonic role seen in the earlier houses. In other areas walls rise uninterrupted to meet the ceilings; in the gable ends of the living and dining space they terminate in triangular shapes at the lower edge of the high slit windows.

Also in 1959-1960, Bernoudy-Mutrux-Bauer designed a house for Dr. and Mrs. Fred Tietjens in Jefferson City on a dramatic site overlooking the Missouri River. The drawings give both "Tree House" and "Hillside House" as titles for this project. Although preliminary sketches were not done by Bernoudy, the house is typical of the work of the firm at this time.

4–65. Childress house, living room.

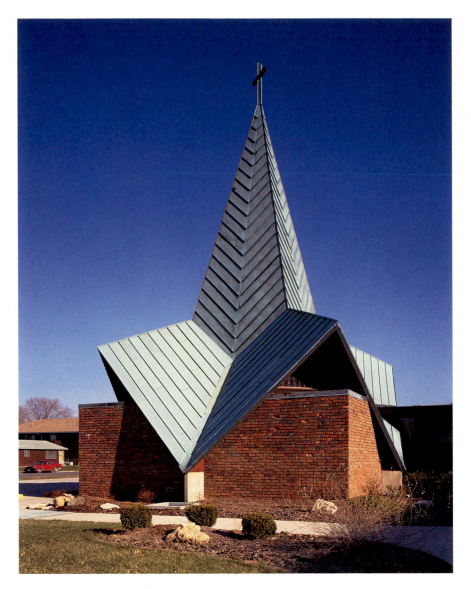

4–66. First Methodist Church, chapel.

When the congregation of the First Methodist Church in East Alton, Illinois, decided to build a large new church complex in 1958, the architectural commission came to Bernoudy-Mutrux-Bauer through Hank Bauer. He had grown up in Alton and attended the church along with other members of his family. The plan included a large educational wing, offices, social rooms, a chapel, and a large sanctuary. When construction began in 1961 the congregation lacked sufficient funds for the entire complex, and construction of the sanctuary was postponed. When the sanctuary was finally added in 1986, it was built to a different design by another architect, John Rapp. The original chapel is a small, centralized building under a dramatic roof (Figs. 4–66, 4–67). The plan is square, measuring thirty feet on each side; the building is entered at a corner and organized internally on the diagonal. High brick walls cut off any view of the outside. In the lower zone of the dramatic roof, four gables rise over the four corners of the square plan from low piers outside the center point of each wall. They cover the interior space with eight sharply faceted ceiling planes. Under the gables above the tops of the brick wall, triangular stained-glass windows illuminate the interior, reflecting the warm soft colors of the brick walls and the natural finish of the wood decking of the roof. The interior, strongly focused in on itself, is an arresting space and yet one of repose. The lower zone of the roof in turn carries a steeply pointed spire that rises in alignment with the large square plan of the chapel below. The twelve surfaces of the roof are covered with copper, and the pattern of the standing seam joints of the copper sheathing enlivens the roof's strong geometry.

The original sanctuary, which was not built, was also designed on a square plan (Fig. 4–68). Four large piers, set in from the corners, would have created the form of a large Greek cross, an ancient church plan. The piers were to carry a balcony around three sides, while on the fourth side was to be a raised platform for the chancel. In plan this unbuilt sanctuary bears a striking resemblance to Frank Lloyd Wright's Unity Temple of 1904 in Oak Park, Illinois, a building Bernoudy certainly had seen numerous times during his visits to Chicago. The two would have been different in elevation, however. Wright's church rises as a cube of space with a flat skylight in the roof, while the Alton design called for a tent-like roof rising to a peak over the center.

4–67. BELOW. **First Methodist Church, chapel interior.**

4–68. RIGHT. **First Methodist Church, plan of the unbuilt sanctuary.**

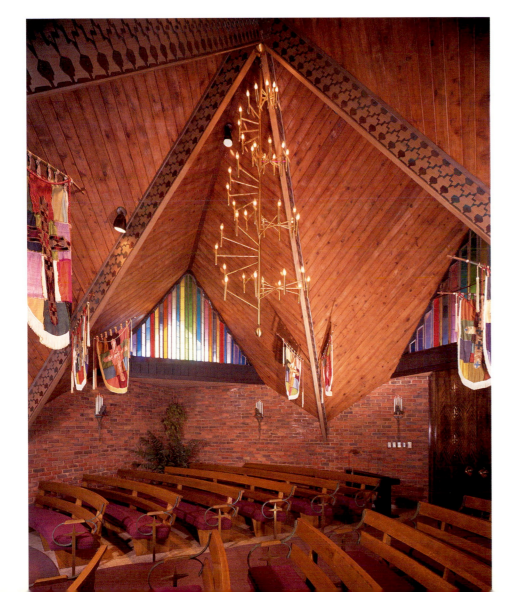

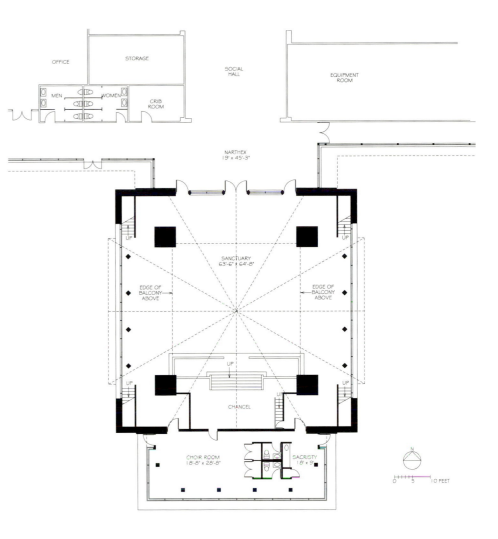

The chapel at First Methodist Church could be considered a small-scale study for the most admired religious project of the Bernoudy-Mutrux-Bauer firm, Temple Emanuel on Conway Road in the St. Louis suburb of Creve Coeur (Fig. 4–69). Temple Emanuel was organized in 1956, the fifth Reform Jewish congregation in St. Louis and the first new one in seventy years. In 1960, when the congregation had grown to the point that it could begin seriously to plan for a new place of worship, a building committee was named with Arthur Monsey and Paul Ullman as cochairmen. Monsey was a professional engineer, and through his acquaintance with Edouard Mutrux, the commission for the new temple came to Bernoudy-Mutrux-Bauer.[24] In April 1961, as architectural work progressed, Arthur Scharff Jr. became president of the congregation.[25] In June 1961, Dr. Joseph R. Rosenbloom, who had been the rabbi of Adath Israel Temple in Lexington, Kentucky, came to St. Louis to become the new rabbi of Temple Emanuel, a post he still held in 1998. He arrived in time to participate in the design and construction of the new building. In December 1961, Monsey commissioned a house for himself and his large family from Bernoudy-Mutrux-Bauer, a project that Mutrux designed.

The congregation had acquired 8.6 acres of land on the south side of Conway Road, just west of Ballas Road, on October 20, 1960. The plans for the new building were approved by the congregation in August 1961, and ground breaking occurred on September 24, 1961 (Figs. 4–70, 4–71). As parts of the new building became ready, they were put into use. In March 1962, Rabbi Rosenbloom moved into his new office. Steady progress was made during the summer of 1962, and on October 7 the Sunday school, an important activity of the congregation requiring a major portion of the new building, was ready. A cornerstone-laying ceremony took place on October 21. A formal dedication service for the congregation was held on Friday evening, January 25, 1963, and a public dedication ceremony on the following Sunday afternoon.

The brick sanctuary, on a hexagonal plan carrying a high, dramatically faceted roof covered in copper, now with a green patina, recalls the little Methodist chapel in East Alton (Figs. 4–72, 4–73). From the sanctuary, two projecting wings originally contained seventeen classrooms, offices, a library, a kitchen, and a large social hall. The six brick walls of the sanctuary rise to high-pointed gables containing circular windows. The six

principal roof beams of laminated wood rest on the peaks of these gables and curve up sharply at midpoint, converging at the peak of the roof. Secondary beams run from the midpoints of the principal beams down to the junctions of the six faces of the brick walls. Exposed wood planking completes the ceiling surfaces. This system of wood framing and decking was employed widely at this time and was available from several major fabricators.[26] Even geometrically elaborate roofs like this were reasonable in cost. In this case, the roof was supplied by the Weyerhaeuser Company under the trade name Rilco. The components were made in the Weyerhaeuser factory in Albert Lea, Minnesota, and shipped to the site ready for erection. The entire roof frame was erected with one light crane and a minimum of scaffolding in just a little more than two days. The building, measuring 23,740 square feet, cost a total of $326,577.00, or $13.76 per square foot.

The sanctuary has a very large balcony to accommodate the greater number of worshipers who attend services on High Holy Days. Rabbi Rosenbloom explained, "The sanctuary of our new temple was carefully designed to provide a warm, intimate atmosphere for our relatively small congregation. There are only 150 seats in the downstairs area, and from here, worshipers can follow the soaring wood beams right to the apex of the synagogue without being aware of the 250-seat balcony above. . . . [the] laminated beams and exposed wood deck are finished natural, adding an extra touch of warmth to our sanctuary. The six-sided structure forms a Star of David and it is also reminiscent of the 'tent of meeting' in which the Ark was carried in the wilderness."[27]

The interior focuses on the familiar ritual furnishings of Reform Jewish synagogues (Figs. 4–74, 4–75).[28] A large, carefully finished wood ark is placed against one brick wall with a wood lattice continuing left and right across the wall. Kurt J. Matzdorf, a silversmith from New Paltz, New York, crafted the decorative work, including the Ten Commandments on the doors of the ark and the eternal light that hangs in front of it, working closely with Mutrux and Rosenbloom on the design. On the bema, or raised platform that extends out from the ark, stand a pulpit and the table from which the Torah scrolls are read. Jean Mutrux did custom cabinet work for the project. Candle stands and four large chairs complete the furnishings of the area, sometimes called the altar in Reform practice.

4-69. Temple Emanuel.

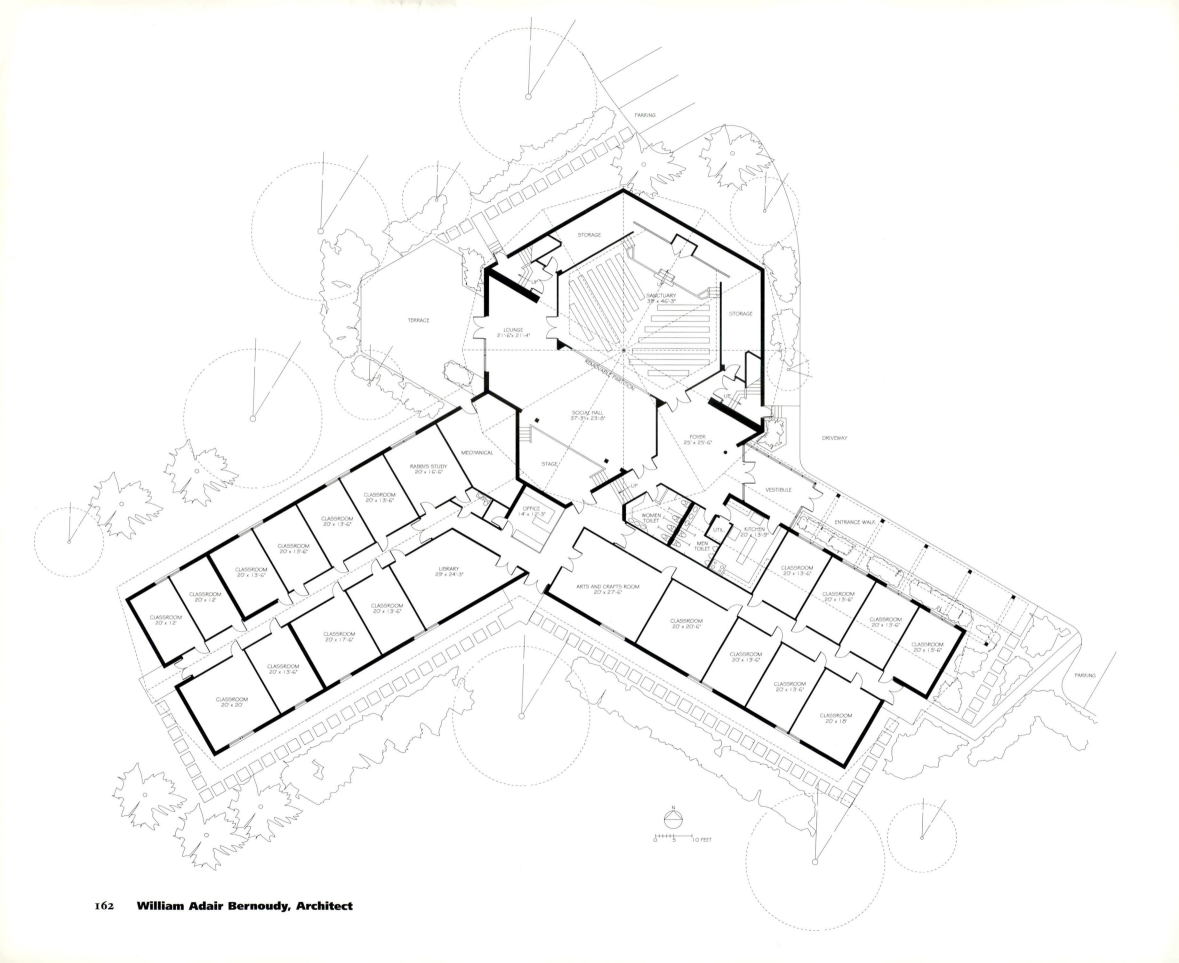

PARKING

STORAGE

SANCTUARY
39' x 46'-3"

STORAGE

TERRACE

LOUNGE
21'-6"x 21'-4"

REMOVABLE PARTITION

UP

UP

SOCIAL HALL
37'-3"x 23'-8"

FOYER
25' x 25'-6"

DRIVEWAY

MECHANICAL

STAGE

UP

VESTIBULE

RABBI'S STUDY
20' x 16'-6"

CLASSROOM
20' x 13'-6"

CLASSROOM
20' x 13'-6"

OFFICE
14' x 12'-3"

WOMEN
TOILET

UTIL.

KITCHEN
20' x 13'-9"

ENTRANCE WALK

CLASSROOM
20' x 12'

LIBRARY
29' x 24'-3"

MEN
TOILET

CLASSROOM
20' x 13'-6"

CLASSROOM
20' x 12'

CLASSROOM
20' x 13'-6"

ARTS AND CRAFTS ROOM
20' x 27'-6"

CLASSROOM
20' x 13'-6"

CLASSROOM
20' x 17'-6"

CLASSROOM
20' x 13'-6"

CLASSROOM
20' x 20'-6"

CLASSROOM
20' x 13'-6"

CLASSROOM
20' x 20'

CLASSROOM
20' x 13'-6"

CLASSROOM
20' x 13'-6"

CLASSROOM
20' x 18'

PARKING

N

0   5   10 FEET

162 William Adair Bernoudy, Architect

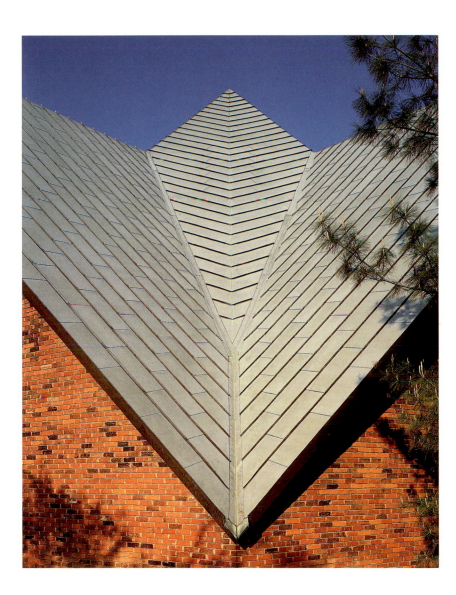

4–70. LEFT. Temple Emanuel, plan.

4–71. ABOVE. Temple Emanuel, aerial view.

4–72. RIGHT. Temple Emanuel, roof detail.
Photograph ca. 1990 by Robert Pettus.

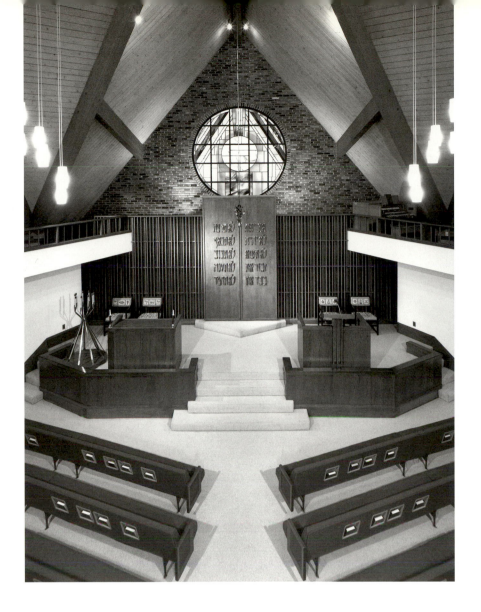

4–73. LEFT. Temple Emanuel, interior.

4–74. ABOVE. Temple Emanuel, bema.

4–75. RIGHT. Temple Emanuel, detail of direct and indirect light fixtures.

In February 1965, the board of the congregation voted to add four classrooms according to construction plans by Bernoudy-Mutrux-Bauer. The new rooms were ready for the opening of the Religious School the following September. In 1965 the state of Missouri condemned part of the grounds, including a portion of the parking area, for the construction of the new outer-belt highway (now known as I–270). This led to an extensive new landscaping plan, prepared by Edouard Mutrux and landscape architect Robert Goetz. In 1967 a new vestibule was added outside the main entrance to make the foyer more comfortable in cold weather. By this date the Bernoudy-Mutrux-Bauer firm had been dissolved, and for the vestibule project the congregation turned to Mutrux rather than Bernoudy.

Many attractive works of art have been added from time to time, often as gifts. In the spring of 1964, Isabel and Howard Baer gave a large wood carving of a hand by the sculptor Clark Fitzgerald, which was placed on the east side of the temple on the advice of the artist and Bernoudy. In 1966 new tapestry covers for the four altar chairs, made by four women of the congregation, were dedicated. With rich symbolism, the designs are based on floor mosaics in a fourth-century synagogue in Israel. In 1968 an art committee was formed to determine the appropriateness of adding stained-glass windows for the sanctuary. It recommended extending an invitation to Margaret Traherne, an English artist who had designed windows for cathedrals in Coventry, Liverpool, and Manchester. She came to St. Louis as the guest of Mr. and Mrs. Howard Baer, and the congregation commissioned her to design, execute, and install the windows, which were dedicated on January 18, 1970. Bernoudy was said to have been inspired to design colored-glass screens later in his career from watching Traherne at work.[29] New candlesticks for the sanctuary were given in honor of the dedication of the windows. Also in 1968 the congregation acquired a menorah, handwrought of bronze and gold-plated, created by Heikki Seppa of the art faculty at Washington University.

Wright designed only one synagogue during his career, the Beth Sholom Synagogue in Elkins Park, Pennsylvania.[30] He completed his design in 1954, and the building was dedicated in 1959. It was published widely, and the members of the Bernoudy-Mutrux-Bauer firm must have known about it. There are some similarities between the two buildings—in their centralized form with abstract reference to the Jewish tradition of tents as places of worship, in the ritual arrangement of the interiors, and in the six-sided plans. But Beth Sholom Synagogue is much larger than Temple Emanuel, seating 1,030, and its great, high roof is made of glass and metal. A closer parallel to Temple Emanuel can be found in the work of Pietro Belluschi, one of the founders of the Pacific Northwest School of modernism who was known for his religious buildings.[31] His first synagogue was Temple Israel in Swampscott, Massachusetts, built in 1953–1956. It does not have as dramatic a roof form as does Temple Emanuel, but it does incorporate a centralized space within a six-sided plan, has a similar interior arrangement and furnishings, and has high windows on its six walls filled with translucent tinted glass. But more important is the character of the interior, similar to those of the much admired churches Belluschi had been building since World War II. In both Temple Israel and Temple Emanuel, the natural finished wood of the laminated beams and the roof decking, the screens and the walls of richly textured brick, the sensitively distributed light, and the strategic contrast of a few liturgical features and objects create quiet, serene spaces focused on worship.

During the 1940s and 1950s architects had successfully addressed the challenge of creating beautiful and appropriate religious buildings using the forms and ideas of modern architecture. A growing number of built examples reflected the consensus that had developed from lively discussions among architects and theologians at conferences and in publications. In 1962 Albert Christ-Janer and Mary Mix Foley richly summed up this important milestone in the evolution of the modern movement in a book with the appropriate title *Modern Church Architecture: A Guide to the Form and Spirit of 20th Century Religious Buildings.*[32] Temple Emanuel takes its place handsomely in the mainstream of this movement in religious architecture, the range of which can be seen in two St. Louis religious buildings built at the same time as Temple Emanuel and both designed by Hellmuth, Obata, and Kassabaum. Temple Israel is a large, clean-lined, horizontal building. Here the architects solved the problem of large attendance on High Holy Days with a folding wall between the sanctuary and an adjoining auditorium. In contrast to the static, all-purpose forms of Temple Israel, the St. Louis Abbey (better known by its earlier name, the Priory Chapel) engages in a kind of structural gymnastics with a triple tier of thin-shell concrete vaults. Between them, and emphasizing the creation of a numinous atmosphere, lie buildings like Temple Emanuel. The St. Louis building that most fully represents the modern movement in ecclesiastical architecture—especially in its parabolic plan—is Resurrection Roman Catholic Church of 1952, by Joseph D. Murphy of the firm Murphy and Mackey.[33]

A similar consensus had formed in residential architecture. Gone were the old polemics of the 1930s when Bernoudy first became an advocate for Organic Modern architecture. At that time he could draw sharp distinctions both between it and traditional revivalism and between it and the new modernistic International Style. In the late 1930s one had to seek out an architect to design a modern house, and it was a pioneering gesture to do so. But by 1960 it was hard, but not impossible, to find an architect who would do a sophisticated, well-informed design in one of the revival styles. And by 1960, that distinction between the Wright tradition and the architecture of the International Style, which had seemed so clear earlier, had been bridged in many accommodating ways. In the United States a number of regional schools had developed—the Bay Region style, the Pacific Northwest style, the Bloomfield Hills style, the New Canaan style, and others—which had explored the middle ground,

and out of that process a consensus was appearing. At the same time, something similar was happening in Europe, in the form of a renewed appreciation for Scandinavian architecture and design. The big challenge now seemed to be to consolidate the gains of the modern movement and sort out its failures—failures of careless plans, tricky elevations, technological exhibitionism, wasteful gadgetry, deplorable craftsmanship, and a mindless reliance on architectural clichés.[34]

In *Contemporary Houses, Evaluated by Their Owners,* published in 1961, Thomas H. Creighton and Katherine M. Ford argue that modern houses are not simply a matter of flat roofs and innovative construction systems, and they identify five basic traits by which modern houses should be identified: (1) openness of planning, with space flowing from one area to another; (2) openness to the outdoors through the use of glass walls; (3) a flexibility in function that reflects the freedom and informality of modern family life; (4) materials and finishes chosen for their natural color, texture, and warmth, rather than interiors decorated through applied and added means; and (5) the elimination of architectural ornament—no moldings, no trim, no references to older styles—to provide a simple, neutral background for the objects and activities the owners might introduce.[35] Although these concepts sound as if they were derived from the Wright tradition, every example illustrated in the book is by an architect grounded in the tradition of European modernism and the International Style. (The one St. Louis architect included was Harris Armstrong.) It is also important to remember that, through the influence of Walter Gropius, the curriculum of the Bauhaus had taken over nearly every school of architecture in the United States by this date. But the machine-age aesthetics that earlier had seemed to be at the heart of the European modern movement had now become just a part of it, and it had even become common to question the historical accuracy and pertinence of the term *International Style.*

4–76. Horan house, view from the living room to the entry.

The decade from 1955 to 1965 was a busy one for Bernoudy, as the Bernoudy-Mutrux-Bauer firm averaged more than seven projects a year, nearly all of them houses. During these years the firm's handling of Wright's Usonian themes evolved, sometimes toward the use of more open and unarticulated space or toward an openness to the outdoors at the level of the trees rather than at ground level, at other times toward a more elegantly formal plan and away from the flowing open plan, and at still other times toward richer finish detail and sumptuous materials. The houses designed from 1960 to 1965 play rich variations on these themes.

A house built for Mr. and Mrs. John J. Horan in Creve Coeur, a St. Louis suburb, in 1960 offers an interesting example of geometrical lattice-work motifs in garden walls and balcony railings seen against the rich texture of brick walls and walks (Figs. 4–76, 4–77, 4–78, 4–79). The house fits into the sloping topography, providing a range of relationships to the outside, from the walled entrance court, a private outdoor space, to the bedroom that opens not only to a balcony but also to the treetops through a large fully glazed gable in the sloped ceiling above the light shelf.

4–77. Horan house, entrance walk.

4–78. LEFT. Horan house, master bedroom and deck.

4–79. BELOW. Horan house, exterior rear and side view.

A house designed for Dr. and Mrs. Alex H. Kaplan was built in Ladue by Rufkahr Construction Company in 1960–1961 for $53,490.00. It is beautifully maintained and furnished by its second owners, Kyrle and Ann Boldt. It is gently wedded to a rising site, providing surprising privacy to an unexpectedly large entrance terrace (Figs. 4–80, 4–81, 4–82, 4–83).[36] The old theme of low ceilings at door height contrasting with high ceilings that follow roof pitches is here interpreted with new freedom, even a playful quality, over the open plan of the living room, dining room, and entry hall. Especially impressive are the fine materials used for the trim and the high quality of the details, which are carried through harmoniously in the built-in furniture, especially in the dining room. These effects are accented by attention to refinements such as the large panes of glass that are stopped directly against the brick or against the ceiling plane.

4–80. Kaplan house, boxed column supporting the roof.

4–81. LEFT. Kaplan house, view from the entry, looking toward the living room and the kitchen on the left.

4–82. ABOVE. Kaplan house, living room.

4–83. RIGHT. Kaplan house, dining room with built-in buffet.

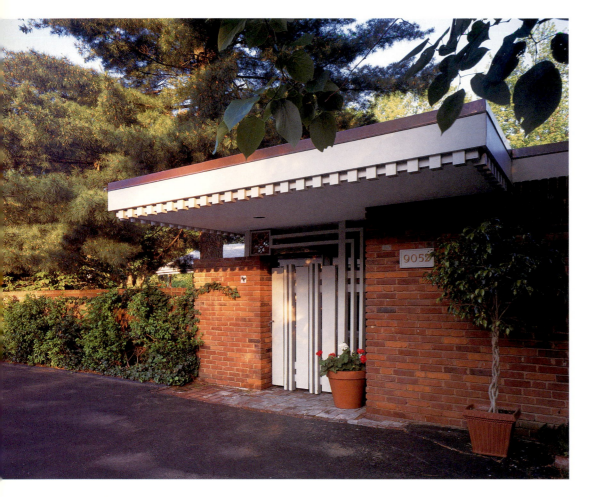

4–84. King house, entrance gate.

Many features seen in the Horan and Kaplan houses are evident, too, in a house designed for Mr. and Mrs. Clarence H. King in Ladue (Figs. 4–84, 4–85, 4–86, 4–87). The plan for this house carries further the extended, spread plan of the Grand house, admitting light from many directions throughout the house. The house was built in 1960 and immediately enlarged with the addition of a studio room in 1961–1962. Bernoudy explained that the Kings "specified a house that would be flooded with daylight and be devoid of glare. For this reason, the house is built around several small private gardens to take advantage of all exposures and to insure maximum privacy. The house proved to be such a haven for nearby grandchildren that the studio room was added where they spend many hours painting and making music" (Figs. 4–88, 4–89, 4–90, 4–91, 4–92).[37] In no other house has Bernoudy realized such a subtle and richly varied integration of interior and exterior spaces that truly enchant the viewer.

4–85. King house, gate from entrance walk.

4-86. LEFT. **King house, entrance walk and terrace.**

4-87. BELOW. **King house, plan.**

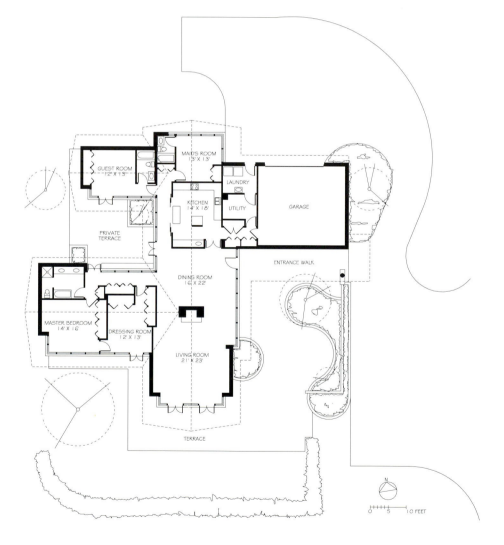

4–88. King house, living room terrace detail.

4–89. LEFT. King house, view from the main entrance past the dining room looking toward the living room and the adjoining terraces.

4–90. ABOVE. King house, living room terrace.

4–91. RIGHT. King house, private terrace.

4–92. King house, studio room addition.

4–93. LEFT. Forrestal house, living room.

4–94. BELOW. Forrestal house, bathroom with a high level of detail and finish.

A new feature was added in the flat-roofed house designed for Mr. and Mrs. Dan J. Forrestal in 1960–1961 (Figs. 4–93, 4–94). Immediately above the light shelves that extend part of the way around the interior spaces are tall rectangular windows that reach from the light shelves to the ceiling plane. Their architectonic ornamental character, almost like oversize dentils, is echoed on the exterior by sharply projecting, geometrical stone sills.

4–95. Messing house, view from dining room toward living room.

The houses with more formally, axially organized plans, beginning with the Guthrie house, have fireplaces arranged symmetrically, on axis. This allowed the fireplace to become a focal point for geometrical elaboration, a tendency that reached a new level of development in the house built in 1960–1962 for Mr. and Mrs. Roswell Messing in Westwood (Fig. 4–95). The fireplace in this house rests on a broad tiled hearth raised above the floor. The exposed brick of the fireplace is reduced to two large piers that rise to the high ceiling. The projecting wood mantel shelf has become a large projecting rectangle with stepped face, edged with metal, while the space above, recessed between the brick piers, is faced vertically with boards. The geometrical theme finds expression elsewhere, too, especially in the embellishment of the facing boards on the edges of the light shelves. The contract between the owners and the architects specified a budget of $70,000 for this house, but the owners' contract with the Emert Contracting Company for its construction was for $104,666.

Malinmor, near Eolia in Pike County, was the country estate of Mr. and Mrs. Fristoe Mullins of St. Louis, a 2,100-acre farm where they raised prizewinning registered Hereford cattle. In 1961, Bernoudy-Mutrux-Bauer designed a 15,000-square-foot house for the farm, the largest residence in Bernoudy's entire career (Fig. 4–96). The house is sited at the top of a hill, something Wright cautioned against, saying a building should be of the hill, not on it. The approach, through an entrance gate that announces the architectural themes of the house, is formal, with the straight road rising gradually for one-quarter of a mile before reaching the house. The entrance to the house is from the side on a strong cross axis that provides the main line of circulation. At the center of the house the cross axis intersects a main axis on which are placed the principal rooms and the large swimming pool. The main axis continues beyond the pool in the form of a long view to the south over the beautiful, rolling farmland. The scale is large. Surprisingly, aluminum windows are used throughout, including aluminum window walls at the front entrance, the north facade, and the

4–96. Malinmor, the Mullins house, from the south.

4–97. Malinmor, stairway with brushed
aluminum railing.

main south facade facing the pool and for interior details (Fig. 4–97). Occasionally the Bernoudy firms designed creative bathrooms with luxurious materials and fixtures for larger houses with adequate budgets. The ultimate example is found here in a large marble bathroom with a sunken L-shaped bathing pool that looks out to a private walled garden. The brick house has low hipped roofs hovering above flat roofs with compound layered soffits. The Oriental character of these compound roofs is most effective in the small brick garden houses to the sides of the swimming pool (Fig. 4–98). In 1994 the Mullins family sold the house, farm structures, and most of the acreage to Malinmor Hunt Club, Inc., an exclusive sporting and shooting club.

4–98. Malinmor, garden house alongside the swimming pool.

4–99. Symington house, entry.

The fine Oriental art collection of the Symington family set the mood for both the architecture and the landscaping of the family's Ladue house (Fig. 4–99). Mr. and Mrs. Stuart Symington Jr. interviewed several architects, including Harris Armstrong, Ralph Cole Hall, and Isadore Shank, before commissioning Bernoudy in 1961. Janey Symington had been introduced to Bernoudy many years earlier by her father, Sidney Studt, the developer of the area of Clayton in which Bernoudy opened his Forsythe Walk office. The Symingtons also knew about the reputation of the Bernoudy-Mutrux-Bauer firm for going way over budget. They gave Bernoudy a budget of $45,000. The final cost of the house was $85,000, what they had privately been prepared to spend from the beginning.

The Symingtons' stress on economy led to the simple rectangular shape of the house (Fig. 4–100). Although the interior has the familiar low ceilings, they are higher than usual to be in scale with the client's height. The house, placed on a falling site, is one story high on the west, entrance side but a full two stories high on the east side, where a lower level is on grade. All of the principal rooms—dining room, living room, study, and master bedroom—are on the east side of the upper floor, and all open to a porch that extends the full length of the house at tree-branch level (Figs. 4–101, 4–102). The Japanese character is found in the serene simplicity of the house and suggested more specifically in many details such as the lattice motifs of the stairway and the balcony railing, the shoji at the entry, the attention to detail in the interior trim and the built-in furniture, the landscaped drainage system that allows roofs without gutters, and the garden (Fig. 4–103). At the same time, the house was also designed to accommodate American antique furniture nicely, especially a large breakfront in the dining room.

4–100. ABOVE. Symington house, east porch view.

4–101. RIGHT. Symington house, view from entry toward living room.

4–102. LEFT. Symington house, master bedroom.

4–103. RIGHT. Symington house, Japanese garden and fountain.

4–104. Mathews house, balconies.

On July 1, 1962, the members of the Bernoudy-Mutrux-Bauer firm entered into a new partnership agreement.[38] Donald W. Lehman, who had served an apprenticeship at Taliesin and was a registered architect, became a full, equal partner with William Bernoudy, Edouard Mutrux, and Henry Bauer. The firm's name remained Bernoudy-Mutrux-Bauer, although by 1965 Lehman's name had been added to the letterhead. Copies of correspondence from Lehman appear in project files beginning in 1962 and indicate that he was active in all phases of projects from preliminary design to construction management.

Wright's Broadacre City was never built, but as an idea it had some influence. The area around Taliesin in Wisconsin, for example, came to resemble part of this vision over the years as members of the Taliesin community acquired surrounding lots and built houses. Certainly the Broadacre idea was prophetic, describing what would develop in suburbs such as the ones around St. Louis where the Bernoudy-Mutrux-Bauer houses were going up. The community ideals behind Broadacre City also occasionally came into play. One instance occurred in Columbia, Missouri, in 1963 when three families bought a wild tract of land on two sides of a deep valley, set aside three building sites for themselves, and created a nature preserve of the rest, surrounding the building sites. Two of the three families commissioned houses from Bernoudy-Mutrux-Bauer, having admired the firm's earlier work in Columbia.

For both Paul W. and Gertrude Mathews and William and Nina Elder, falling sites were used to make the upper floors of two-story houses the principal floors, with the main rooms opening out to balconies up in the trees, as in the Symington house but in a wilder setting (Figs. 4–104, 4–105). The costs were watched closely, and both projects came in close to budget. The Mathews, for example, had specified a budget of $50,000, and the contract for construction came in at just under $52,000. Don Lehman and Bernoudy were principally responsible for these two

4–105. Mathews house, living room.

projects, and both clients expressed gratitude for their work. Nina Elder wrote to Lehman, "With your and Bill's wonderful guidance we have something of lasting beauty which we shall enjoy more each day of our lives. I only wish I could adequately tell you how appreciative and grateful we are to you both." Gertrude Mathews wrote to Bernoudy and Lehman: "Let me try to tell you how good we feel about this place, and how grateful we are to have been led to your door. Word flies about town that the Mathews' home is something to see! The Negro truck operator comes *in person* to collect his bill . . . the minister cancels a previous engagement to come to a 'Crossroads Africa' report in our living room . . . the painter, returned to finish the buffet, says three times over, 'It sure is nice!' And we feel over and over how right is the house for the trees, the trees for the house, the slopes, the protection from rain at the same time that you're part of the storm through your windows; the moon glimpsed recently from one window or porch point to another, as the hours command. It's pretty heavenly."[39]

Balcon Estates in Creve Coeur was conceived as a controlled development of homes in the medium-to-high price range—$50,000 to $70,000—all required to be architect-designed. Clients could choose from a list of six firms: Harris Armstrong, Gale and Cannon, Isadore Shank, Shapiro and Tisdale, Architectural Design Associates, and Bernoudy-Mutrux-Bauer. Mr. and Mrs. Maurice Hirsch commissioned their house in Balcon Estates from Bernoudy-Mutrux-Bauer in July 1963. Mr. Hirsch was related to the Messings, whose Bernoudy house had been completed the year before, and the Hirsches believed Bernoudy to be the finest house architect in the area.[40] The following February, plans were submitted to the Board of Trustees of Balcon Estates for approval. The contractor, Karl Flach, submitted a final statement in January 1965 showing a total cost of $81,525.28.

Once again the firm designed a house for a hillside site, with the principal rooms on the upper floor (Figs. 4–106, 4–107, 4–108). In this case, however, the entrance at the northeast corner is on the lower level, leading into a generous hallway with a dramatic, skylighted stair leading up to the main floor. The white steelwork now on the stairway was originally black, and the interior trim—now white—originally had a natural finish. The main rooms—dining room, living room, master bedroom—open to

balconies on the north-facing, two-story front side of the house and open directly out on grade to the private backyard on the south. In addition to the open quality of the large windows on both exposures, these rooms have the open spatial quality typical of most of the houses designed by Bernoudy-Mutrux-Bauer during the 1960s with skylights above the level of the light shelves. The circular fireplace is as unusual and striking a feature as the stairway. The unusual location of the main entrance on the lower level was not entirely successful. In 1968–1969, the owners went back to their architects and builder and had a new, formal entrance added on the east side of the house at the upper level, leading more directly into the living room. It replaced a secondary entry and mudroom that led to the kitchen, originally meant just for the family but often used by visitors as well. The exterior woodwork was stained a blue-green.

4–106. Hirsch house.

4–107. LEFT. **Hirsch house, entry stairway.**

4–108. BELOW. **Hirsch house, living room.**

4–109. Graul house, aerial view.

Sherwood Lake in Overland, a St. Louis suburb, was planned in the early 1890s and filled by 1897. The area around the lake was subdivided and development began in the early 1930s. The house built here for Dr. and Mrs. Walter Graul in 1963 reverts to earlier themes in Bernoudy's architecture (Figs. 4–109, 4–110). These themes are apparent in the organization of rooms and circulation patterns, the position of the fireplace, and the contrast between high-pitched ceilings under hip roofs and the low ceilings of extended light shelves continued by the soffits of deep eaves outside. Most striking is the pattern of batten strips on the ceiling, a detail characteristic of Wright's early work and something Bernoudy would have first seen when he went to Taliesin in 1932 (Fig. 4–111). Another notable feature is the tall window in the corner of the stairwell, with a cascade of small panes of mitered glass carried in heavy mullions, calling to mind mullion designs going back to the Talbot house, Bernoudy and Mutrux's first design. More similar to other projects of this period is the way the firm used a rolling site in the development of the house, with the living room and dining room opening to a large balcony rather than to a terrace (Fig. 4–112). Most ingeniously, the swimming pool is terraced into a falling site, its curves picking up the form of the land and serving as a foil to the rectangular geometry of the house. Originally the bedrooms formed a bridge over a terrace on the lower level that opened to the swimming pool. The terrace has since been enclosed.

4–110. BELOW. **Graul house, plan.**

4–111. RIGHT. **Graul house, living room.**

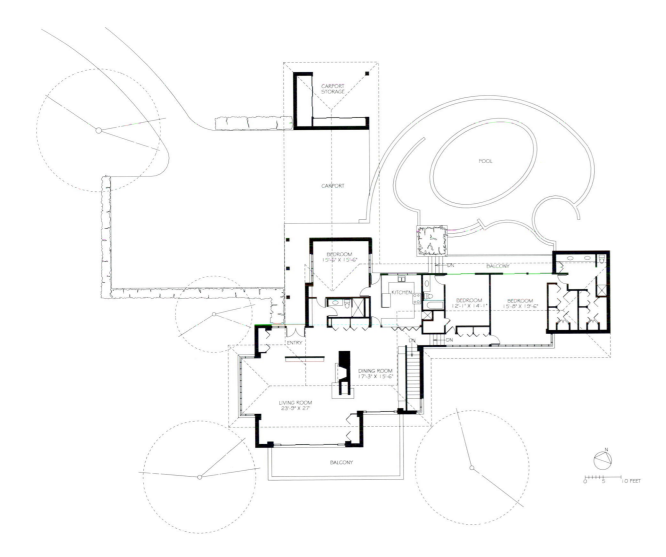

4–112. Graul house, from the southeast.

Mr. and Mrs. John T. Rogers brought unusually well-developed and detailed drawings that they had prepared of what they wanted when they commissioned a house from Bernoudy-Mutrux-Bauer in 1962. The result was a design unique among Bernoudy's work, strongly focused on a circular living room (Figs. 4–113, 4–114, 4–115). It took extensive redesign to scale back the project to keep the cost below $100,000. In May 1963 a contract was awarded to Rufkahr Construction Company, which completed the house a year later. The circle of the living room is defined by brick partitions set within a larger polygonal form containing circulation areas. The low ceilings around the perimeter give way to a higher ceiling in the form of a low saucer-shaped dome with a skylight at the center. Wright occasionally had used circular forms, but in his residential designs he nearly always played off segments of circles against each other. One of the earliest examples of this use of circular forms was in the second Jacobs house of 1944, mentioned earlier in connection with the Pinkney house by Bernoudy-Mutrux. Wright's Friedman house in Pleasantville, New York, of 1948 has a circular living room, but with a separate circular chimney mass rising within it and an intersecting circle of smaller radius projecting into the living room as a balcony. Wright's last residential design, the Lykes house in Phoenix, sketched in 1959, the year of his death, and built in 1966–1968, is closer to the design used for the Rogers house, but a strong intersecting smaller circular form, providing a back wall for the fireplace, sets it apart, too. Thus Bernoudy's design does not closely follow any of Wright's houses, and if he had Wright's work in mind, it could just as well have been the better-known Morris Gift Shop in San Francisco or even the Guggenheim Museum in New York.[41]

4–113. Rogers house, exterior view.

4-114. LEFT. Rogers house, circular living room.

4-115. BELOW. Rogers house, fireplace.

4-116. RIGHT. Larner house, exterior view of foyer.

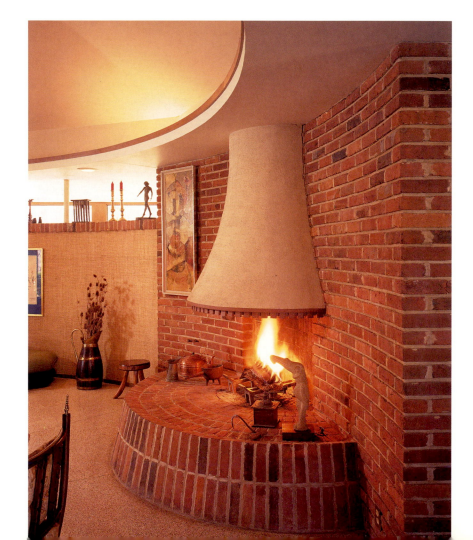

The house built for Irvin and Sara Larner in Frontenac, a St. Louis suburb, in 1963–1964 once again takes advantage of a falling site, with the living room, dining room, kitchen, and master bedroom on the upper level (Figs. 4–116, 4–117). The entrance is at a split level, and the lower perimeter ceilings of the upper level carry forward over the entry hall as a high ceiling. The simple elegance of the entry continues in the attention given to fine materials, beginning with the green slate floors of the entry hall and the mitered glass corners in the entry hall and the living room. It continues further with carefully detailed wood trim, wood floors, and shoji in principal rooms, all played off against reused brick. The design again used gable-on-hip roofs, with large windows high in the gables. An unusual feature in the living room is a ridge beam that runs the length of the gable roof, elegantly encased in wood to match the other wood trim, but terminating at the gable window with no visible means of support.

The house was built by the Rufkahr Construction Company for $85,390. The specified budget in the contract between the owners and Bernoudy-Mutrux-Bauer, which Bernoudy signed, was $70,000. Judging from the project file, this escalation in the cost was a particularly sore point. As a result, Bernoudy reduced the architectural fee to $8,000, $539 less than the contracted 10 percent, something the firm could ill afford. The house is beautifully maintained and appreciated by its third owners, Mr. and Mrs. Robert F. Deubel, who had lived earlier in another Bernoudy house on Dielman Road.

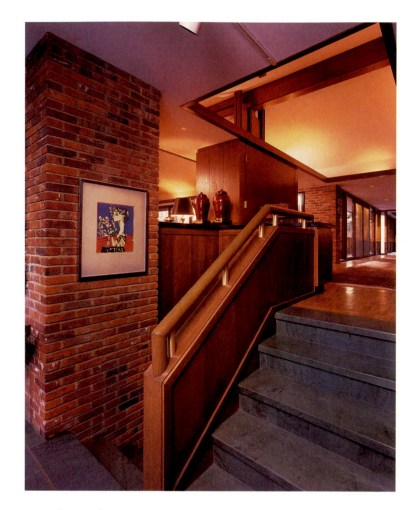

4–117. Larner house, entry.

The Bernoudy-Mutrux-Bauer firm occasionally did commercial or institutional work and wanted badly to do more for financial reasons. But the firm met with limited success, as seen with the project for Harry Lenart. A small veterinary clinic on Manchester Road, built in 1957, is a simple concrete-block building that survives in rather shabby condition. It usually fell to Mutrux to take charge of these initiatives.

The firm's most interesting commercial project was a design for an apartment tower in Galveston, Texas. The project was presented to the local community in a well-publicized event in 1963.[42] Bernoudy attended the reception and exhibited a model of the proposed $3 million building (Fig. 4–118). The building, which was to be called University Tower Apartments and rise twenty stories high—which would have made it the tallest building in Galveston—would have had 104 apartments ranging in size from one to three bedrooms, with every apartment having at least one balcony. In contrast to most tall buildings of the day, which reflected the pure forms of Mies van der Rohe's architecture, this design called for a variety of facing materials in contrasting colors and made use of stacked balconies to achieve richly articulated facades—more like Wright's 1953 Price Tower in Bartlesville, Oklahoma.[43] Designing tall buildings outside the Miesian idiom was a difficult challenge at this time, and this was certainly a more successful attempt than most. A less successful example is the Lincoln Tower project of the same time in Louisville, Kentucky—designed by Wright's successor firm, Taliesin Associated Architects—which is overwhelmed by its fussy decoration.[44] Although the Galveston newspaper announced that test borings would soon begin, the Galveston project did not go ahead. The developers were a group called the 304 Corporation, which consisted of three St. Louisans—Bernoudy, an engineer named Paul Londe, and Al Gerber, a retired manufacturer—and a group of investors from Galveston.

David Wheatley was another St. Louisan Bernoudy had sent to Taliesin, and who came back and worked for him briefly in 1967. In 1963, when Wheatley was still at Taliesin, Bernoudy wrote him: "We keep busy but make very little money—I'm afraid architects cannot survive today on residential work so, we are hoping to ease into some commercial project. We are about to start construction on a motel in Clayton so, we have hopes."[45] The project that did go ahead was a hotel for Ramada Inns called Clayton Square Motor Lodge on North Meramec in Clayton, now the Daniele Hotel. At a meeting in October 1963, Ramada Inns agreed

4–118. Bernoudy with the model for the University Tower project, Galveston, Texas, *Galveston Daily News,* February 2, 1963. Photo courtesy *Galveston County Daily News.*

to construct a forty-four-unit hotel, with Paul Londe and Associates as engineer and Bernoudy-Mutrux-Bauer as architect. In a switch from normal practice, Ramada contracted with the engineer, Paul Londe, who in turn subcontracted with Bernoudy-Mutrux-Bauer for architectural services, at a fee of 6 percent of the construction cost. Out of that, the architects were to retain Londe's firm for mechanical and electrical engineering services. They had no responsibility or control over interior design, for which Ramada Inns contracted separately. The hotel was completed in 1965, and again, Mutrux handled the project for the firm. Bernoudy had serious reservations about the compromises involved in moving in this direction, even though the firm could not be profitable designing the houses on which its reputation was based. He took a short holiday to San Francisco to mull over the problem and discuss it frankly with an architect friend and former Taliesin fellow, Henry Herold, who believes that the Ramada project was a major factor in the breakup of the firm that followed soon afterward.[46]

Even though the firm may not have been profitable, its reputation for houses was high, and good commissions continued to come. A large house designed for Mr. and Mrs. Erwin Bry in Ladue in 1964 recalls earlier themes in the work of Bernoudy-Mutrux-Bauer (Figs. 4–119, 4–120). The asymmetrical plan, the fireplace set toward a corner of the living room, the spatial continuity of the dining room, living room, and entry hall, and the stair placed against the broad back of the fireplace are all classic features of the work of the firm and in the Wright tradition. So, too, are the unbroken light shelves at doorway height with strong, simple wood fascias, set off against the higher-pitched ceilings (Fig. 4–121). The raised ceilings are decorated with the same batten strips that reappeared at the Graul house, which emphasize their caplike quality. The large oval

4–119. ABOVE. Bry house.

4–120. RIGHT. Bry house, plan.

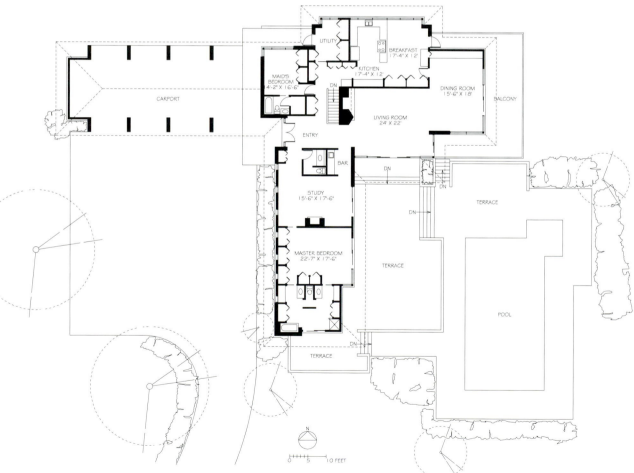

4-121. Bry house, living room.

4–122. Bry house, balcony detail.

motif that appears in the balcony railings (Fig. 4–122) and the stair railing inside is more unusual and reappears as a relief panel on the entrance doors. The house is set into a gently rolling site. The living room, study, and master bedroom on the main floor open directly to a terrace, which steps down to a lower terrace and swimming pool following the falling grade, while the dining room opens to a balcony where the ground has dropped, exposing a lower level at grade.

The Gallup house in Creve Coeur of 1965–1966 is unusual in several respects, especially in the open spatial character of its principal rooms (Fig. 4–123). These consist of a combined living and dining space and a combined family room and kitchen space in a rectangular plan, twenty-eight feet by thirty-eight feet. Above the low-pitched hip roofs around the perimeter, a second hip roof rises to provide a zone for clerestory windows that are open to both spaces below. A brick fireplace at the center rises the full height of the interior to help support the exposed heavy timber framing and the wood decking of the upper roof. A bedroom wing is up half a flight, and a playroom, offices, and basement are on two levels below the main floor. Although the subdivision was restricted to one-story houses, this two-story, four-level house was so deftly designed and fitted to its landscape that the trustees, who thought it would be the most beautiful house in the area, overlooked the restriction and approved the design.

The project was primarily in the hands of Mutrux because the owners had limited the budget to $35,000, and Bernoudy was more interested in projects with larger budgets. Bernoudy did review the design. Both Allan Gallup, a civil engineer and an attorney specializing in construction law, and Ruth Gallup played an active role in the design development with Mutrux. Early designs show the inset corner windows that are typical of much of Bernoudy-Mutrux-Bauer's work, one of those Wrightian features that the firm used to get away from boxlike interior spaces. In the interests of simpler construction and increased interior space, the final design eliminated the corner windows and incorporated other simplifications in both details and materials. Thermopane windows were used throughout, and the house has performed well. Oak flooring, one of the features reluctantly given up, has been added over the years. By August 1966, when the Gallups moved in, the Bernoudy-Mutrux-Bauer firm had closed, and Mutrux turned over all the construction drawings and records to the owners.

4-123. Gallup house.

4–124. LEFT. Conreux house.

4–125. BELOW. Conreux house, living room.

In 1965–1966, Jack and Loraine Conreux built one of the first houses in a new development on Thornhill Drive in the St. Louis suburb of Town and Country. They had not known Bernoudy but sought him out based on his reputation as the best architect for their hilltop site. He made dramatic use of it, presenting an angled front wall under the sweep of a high gabled roof as a climax to the rising hill and a greeting to those who pass by or arrive at the house. The entrance is to the side of this front part of the house, which contains a living room, dining room, kitchen, and breakfast room around a utility core (Figs. 4–124, 4–125). A two-story wing runs to the rear with a study and bedrooms up half a flight from the entrance and the basement and garage down half a flight. The roof level of the bedroom wing carries forward over the front part of the house, creating a high, open space for the principal rooms. This high space is dramatized by the exposed heavy wood construction of the roof, more developed than anything seen before in the residential work of the Bernoudy-Mutrux-Bauer firm. The principal longitudinal girders measure six inches by six inches and are spaced eight feet on center, carried on six-by-six-inch posts. They in turn carry secondary beams, either four by eight inches or four by ten, spaced six feet on center. The beams carry exposed two-by-six-inch tongue-and-groove roof decking. Between the decking and the exterior cedar shake shingles are two inches of rigid insulation. This heavy post-and-beam construction was widely used at the time, inspired by Japanese carpentry on the West Coast and the tradition of Colonial American architecture in New England.

The early drawings for the Conreux house are dated June, July, and August 1965. They still carry the Bernoudy-Mutrux-Bauer name, but neither Mutrux nor Bauer took part in the project. Loraine Conreux remembers working with Don Lehman and Richard Arenson, a new employee of the firm, in addition to Bernoudy. The Conreuxs, knowing Bernoudy's reputation for exceeding the budget, gave him a smaller figure than their actual budget and came out about right. A contract was signed on November 22, 1965, for $96,775.21. Loraine Conreux represented the family, watching the job closely, even though their highly competent contractor, Karl Flach, did not like dealing with a woman. The Conreuxs moved in on January 13, 1967.

A house Bernoudy designed for Dr. and Mrs. Bert H. Klein in the St. Louis suburb of Huntleigh, which beautifully embodies many of the innovations of the prior decade, was also underway as the Bernoudy-Mutrux-Bauer firm was breaking up. Like so many of the firm's houses, this two-story house is set in a falling site, with the entrance at a split level and the principal rooms on the upper level (Figs. 4–126, 4–127). The breakfast room, living room, study, and master bedroom open to a balcony up in the trees, while additional bedrooms and the family room on the lower level open to the backyard under the balcony (Figs. 4–128, 4–129, 4–130). The plan of the living room with its large brick fireplace is symmetrical with a strong sense of axiality, a recurring theme that goes back to the Guthrie house. Emphasizing this symmetry, the unbroken gable roof, framed in heavy timbers and sheathed in wood decking, extends from the entrance to the rear balcony. The roof is similar to that of the Conreux house, but simpler and more resolved in relation to the plan it shelters. The clarity of the gable roof and the serene sense of shelter it conveys are emphasized by the unbroken line of the light shelf above which the roof rises and by the full glazing of the gable ends. The theme is continued by the long pent roof along the entrance facade, which welcomes visitors as they step down under its shelter upon arriving. Brick is in evidence in the garage and the terrace walls, but the house is primarily of frame construction, vertically sheathed on the exterior.

Careful attention was paid to detail, beginning on the exterior with the slightly projecting brick base course on which the wood sheathed walls rest, a detail that goes back to the earliest work of Bernoudy-Mutrux. The plan is developed on a four-foot-square module. The walls are faced in carefully selected woods: pecky cypress in the study in random widths, five and a half inches to eleven and a half inches with a three-quarter-inch V-joint; pecan with a walnut inlay in the dining room and hall. The architect's services included the design of built-in furniture and the selection of furniture, fabrics, drapes, wall coverings, and carpets. Fabrics and wall coverings were heavily textured and tended toward earthy reds and greens.

4-126. LEFT. Klein house, entry.

4-127. BELOW. Klein house, plan.

4-128. RIGHT. Klein house, balcony.

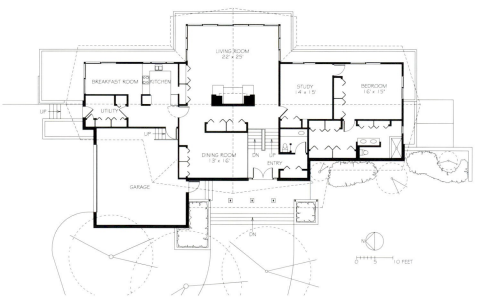

The Kleins and Bernoudy-Mutrux-Bauer completed the standard AIA agreement on November 25, 1964, at the usual 10 percent fee. The preliminary designs were accepted at a meeting on February 24, 1965, with an estimated construction cost of $97,000. In July a contract with Rufkahr Construction Company for $109,270.76 was signed, and the house was completed a year later. Charles Klein, the son of the owners, worked for Bernoudy following his graduation from Washington University, and he did some work on this house when it was well along. He remembers that Hank Bauer and Don Lehman developed the project and prepared the construction drawings and documents after the preliminary design stage.[47] After ten years, Eugene and Jane O'Neill acquired the house; they still live in it and are preserving it with the care it deserves.

Hank Bauer precipitated the impending breakup of the Bernoudy-Mutrux-Bauer firm. With four children to send to college, he simply could not afford to stay in the firm. He called a meeting of the four partners to say that he was leaving, and Mutrux and Lehman made the same decision. Bernoudy was willing to admit that he could afford to continue with the kind of residential work they had been doing.[48] Charles Klein and Dick Arenson remained with Bernoudy in a new firm called Bernoudy Associates. Klein stayed just nine months before being drafted into military service, but it was an important experience. Sixteen years later he wrote Bernoudy, "Your influence on me, both professionally and personally, is still strong and it has certainly made me a better architect."[49]

4–130. Klein house, entry hall.

4–129. Klein house, living room.

As early as 1961, Bernoudy had begun work on another project for his good friends the Pulitzers, a town house on Westmoreland Place. Because the Pulitzers wanted to be able to accommodate their art collection adequately, the house was also conceived of as a private museum. It was not built, but it was published in *House Beautiful* in 1965, as the Bernoudy-Mutrux-Bauer firm was breaking up.[1] Strikingly different from what had come before, it signals the beginning of Bernoudy's late career.

The *House Beautiful* article opens with a quotation from Bernoudy: "With today's emphasis on suburban living, it is distinctly a refreshing experience to be asked to design a town house." Time after time Bernoudy had responded creatively to a specific landscape, but here the site offered nothing. The lot was flat and treeless, confined on three sides by an eight-foot-high brick wall, and measured only one hundred feet by two hundred feet, less than half an acre. But the context offered everything: "a venerable private street . . . three-storied houses of an elegant vintage, the mood—if not the idiom—was indicated."

The design went through different versions, all formal. The final, published one (Fig. 5–1) called for a building of large scale, made of old brick with hammered limestone trim, windowless on the north, street face. The structure would have been monumentally massed in large blocks, absolutely symmetrical with the circulation organized along a central axis. Two two-car garages were to have faced each other, framing a thirty-five-foot-wide entrance court sheltered by a shallow vaulted roof hovering on invisible supports from garage to garage. The two-story mass of the house would have risen behind. Along the central axis, through the entrance court, one would have gone up four broad steps in the rectangular entrance garden to the front door, into a broad foyer measuring thirty-one feet by twenty-one feet, with the library to the left and the dining room to the right, and a living room, thirty-seven by thirty-one feet, directly ahead. Bedrooms would have been on the second floor, a master bedroom above the living room and of the same size. A skylighted gallery was to have run around three sides of the second-floor area above the foyer, open to the foyer below and fitted with cases for the storage and display of prints and drawings. The ceiling heights of the main first-floor rooms would have been sufficient to allow mezzanines above the service rooms for the storage of artworks in addition to the storage space in the basement. The major rooms would have looked out to the south through tall arched window openings fitted with bronze window sash,

5–1. Pulitzer house-museum project. Bernoudy Archive, West Campus Library Annex, Washington University, St. Louis.

overlooking what Bernoudy called "a small, disciplined water garden . . . a setting for sculpture," still oriented along that irrepressible central axis.

In the more formally axial schemes of the previous decade, beginning with the Guthrie house, the open plan and the Wrightian sense of flowing space remained vivid, creating the elegant interpretation of Organic Modern architecture that is one of the best themes of the Bernoudy-Mutrux-Bauer years. For the Pulitzer project Bernoudy turned his back on the open plan, which Wright had described as breaking the box of interior space. Rather, for the Pulitzer project Bernoudy chose the discrete, cubical spaces of traditional architecture and disposed them with all the formality of a Beaux Arts scheme. The project was not carried out, but in a sense it has come to fruition in 1999 with a building for the Pulitzer Foundation in the Grand Center arts district in St. Louis, designed by the distinguished Japanese architect Tadao Ando. Although Bernoudy did not get to build his Pulitzer house, it was followed immediately by a similar project that was built.

The house Bernoudy designed in 1966 for Mrs. Marie Williams shows much traditional formality and deliberately evokes Italian architecture. The drawings call it not the Williams house or residence but the Williams "villa," and it is entered through a "loggia" that surrounds an "atrium" (Figs. 5–2, 5–3, 5–4). Even though the house is located in the St. Louis Country Club grounds, the interior relates to the outside only through the small formal garden framed within the loggia, with the controlled views beyond that framed by the arches of the loggia (Figs. 5–5, 5–6, 5–7). The brickwork throughout is different, not just in its traditional arcaded design but also in its traditional detailing with corbeled cresting and with both the vertical mortar joints and the horizontal ones raked out. Flush vertical mortar joints combined with deeply raked horizontal ones to create a subtle shadow pattern of horizontal lines had been a hallmark of Bernoudy's work since the Talbot house, just as it had been of Wright's work since the beginning of the century. But now horizontality was not a theme. The traditional motifs of the exterior of the house are echoed in the formality of the interior, where they are elegantly articulated in the generous use of moldings, some with traditional profiles and others with interesting adaptations (Figs. 5–8, 5–9).

Mrs. Williams had admired a similar house, built shortly before hers and designed by another well-known St. Louis architect, Fred Dunn.[2] Bernoudy happily took the Dunn design as his model. In an ironic twist, years earlier he had recommended Dunn to a friend who had wanted to build a traditional house. Bernoudy had felt then that it would be "morally irresponsible" for him to design a traditional house given his philosophical commitment to modern architecture.[3] But twenty-five years later he was quite willing to do a resonantly traditional design with great skill and taste. By 1966, Frank Lloyd Wright had been dead for seven years, Bernoudy had almost no contact with Taliesin, and he had, after all, been a faithful exponent of the Organic Modern architecture of the 1930s for three decades. His identification by *House Beautiful* in 1965 as one of six emerging leaders in American architecture must have added to his confidence in exploring new themes.[4] Works by all six architects were featured in a portfolio section of the magazine. Bernoudy was represented by the Pulitzer town house and private museum, while the works of the other five architects were all uncompromisingly modern designs.

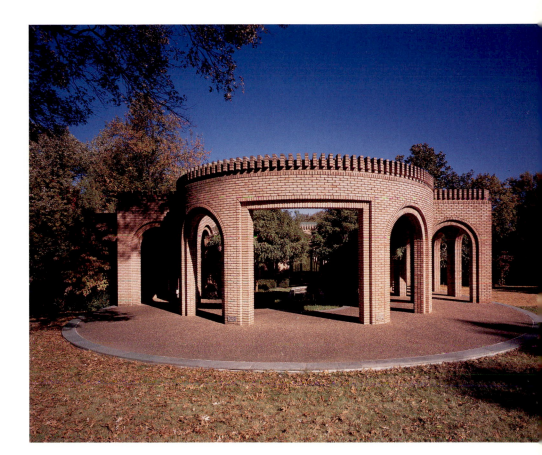

5–2. Williams villa, the loggia.

5-3. LEFT. Williams villa, the atrium. Photograph ca. 1990 by Robert Pettus.

5-4. RIGHT. Williams villa, aerial view.

5–5. LEFT. Williams villa, atrium detail.

5–6. BELOW. Williams villa, plan.

5–7. RIGHT. Williams villa, view from the living room to the atrium.

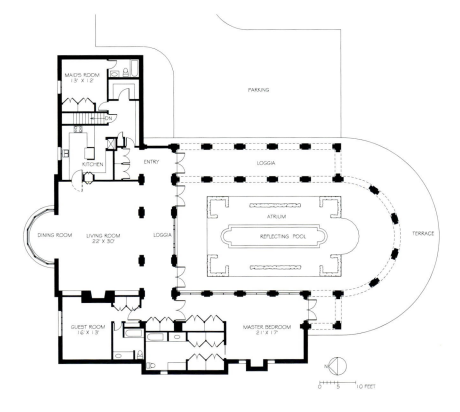

5–8. LEFT. Williams villa, living room from the entry loggia.

5–9. RIGHT. Williams villa, interior detail.

5–10. Second Wolfson house.

It was time for something new. Modernism in general was being closely scrutinized by architects and critics, and important departures from the modern tradition were being tried, the first steps in what would soon be called postmodernism. In 1966, Robert Venturi published the first major theoretical argument for a postmodern architecture, *Complexity and Contradiction in Architecture.*[5] Bernoudy seems to have been moving into his own postmodern period with projects like the Pulitzer town house and private museum and the Williams villa. He did not banish Organic Modernism from his repertoire but kept it as just one of a number of options of amazing variety in his late work. This is not to

say that Bernoudy was ready to embrace all of the revolutionary new movements of the moment. A member of the British Archigram group lectured at Washington University at this time. The wildly improbable work of this group was to serious architecture about what Pop Art was at that same time to serious abstract painting, painting of the kind found in the Bernoudy collection. The lecture examined the work of the Archigram group and Brutalist architecture, another alternative to modernism. Bernoudy held a reception at his house following the lecture, but it put his good manners to a severe test. Outraged, he kept asserting that the architect's responsibility still was to create beauty for the client.[6]

At the same time that Bernoudy was exploring these new directions, he designed a large, exquisitely finished house, very much in the Bernoudy-Mutrux-Bauer tradition of the previous decade, for Robert and Ethel Wolfson in Ladue. The house is beautifully and appropriately maintained and furnished by its current owner, Martin Green. The Bernoudy-Mutrux firm had built an earlier house for Wolfson in 1953–1955. In February 1965, he signed an agreement with Bernoudy-Mutrux-Bauer for a new house. By the time the house was finished late in 1966 the firm had been dissolved, and the distribution of the payments for professional services for this project was the last administrative vestige of the old firm.

Preliminary designs with an estimated cost of $146,000 were accepted in April 1965, and the authorization to proceed with working drawings to be completed two months later was signed by Wolfson and Bernoudy. The cost estimate was based on a comparison with the nearby Bry house, which was similar in size and detail and had been bid just a year earlier. The Bry house had cost $18.60 a square foot, and the figure of $146,000 for the Wolfson house was based on the assumption that it could be built for $20.00 a square foot. But by the time the project went ahead, because the owners made no compromises in choosing elegant details, materials, and finishes, the actual cost was $206,787.

The long, low, one-story brick house under broad hip roofs sits on a slightly declining site (Figs. 5–10, 5–11). The principal rooms are axially arranged at the center—the main entrance porch, doorway, and hall leading to the living room and brick terrace beyond, with a study to the right balancing the dining room to the left (Figs. 5–12, 5–13, 5–14). The broad fireplace is on axis between the entry hall and the living room, with three steps down on either side giving added height to the living room even as its ceiling follows the slope of the roof upward. Several different ceiling slopes converge at the center, their geometrical configuration augmented by patterns of applied wood trim, a decorative detail that goes back to Bernoudy's earliest work but had never before been so richly developed. Extending from this symmetrically organized center is a bedroom wing on the right; on the left is a detached wing for the garage, a guest suite, and a summer pavilion that opens to a lower terrace and swimming pool (Fig. 5–15).

5–11. Second Wolfson house, aerial view.

5–12. LEFT. Second Wolfson house, living room and the entry beyond.

5–13. ABOVE. Second Wolfson house, entry, with one of the early planter stands.

5–14. RIGHT. Second Wolfson house, view from the living room toward the dining room.

A late furniture design that gives expression to the theme of elegance is seen in the circular living room table clustered with three smaller tables (Fig. 5–16). With their sensuous curves and polished metal and glass finishes, the tables offer a contrast to the Wrightian geometry of the planter stand in the entry. The fireplace chimney, broadened above the ceiling to the full width of the living room and entry hall, emerges above the roof, marking the center axis. The chimney's broad mass, emphasized by the unusual battered slope of its sides, decisively anchors the whole composition. A similar detail on a smaller scale does the same for the summer pavilion. Wright occasionally used battered chimneys, but never in such an effective way.[7] The paneled, domed ceiling of the summer pavilion echoes the outward curve of the latticed window—a new and very effective design element (Fig. 5–17).

5–15. ABOVE. **Second Wolfson house, swimming pool and summer pavilion.**

5–16. RIGHT. **Second Wolfson house, living room table.**

5–17. Second Wolfson house, summer pavilion interior.

5–18. LEFT. **Hoblitzelle house.**

5–19. BELOW. **Hoblitzelle house, deck.**

The house designed by Bernoudy Associates for Mr. and Mrs. George Hoblitzelle in Augusta, Missouri, in 1966 is set into the side of a high hill to take advantage of magnificent views across the Missouri River valley (Figs. 5–18, 5–19). The simple cube of this two-story house is enlivened with insets and projections, mitered glass corner windows, balconies, and a broad gabled roof whose gables are filled with glass. A collection of Western and decorative art of the present owner of the house, Joseph Meiners, points up the rustic theme in the architecture, setting this house apart from Bernoudy's other work (Figs. 5–20, 5–21).

5–20. Hoblitzelle house, entry.

5-21. Hoblitzelle house, living room.

In 1966 Mr. and Mrs. Harry O. Schloss engaged Bernoudy Associates to design additions and alterations to their residence in Creve Coeur (Figs. 5–22, 5–23). The design of the new porch shows a variation on the strongly geometrical version of Oriental latticework that was one of the recurring themes in Bernoudy's work. Helping on this project was a new employee of the firm, Barry W. Evens, a designer who had joined Bernoudy and Arenson. During its first years the new Bernoudy Associates firm received a number of such small commissions, as well as others that involved only interior decoration projects. Richard Arenson was responsible for most of the latter and at times was identified as being in the interior design department of Bernoudy Associates. The firm handled a variety of lines of modern furniture and furnishings, carpets, wall coverings, upholstery, and drapes, with sources all around the country. Arenson would occasionally take clients to the Merchandise Mart in Chicago to select items for their residences.

5–22. Schloss house, deck.

5–23. Schloss house, porch addition.

Thomas H. Saunders, another Taliesin-trained young architect, joined Bernoudy Associates in August 1967.[8] Saunders was from Nebraska, and after two years at the University of Nebraska had joined the Taliesin Fellowship, where he stayed from 1961 until 1967. Saunders knew about Bernoudy through David Wheatley, another Taliesin student who had worked for the Bernoudy-Mutrux-Bauer firm. Saunders came to St. Louis for an interview with Hellmuth, Obata, and Kassabaum, but when Bernoudy also offered him a position and was willing to match the salary, Saunders accepted. He stayed with the firm until 1970 but continued to collaborate after that and remained a helpful friend to the end of Bernoudy's life. Bernoudy had able associates in his new firm, especially in Saunders with his Taliesin background, but they were much younger than he was and certainly did not have the experience of his prior partners. By the end of the sixties, the volume of work had declined significantly, averaging just one or two commissions a year until the last in 1985. By then Bernoudy was seventy-five years old and not in good health. In spite of the much reduced production, the firm designed some wonderful projects during those years, including a few large ones. To manage them Bernoudy found it necessary to contract with other architects for help with the construction drawings and the supervision stages of the architectural work.

Some of these later projects continue the familiar themes of Bernoudy's earlier work. A house built for Mr. and Mrs. Robert Phillips in Ladue of 1968–1969, for example, is a long, one-story brick house with low hip roofs; deep eaves continue on the interior as light shelves, giving way to higher ceilings that follow the pitch of the roof (Fig. 5–24). A distinctive element is found on both the exterior and interior in the large square panels made of overlapped wide boards, stepped out toward the center (Figs. 5–25, 5–26). They rise to the soffit of the eaves on the exterior and from the floor to the light shelves on the interior.

5–24. Phillips house.

5–25. LEFT. Phillips house, detail of panels.

5–26. BELOW. Phillips house, interior panels.

A large, glassed-in room that Marjorie Hankins commissioned in 1972 quite literally grew out of an earlier project, the house that the Bernoudy-Mutrux firm had designed in 1948 for Mr. and Mrs. Donald Grant (Fig. 5–27). The Grant house, planned in connection with the Klyman house next door, has been altered extensively over the years. The Hankins addition, with its heavy timber framing and roof decking, picks up Bernoudy themes from the 1960s, but the wood is silhouetted by the extensive use of glass, and the room stands like an intriguing open frame in its landscape setting. The slight asymmetry of the frame allowed for a heightened southern exposure.

5–27. Hankins addition to the Grant house.

5–28. Portnoy house, entrance porch.

The approach to the house built for Mr. and Mrs. Allen J. Portnoy in Ladue in 1971–1973 recalls the second Wolfson house, but in a larger version with more elaborately developed detail (Figs. 5–28, 5–29). To the rear, the house steps into the dropping hillside with the natural ease that had always been one of Bernoudy's great talents, but here the roof parallels the slope of the hill in a distinctive way. The final billing from the Rufkahr Construction Company showed a cost grown to $345,067 from the original estimate of $300,000. Bernoudy agreed to accept as his fee 10 percent of the estimate rather than of the actual cost.

5–29. Portnoy house, main door.

Two other projects from these same years could hardly provide a stronger contrast. Bernoudy designed a major addition to the residence of his good friends Stanley and Alice Goodman in Ladue in 1967–1968 (Figs. 5–30, 5–31). Stanley Goodman had succeeded Morton D. May at the May Company and was a noted patron of the arts and an accomplished musician. The addition consists of a sunroom or orangery added to the rear, south side of a two-story brick house. Opening to an oval pool, it is done in steel, glass, and Plexiglass in a black-and-white color scheme. The black slate of the orangery floor continues to the pool deck, where it frames panels of a white pebble aggregate. The simple, symmetrical, three-bay organization derives from the three doorways between the orangery and the existing living room. The doorways have paired plate-glass doors on sliding tracks, so that the whole could be thrown open for the famous Goodman musical evenings. The six glass lamps suspended from the beams that project from the steel columns were acquired in Thailand.[9] The elegant classicism in this hard, minimalist design comes closer to the contemporary architecture of Ludwig Mies van der Rohe or Philip Johnson than to anything Wright ever did.

5–31. Goodman sunroom addition, interior view.

5–30. Goodman sunroom addition.

5–32. Yalem pavilion. Photograph ca. 1974 by Norman McGrath, courtesy the photographer and Joseph Braswell and Associates.

A second project, a collaboration with Joseph Braswell, an interior designer from New York, is even more surprising. Braswell had designed interiors for Mr. and Mrs. Charles Yalem some eight years before, and they returned to him in 1971 for a garden pavilion addition (Fig. 5–32).[10] He sought out Bernoudy to design the hexagonal pavilion and took his inspiration for the interior design from a rococo teahouse at Sans Souci in Potsdam, Germany, built for Emperor Frederick II in the eighteenth century. The theme is exotic, to say the least, and Bernoudy's pavilion with its Oriental, copper-clad dome picks up on the rococo motif, although it owes more to a pavilion he would have known well, the Music Stand in Tower Grove Park of 1872 designed by Eugene Greenleaf, than it does to Sans Souci. Braswell's interiors—palm-tree columns and Chinese red-lacquer paneling, furniture, and furnishings—were all fabricated or purchased in New York and shipped to St. Louis for installation in Bernoudy's architectural shell. Braswell remembered the team effort with pleasure: "Ideas sprang from one head to another. All in all it was a collective activity."

These years also brought commercial and institutional commissions to Bernoudy Associates. Although there were more of these than before, they were mostly modest in size and would not have solved the financial problems that led to the dissolution of the Bernoudy-Mutrux-Bauer firm. Work on a permanent replacement for the temporary shell designed in 1952 by Bernoudy-Mutrux for Washington University's Little Symphony Association was begun in 1964 by Bernoudy-Mutrux-Bauer, but by the time the project was completed in 1966 it had been taken over by Bernoudy alone (Fig. 5–33). The design of the Beaumont pavilion is another fully successful effort, sympathetically adapting the traditional forms of the Wright tradition to a very different setting by using the same materials, colors, and textures as the surrounding buildings.

5-33. Beaumont pavilion, Washington University.

5-34. Gertrude and William Bernoudy in the garden of the Catlin house in 1963. Photograph by Ed Meyer for the *St. Louis Globe-Democrat,* April 22, 1963, courtesy St. Louis Mercantile Library, University of Missouri–St. Louis.

William and Gertrude Bernoudy maintained a significant presence in the cultural and social life of St. Louis, actively supporting the museum, the symphony, the zoo, the Artists' Guild, and numerous charity events. Gertrude Bernoudy was celebrated for her beauty and sense of style, and together they made a glamorous pair who were as likely as anyone to be included in the photographs accompanying newspaper accounts of art and charity events (Fig. 5–34). A few years after her arrival in St. Louis, Gertrude appeared posed on the steps of the City Art Museum with her dog in a full-page advertisement for the Famous-Barr department store above the caption, "St. Louisans would know her anywhere, The Famous Woman, and the fashions she makes famous. Identifiable with immense chic is Mrs. William Bernoudy." When *Life* magazine covered the Spanish Masked Ball in 1958, it was the Bernoudys who were in the picture.[11]

Because of her work at the Valentin Gallery and her art collection, Gertrude was accepted as an authority on collecting and exhibiting art. The Bernoudys' personal friendships with famous artists, including Marino Marini, Jean (Hans) Arp, Jacques Lipchitz, Oskar Kokoschka, Max Beckmann, and Henry Moore (Fig. 5–35), among many others, as well as with celebrities in theater, music, and dance, only added to their reputations as experts in artistic matters.[12] Within weeks of settling into the Bernoudy house on Litzsinger Road, Gertrude served on a jury with Charles Nagel, Perry Rathbone's successor as director of the City Art Museum, and Kenneth E. Hudson, dean of the School of Fine Arts at Washington University. The three were to select work by local artists for an exhibition at the museum. Nagel wrote her, "It is wonderful that you are generous enough to contribute your sophisticated but detached taste to selecting the best work that we have here in the community."[13] She frequently served on juries for exhibitions, as graciously for shows by schoolchildren as for those by professionals, and she was a favorite at public discussions because she was informed, opinionated, outspoken, and articulate, as well as glamorous. Her remarks at a fine arts sympo-sium organized by Hudson primarily for the Washington University art faculty were quoted at length in subsequent news reports, and Hudson thanked her for her "provocative contributions."[14]

Gertrude Bernoudy could not turn down her husband's friend of many years, Charles van Ravenswaay, who was now director of the Missouri Historical Society, when he asked for her help in organizing the art department for the society's benefit flea market.[15] She also organized a

For Gertrude & Bill
with love from Henry. Much Hadham
1965

5-35. Gertrude and William Bernoudy with the sculptor Henry Moore at his home and studio in England in 1965. Photograph by Charles Gimpel, London, with personal inscription by Moore. Bernoudy Trust Archive.

large exhibition of Asian art at Fort Leonard Wood, Missouri, in 1968. The purpose of the exhibition was to educate American military personnel about Asian culture before they began their tours of duty in Vietnam and East Asia. She lent works of art from the Bernoudys' own collection and was able to borrow others from the City Art Museum in St. Louis, the Nelson-Atkins Museum of Art in Kansas City, and the Boston Museum of Fine Arts, where Perry Rathbone was now the director.

Gertrude and Bill Bernoudy were life members of the Friends of the City Art Museum, and naturally they became friends of Charles E. Buckley when he came to St. Louis in 1964 to serve as director of the museum.[16] A major opportunity for Bernoudy was a commission for a new master plan for the museum during the early years of Buckley's directorship, but nothing came of it. The plan began as a Bernoudy-Mutrux-Bauer project in 1965, and Bernoudy Associates continued to handle related specific projects into 1968. The St. Louis architectural firm of Murphy and Mackey had prepared a long-range development plan in 1959 that retained the formal disposition of Cass Gilbert's original build-

ing with additions in the pared-down expression of the modern movement. In 1954–1955, Murphy and Mackey had been the architects for a new restaurant at basement level that replaced the main south stairway to the museum (the restaurant is now gone and the stairs have been restored) and for an education wing of which only the auditorium survives.

Bernoudy's master plan of 1965 called for increasing the square footage of the museum by 50 percent, to 168,282. The main feature of the plan, as it developed through several schemes, would have been a sculpture court on the north side of the museum in a series of hexagonal terraces down the edge of Art Hill, connected at a lower level to education areas and the basement of the existing museum. One scheme even called for rest rooms and concession booths on a lower terrace for iceskaters and tobogganers. Attention was given to more rationally organizing the support areas—the offices, the library, and the education, storage, and receiving facilities. Bernoudy also prepared studies for new locations for the museum shop. One possibility located the shop above the restaurant with the columns of the south portico glassed in as decorative fea-

5–36. St. Louis Zoological Park, Kiener Memorial Entrance.

tures. Bernoudy Associates did provide new designs for Galleries 6 and 7 that were carried out in 1967 under the supervision of Barry Evens and Richard Arenson, but these designs do not survive. The work in Gallery 7, the Dutch Gallery, included installing parquet floors, repainting the ceiling, adding gold leafing to the capitals, providing new wall coverings, and rewiring.

Buckley began inquiring quietly but widely about architects qualified for museum work in 1968. In 1971, when voters approved the Metropolitan Zoological Park and Museum District, the museum acquired a much stronger base of support and was renamed the Saint Louis Art Museum. That same year the New York architectural firm of Hardy Holzman Pfeiffer Associates was selected to develop a master plan that would provide the basis for major projects during the next decade and a half. Bernoudy's scheme for terracing on Art Hill was filed away and forgotten. The creation of the Zoo-Museum District in 1971 also brought about a change in the governance of the museum, with the creation of an advisory board of trustees in addition to the governing board of commissioners. Bernoudy became a member of the board of trustees in 1978, a recognition of his place in the artistic community that he privately felt should have come to him much earlier.

The Bernoudys were friends of Marlin Perkins, the director of the St. Louis Zoological park. His wife, Carol, and Gertrude had even spent time together on the set of *Wild Kingdom,* his popular television program. The Bernoudys were also friends of the president of the Zoological Board of Control, Howard Baer, who had given one of the parties at which the Bernoudys first met. Perkins and Baer held these positions at the zoo when Bernoudy-Mutrux-Bauer was commissioned to design a new small mammal house in 1965. The firm produced an inventive design that received some publicity and favorable public comment, but the zoo had no funds for the project at the time and it was never built.[17]

In 1966, Bernoudy Associates was commissioned to design a new main entrance for the zoo, the Kiener Memorial Entrance (Fig. 5–36). The design sets a long, gently curved colonnade with seven wide bays, tall and dignified in proportion, in front of a lower serpentine wall with an iron gate at the center. The articulation is simple, almost severe, in the style of the early neoclassicism of the period around 1800. In keeping with that severity and in contrast to Bernoudy's brick houses, the mortar is colored to match the brick and the mortar joints are finished flush with the surface of the brick. The serpentine wall recalls Thomas Jefferson's early neoclassical garden walls at the University of Virginia in Charlottesville; like them, because of the stiffening effect of its continuous curve, the wall can be just one brick thick, even though it rises an average of about eight feet.

In the fall of 1965, the mayor of St. Louis, Alphonso J. Cervantes, asked Charles Buckley and Bernoudy to undertake the decoration of his reception room in City Hall. In November, Bernoudy wrote the mayor congratulating him on his acquisition for the city of the Spanish Pavilion from the 1964–1965 New York World's Fair, which had won the gold medal for architecture at the fair. Bernoudy added that he and Buckley were honored to have been asked to do the office design. After another year and a half, the project finally went forward under the direction of Richard Arenson for Bernoudy Associates. The most important piece was a rug with the seal of the city woven into it, which was custom-made by Vesta S. V' Soske, designers and manufacturers of custom-made rugs in New York, who had occasionally made rugs to Bernoudy's designs for house projects.

There were several other small commercial projects at this time; some of them were not completed, and none of them survive. The Seven-Up Corporation in Clayton commissioned Bernoudy Associates to design a plaza and fountain outside its new office building. The plaza provided a pleasant, small amenity in downtown Clayton during its brief existence. As the glassy, mirror-finished Equitable Building in St. Louis designed by Hellmuth, Obata, and Kassabaum was nearing completion in 1971, Bernoudy Associates was commissioned by the accounting firm of Haskins and Sells to do the interior design of its sixth-floor office, a nicely detailed but rather routine piece of work.

The Bernoudys were close friends of a number of celebrities in the arts, and in 1968 this led to a commission from Margo and Eddie Albert for the addition to their house in Pacific Palisades of a large rehearsal and production studio. Bernoudy made several visits to California at the Alberts' expense, but the arrangements were complicated, involving an independent contractor and a local architect, and the addition finally did not go forward as Bernoudy's project.

Another attractive but unbuilt project of this period was a garden chapel for Memorial Home, a retirement center at Grand and Magnolia in St. Louis (Fig. 5–37). The plan called for two irregular hexagons—a

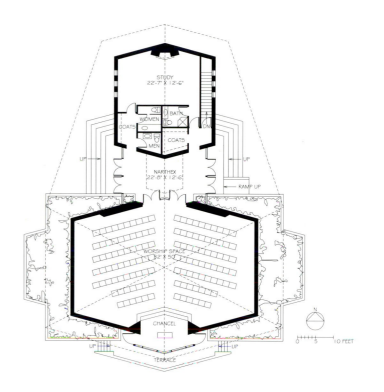

5–37. Project for a garden chapel at Memorial Home.

5–38. United Missouri Bank of Ferguson.

larger one for the sanctuary and a smaller one for utilities and the pastor's study—joined by a narthex. A vast copper roof would cover both hexagons, with the ceiling sloping from a height of twenty feet in the sanctuary to just five feet ten inches at its lowest point, in the study in front of a fireplace. The chapel would have had seating for 126 and with its great sweeping copper roof and hexagonal form recalls Wright's 1947 Unitarian Meeting House in Madison, Wisconsin. The board of Memorial Home could never quite resolve to go ahead with the project. The chapel—like the earlier design for the sanctuary of First Methodist Church in East Alton, which was different but equally interesting and also inspired by one of Wright's buildings—was not built.[18] Together with the completed chapel in East Alton and Temple Emanuel, these designs reflect an extremely creative approach to religious structures.

The United Missouri Bank of Ferguson, now UMB Bank, on Old Halls Ferry Road of 1973–1974 is Bernoudy's most successful surviving commercial work (Figs. 5–38, 5–39). Like the orangery and pool addition to the Goodman house, this design turns to the minimalist, classical tradition of modernism, widely practiced by this date and stemming primarily from the work of Mies van der Rohe. The bank in Ferguson is perfectly symmetrical, with a large, domed skylight centered over the main lobby. The symmetry of the projecting front entrance loggia, all glass and steel, has been compromised by an unnecessary later extension to the right for a ramped entrance that could easily have been designed without disturbing the symmetry. The skylight has a double shell, convex on both the exterior and the interior. The interior, with its weblike metal mullions, has a delicate, suspended quality. This delicate elegance finds additional reflection in the shaped columns that support the skylight opening and in other interior finishes. The original drawings for steel security grilles for the windows show a highly ornamental monogrammatic design abstracted from the bank's initials and a dollar sign, similar to some of the designs Bernoudy was doing for art-glass screens at this time; these grilles are no longer in place.

5–39. United Missouri Bank of Ferguson, interior view.

Marriage to Gertrude had brought foreign travel to Bernoudy's life. Following the honeymoon trip to Japan in 1956 and Bernoudy's first trip to Europe in 1961, they made other trips to Europe, including a visit to Greece in 1965, and traveled often to the Caribbean. Sometimes Gertrude went off on her own. In March 1973 she went by herself on a much different journey—the final step of a long quest for peace from the memories of the horrors visited on her and her family by the Nazis. Irma Turnovská, Gertrude's mother; Žofie Rosenbergová, her nanny; and Hedvika Turnovská, possibly an aunt, were arrested in January, May, and July 1942. They were sent to nearby Terezín (Theresienstadt), which had been converted from a fortress and garrison town to a prison, a central transit point for Jews and other prisoners. Within weeks the three women were sent on separately to death camps. Her father, Richard Turnovský, was sent to Terezín in March 1943, and on to a death camp in December. Gertrude had not returned to Prague since fleeing it in 1939, but that was now her goal. After a short visit with friends, the actor Sam Jaffe and his wife, in London, she went on to Berlin to make her final application for reparations from the German government, expecting five to seven thousand dollars, and to obtain a visa to visit Prague. She stopped in Munich to see relatives, and then went on to Prague. She visited the Jewish cemetery there and arranged to have the names of her family members who were victims of the Nazis added to that of her sister, Ilsa, on the family stone.[19] Then she fled back to London to pull herself together before returning to St. Louis. From London she wrote a long letter to Bill, dated March 29, 1973:

My dearest love,

Well, I did it! I just got back from Prague and I am weeping—but I am so glad I did, I closed the door, the ghost and I will never go back again.

I was at the cemetery the day of my father's birthday [March 27], without even realizing it until today. Strange, isn't it? It was all so neglected and so sad, but I arranged everything to be taken care of, the names on the stone and I think my soul will have more peace.

The city is still so very beautiful, but it is like a phantom, it is dead and so are the people! Everybody bustles around, it is terribly crowded, but everything is grey—no smiles, no laughter, they are all dead, only they don't know it! . . .

I was going to stay another day and when I woke up this morning, I knew I could not stay another hour! But I did what I have done for so many years in my dreams, I walked and walked. It was very strange I found every nook after 34 years and my Czech came back practically flawlessly, nearly better than I spoke it before! *The chapter is closed!* . . .

Did I tell you about Berlin? I am so confused by now, I don't know anymore where I am! All I know is that I want to be with you! *Please* love me, I need you so! I know I am not easy to live with, but I have so many scars and hurts. . . .

. . . These were incredible two weeks—I have to catch my breath! But breath or not, I love you, I love you, I love you!

me.[20]

The money did come through from the German government, eight thousand dollars, and both of the Bernoudys enjoyed a trip to Europe later the same year. Gertrude went on ahead to Berlin in July 1973 to complete the final paperwork and then traveled to a health and beauty spa, a "Schönheitsfarm," in southern Bavaria, to await her husband's arrival. From there she wrote Bill not only of her great love for him and how eagerly she looked forward to his joining her but also complaining about his nagging concern for her good looks. She had gone to beauty spas like this at home, too, but she went on in her letter to assure him that she would "still be the same person, even with wrinkles!"[21]

Bernoudy's residential designs of the late 1970s developed the new themes he had begun exploring with the Pulitzer house and museum project and the Williams villa. In 1975 Bernoudy designed a house for Joseph Pulitzer's brother Michael Pulitzer, then the editor and publisher of the *Arizona Daily Star,* and his wife, Cecille, near Patagonia and Sonoita, Arizona, south of Tucson. Finished in 1977, it carries the formality of the plan of the second Wolfson house further, rendering it in broader, simpler forms (Figs. 5–40, 5–41). In response to its desert setting and in recognition of the traditional adobe architecture of the region, the house is made of stuccoed twelve-inch-thick concrete blocks. The plan is laid out on a four-foot module, or, as a note on the drawings says, using Wright's

5-40. Michael Pulitzer house.

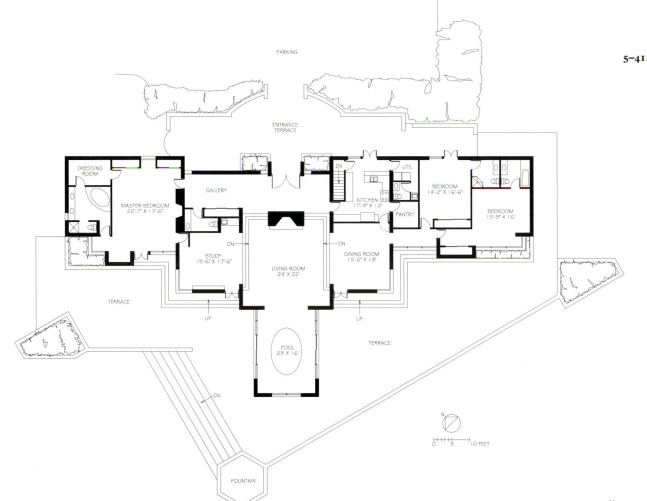

5-41. Michael Pulitzer house, plan.

term, "on a unit system of adjoining 4'-0" x 4'-0" squares." Wright's unit system is followed more rigorously here than in Bernoudy's earlier work (Figs. 5-42, 5-43). The interior faces of all the exterior walls fall on the unit line rather than being centered on it, as do the interior partitions facing the main rooms. When the contract between client and architect was signed in January 1975, the cost for this 4,420-square-foot house was estimated to be $140,000. By the time bidding and negotiating were completed in March 1976, the cost had risen to $246,928.70. When Lou Parrish Builders of Tucson submitted its final billing in May 1977, the total had risen to $306,064. Alvin A. Cullman was involved with the architectural administration of this project, and he continued as a collaborator on principal projects to the end of Bernoudy's career.

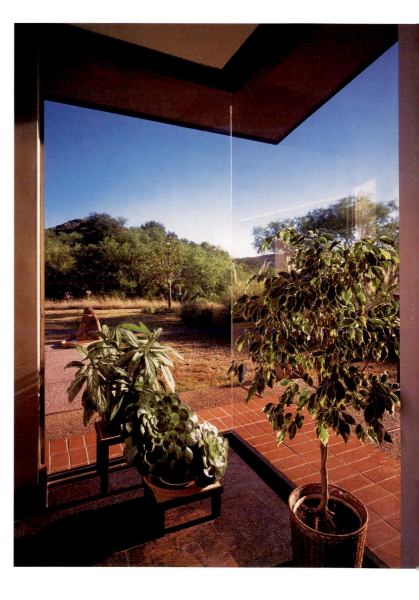

5–42. ABOVE. Michael Pulitzer house, living room.

5–43. RIGHT. Michael Pulitzer house, corner window "breaking the box."

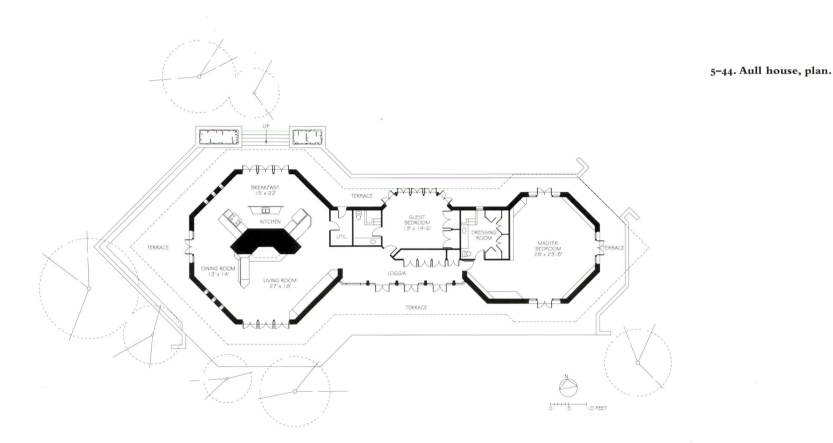

BREAKFAST
15' x 22'

KITCHEN

TERRACE

UP

UTIL

GUEST
BEDROOM
19' x 14'-6'

DRESSING
ROOM

MASTER
BEDROOM
28' x 23'-8'

TERRACE

TERRACE

DINING ROOM
13' x 14'

LIVING ROOM
27' x 18'

LOGGIA

TERRACE

N

0   5   10 FEET

The Pulitzer house offers an interesting contrast to another house Bernoudy designed for a site in Arizona, this one for Mrs. Marie Aull, a Dayton, Ohio, activist in environmental causes who had a ten-acre property in the desert near Sedona (Fig. 5–44). Aull's nephew, Edwin Daniels, a good friend of the Bernoudys, had put them in touch with each other in 1969, and during the following spring, with preliminary designs done, Bernoudy and Aull met at the site and with local contractors. The house would have been built of local stone with battered walls rising from extended angular terraces of similar materials taken from the landscape. The design followed an irregular plan generated by large octagons with walls meeting at angles of 45 degrees and 135 degrees, carrying an undulating hipped roof. Compared with the formality of the Pulitzer house, this de-

5–45. Millard house. Photograph ca. 1984 by Robert Pettus.

sign relates much more closely to Wright's work in the region, such as his own Taliesin West or, much closer in size, the Arnold Friedman vacation lodge in Pecos, New Mexico, of 1945.[22] However, Mrs. Aull lost interest in building on her Arizona property, and the project did not go beyond preliminary drawings.

The design for a house for Mr. and Mrs. John Fouke on Seabrook Island in Charleston, South Carolina, shows a creative response to yet another regional vernacular architecture, this time the beach house of the Southeast. Bernoudy designed a one-story frame house on a raised concrete foundation and with a low-pitched roof. An early scheme included a porch under a deep eave all around the house. But the design was essentially lost as a result of changes made in the course of construction.

Bernoudy first envisioned a low segmental vault form over the entrance court in the design for the Pulitzer town house and private museum in the early 1960s. This form was related in conception to the Roman arches that appeared shortly thereafter in the arcades of the Williams villa and the zoo entrance gates. This form was realized again, prominently, in a house built for Mr. and Mrs. Earl Millard in Belleville, Illinois, in 1977–1978 (Figs. 5–45, 5–46). A low-pitched hip roof emphasizes the length of the house. In striking contrast to it, a cross gable in the form of a low segmental vault, like an oversize pediment, announces the entrance on the approach side and articulates the living room on the garden side. The vault establishes a strong center axis for the entrance doorway and loggia and the living room. The centering of the fireplace

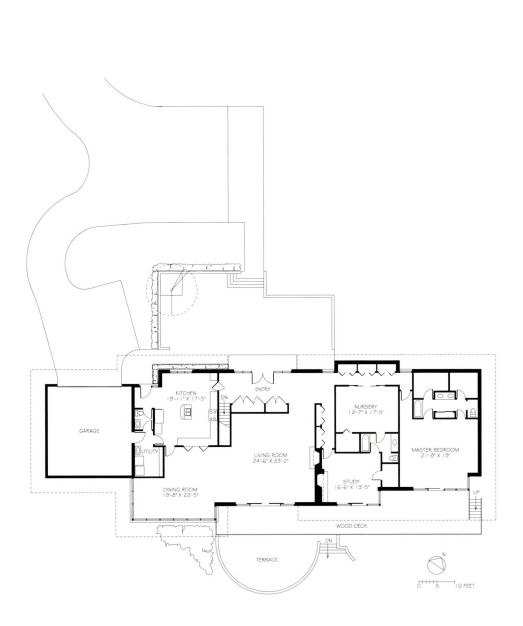

on a side wall creates a cross axis for the living room. A preliminary design shows the springing of the vault at the peak of the hip roof, leaving the vault visually detached from the house and overemphasized. In a quick, conceptual sketch, Bernoudy resolved this awkwardness by pulling the vault down into the zone of the hipped roof, as it was finally built. The curve of the vault is echoed at a smaller scale in the extended decorative motif of the balcony rail (Fig. 5–47). The structure for the vault is provided by laminated timber arches, five inches wide by fifteen inches deep, spaced eight feet on center. Whereas in earlier designs such arches were made a prominent feature in the interior in combination with wood roof decking, they are now concealed by a suspended plaster ceiling. Here Bernoudy presented a pure, abstract arched form, not the structural gymnastics that made it possible, and he must have had one of Wright's late works, the Marin County Civic Center of 1957,[23] in mind. In comparison to the earlier work of each architect, both of these late works are surprising, if not, indeed, a little troubling, given the eloquence with which both men had argued for the natural use of materials. Bauer Brothers Construction Company of Belleville completed the house for a total cost of $221,000. In a serious error in design, essential structural members were not shown on the construction drawings, and their absence was discovered only after the bidding was complete and construction had begun. Bernoudy Associates absorbed the extra cost of $4,619, a sum that represented more than 20 percent of the professional fee.

5–46. Millard house, plan.

5–47. Millard house. Photograph ca. 1984 by Robert Pettus.

5–48. Johnson house addition.

During the 1970s Bernoudy Associates accepted a number of commissions for small projects, additions, and landscaping and pool projects, and the results were often exquisite. In 1974, Mr. and Mrs. James L. Johnson Jr. commissioned an addition and a pool for their house in Ladue, which had been designed by Wesley Wedemeyer and built in the early 1960s (Fig. 5–48). Illuminated panels incorporated in the ceiling and used as a light column in conjunction with a paneled cabinet recall the first Mutrux–Bernoudy project, the Talbot house of 1938–1939. When the project was nearing completion in June 1976, Bettie Johnson wrote to Bernoudy:

> I want you to know how happy I am with the "Bernoudy addition." I knew it would be great but it far surpasses my expectations. It is a happy wonderful place and I am truly thrilled with everything.
> Doing it with you has been the most fun and exciting thing that I have ever done. Sometimes at night when I can't sleep I go down just to look! Thank you so much for your gentle reassurance and interest far and above the call of duty.[24]

A music room addition for Mr. and Mrs. J. A. Van Sant in Ladue, begun in 1977 by Bernoudy Associates with A. A. Cullman as the associate architect, has wood-paneled walls rising to a cornice at window-top height (Fig. 5–49). The cornice, with a convex face like a pulvinated frieze, runs round the room, reminiscent of the familiar light shelves in much of Bernoudy's work. The function of the light shelves carries over, too, as the cornice angles out periodically to form integral light fixtures, which cast light both up and down. The wide vertical boards of the paneled walls are angled out to distribute the sound throughout the room without creating echoes.

5–49. Van Sant house addition.

5–50. Roos pool.

As residential swimming pools became more common, commissions came to Bernoudy Associates for custom-designed pools, something Bernoudy had been creating ever since the spectacular pool he designed for the Pulitzers in 1948. Some were circular, oval, or curved in form, like the one for Lawrence K. Roos in Ladue in 1977, which also incorporated a Jacuzzi (Fig. 5–50). Others, following the model of the Pulitzer pool, were rectangular, like the pool designed for the Ter-Pogossian house in Clayton in 1983, which, like the Pulitzer pool, incorporates a broad waterfall (Fig. 5–51). Invariably these pools enhanced the landscape design through their placement and accompanying terraces and walls.

5–51. Ter-Pogossian pool.

5–52. Kresko pool.

Robert E. Kresko added a pool and pavilion to his house in Ladue in 1982–1983 (Figs. 5–52, 5–53). The house itself had been built about 1924 for Charles Pope O'Fallon.[25] The long, narrow swimming pool serves an important secondary function as a reflecting pool for the domed garden pavilion that stands serenely at one end, like some domestic-size, suburban version of the Taj Mahal, its latticework walls made of wood rather than inlaid marble. Nearby, Bernoudy Associates enclosed a spa with an equally beautiful elaborated arbor or pergola, designed in 1981 for Fielding L. Holmes (Figs. 5–54, 5–55). Here, the arched vault of the Millard house is rendered in an openwork lattice of wood, carried on a stately structure of coupled wood columns and beams.

5–53. Kresko pool from the pavilion.

5–54. LEFT. Holmes pergola.

5–55. BELOW. Holmes pergola detail.

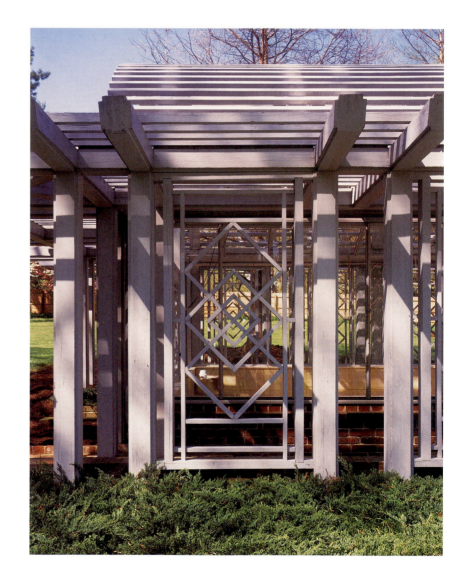

In the Wright tradition, Bernoudy and his partners designed furniture for their houses from the beginning. These pieces were often built in, sometimes freestanding, but always closely related to the architecture. The rich rhythmical patterns of window mullions, built-in or integral lighting fixtures, and custom-designed carpets served as decorative complements within the organic architectural whole. After watching the design and fabrication of the stained-glass windows for Temple Emanuel by Margaret Traherne in 1968–1970, Bernoudy began working in glass as well. The art-glass windows and doors designed by Wright during the early years of his career must have provided a model for Bernoudy as well, although Wright was no longer doing such work when Bernoudy went to Taliesin in 1932 and it was not part of the Usonian program.[26] Bernoudy went well beyond Wright with his freestanding art-glass screens, which were important to their architectural context and sometimes designed for specific buildings but were nonetheless separate from them. Bernoudy compared the distinction to the difference between easel painting and mural painting. To carry the contrast a step further, easel paintings almost never found a comfortable place in Wright's houses, although Wright incorporated decorative mural painting very effectively, whereas easel paintings have been very much at home in Bernoudy's houses.

Bernoudy's art-glass screens share important similarities with Wright's earlier designs in glass. Both avoided pictorial subjects and any suggestion of pictorial space, in sharp contrast to prevailing modes of stained-glass design when Wright was working in this medium. Accordingly, Bernoudy followed Wright's innovation and incorporated glass of varying transparencies so that the form of the panel as a screen of metal supports holding shaped pieces of glass would be unambiguous and the flatness of the material perfectly evident. Wright's early windows had employed highly conventionalized patterns based on plant forms or incorporating totally abstract designs. It was only after he returned from his extended stay in Europe in 1909–1910 that he introduced circular forms into his windows with the commission for the Coonley Playhouse in 1912. The Coonley Playhouse windows were removed and put on the market in the 1950s, and in 1963 the Bernoudys acquired one of them for their own collection.[27]

Bernoudy's own art-glass designs, although much later, began where the Coonley Playhouse windows left off. Wright's designs for the Coon-

5–56. Art-glass screen from the collection of Sally Levy. Photograph 1997 by Sam Fentress.

ley Playhouse windows have been variously attributed to his having seen the early nonobjective paintings of Francis Picabia and František Kupka in Europe, or to his fascination with a parade and its accompanying balloons, flags, and confetti.[28] Bernoudy went quite beyond Wright in the variety of his subject matter, which ranged from purely nonobjective designs, to abstract representations of themes with subjects suggested by the works' titles, such as *Tension* or *Caribbean Sunset,* to identifiable devices wittily used, such as the musical staff and the eighth notes and sixteenth notes incorporated in a screen he designed for Sally Levy on musical and opera themes (Fig. 5–56). Monograms offered another approach. The one designed for Mr. and Mrs. Moscowitz in 1969, mentioned previously, is built on the letters of their name, which can be deciphered with a little patience (Fig. 5–57). It eventually ended up in the Bernoudy collection (see Fig. 3–30).

Like Wright's early examples, Bernoudy's art-glass compositions were designed at the architect's drafting table, with a T-square, triangles, and compasses (see Fig. 5–71). He controlled the proportions through simple geometrical systems, such as a square that would fit in even multiples within the outer frame, which he then repeated, halved, quartered, and doubled. Diagonals might be introduced extending from the diagonal of the square, or the dimension of the square might become the diameter of a circle. This geometrical system was related to the modular system

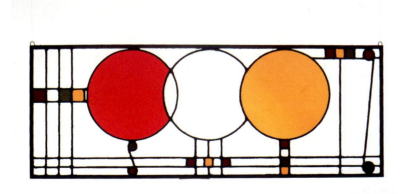

5–57. Moscowitz monogram in an art-glass window. Photograph courtesy Greenberg Van Doren Gallery.

for architectural design, but it allowed a freer, purer, more visible expression of modularity. Wright, and presumably Bernoudy, liked to compare this ordering principle for graphic and architectural design to rhythm in music and, more abstrusely, to harmonic structure. As Wright liked to put it, music and architecture are both "sublimated mathematics."[29] An early set of Bernoudy's art-glass screens was made at the stained-glass studios of the T. C. Esser Company in Milwaukee. Later ones were made by the distinguished St. Louis glass studio of Emil Frei Associates.

Bernoudy's growing reputation for his art-glass compositions and his furniture designs and furnishings culminated in a major exhibition at the Greenberg Gallery in St. Louis in December 1980 and January 1981 (Fig. 5–58).[30] The show focused on the art-glass screens, which sold very well, but it included other types of things as well, including a cast-aluminum planter that was in production briefly in the late 1940s (see Figs. 5–12, 5–63) and the spectacular late furniture design consisting of three small circular tables that fitted under a large one, done in stainless steel, brass, and plate glass (see Fig. 5–17).

In 1982 William Adair Bernoudy was elected to the College of Fellows of the American Institute of Architects and could add the professional honorific FAIA to his name. Bernoudy and Mutrux had joined the AIA, the major professional organization for architects, in 1959, and they both participated in the activities of the strong St. Louis chapter, which had been founded in 1891.[31] For health reasons, Bernoudy was unable to travel to Honolulu for the AIA's annual national meeting in order to receive his FAIA medal; instead, it was presented to him at a special gathering of 160 members and guests of the St. Louis chapter on May 22. The citation reads, "A career of modest but solid professional and public service is matched by William A. Bernoudy's achievement in design. His original inventive work in domestic architecture is both individual and reflective of the strong traditions of the Middle West." At the time the AIA had 38,000 national members, and fewer than 1,000 architects had been recognized with this, the organization's highest honor. Bernoudy's nomination was sponsored by the St. Louis architect J. Robert Green and came with the endorsement of both the St. Louis chapter and six individual chapter members. In addition to the nominators, his references were three prominent St. Louis architects, Gyo Obata, George Kassabaum, and Betty Lou Custer, two St. Louis clients, Stanley Goodman and James Van Sant, another Taliesin fellow, the architect Aaron Green

5–58. Exhibition of Bernoudy art-glass works at the Greenberg Gallery. Photograph courtesy Greenberg Van Doren Gallery.

from San Francisco, and a Los Angeles architect then beginning to emerge as a major international figure in the field, Frank O. Gehry.[32]

Bernoudy was nominated in the areas of design and service to the profession. His nominators mentioned his contributions to arts and cultural organizations in St. Louis and the extraordinary quality of the Bernoudy art collection. But under the heading of service they emphasized his major role in the preservation of the Wainwright Building. The Wainwright, Louis Sullivan's great masterpiece, had been the focus of the tour of downtown St. Louis that Bernoudy arranged for Frank Lloyd Wright in 1939. It is known and admired by architects and lovers of architecture throughout the world for its preeminent place in the history of tall buildings. But it became caught in the general financial

decline of the city's central business district, and by 1972 its survival was seriously threatened. Its ultimate preservation by the state of Missouri resulted from a complex process involving many supporters, but a key early step came when Bernoudy contacted James Biddle, the president of the National Trust for Historic Preservation in Washington, D.C., and persuaded him to use emergency funds from the trust to purchase an option on the building. That provided the necessary time for Missouri's governor, Christopher "Kit" Bond, and other state officials, working with many concerned citizens, to put together a plan to create a new state office building complex on the block incorporating a restored Wainwright Building.[33] The result remains a landmark in the history of the preservation movement.

Bernoudy was especially pleased that the AIA recognized him in the category of design. The nomination, of course, stressed his role in the community as an exponent of Wright's principles, but it nicely distinguished Bernoudy's approach from Wright's, noting that Bernoudy's "work reflects the belief that the design should be shaped by the client's needs rather than the architect's whims, as Mr. Wright was sometimes prone to do." A portfolio of photographs accompanied the nomination. Although only five houses were included—his own house, the Bry residence, the second Wolfson residence, the Williams residence, and the Millard residence—the illustrations chosen appropriately surveyed his design career.

Frank Peters, the arts editor for the *Post-Dispatch,* devoted a full page to Bernoudy and the FAIA award.[34] Peters interviewed Bernoudy and his partners, and the story he wrote was the most authoritative, detailed, and reliable piece about Bernoudy published during his lifetime. As news of the FAIA award spread nationally through AIA outlets, some old friends from Taliesin days sent their congratulations. In his reply to Bradley Ray Storrer, then practicing architecture in Mississippi, Bernoudy sent a copy of the article by Frank Peters. Storrer wrote back about his pleasure in reading it, especially in seeing a photograph of Bernoudy with a cigarette as a glamorous prop because it recalled a photograph by Yousuf Karsh of Wright with a cigarette, even though Wright always insisted he did not smoke. Storrer confessed that he was not sure what was happening in architecture, that for him the "International Style was at least understandable, but Post-Modernism makes no sense at all." He continued: "I can understand your lack of desire to visit Taliesin. I would like to visit, but I, too, could not face Mrs. Wright. I feel very strongly that Mr. Wright did not want a 'school' to be created after he died, but that is exactly what has been done."[35]

Another recognition came to Bernoudy in 1984, an invitation to spend the month of October as a visiting artist in residence at the American Academy in Rome. The American Academy had been founded in 1894 as a center for the study of art amid the incomparable artistic traditions of Rome. Charles Follen McKim, one of the founders and the first president, was the senior partner in the influential architectural firm of McKim, Mead, and White, which exercised great leadership for eclectic architects during the early twentieth century and which from Wright's point of view epitomized everything wrong with American architecture. The academy includes students in classical studies and art history as well as architecture, painting, sculpture, music, literature, and landscape architecture. By the time Bernoudy went there, the McKim, Mead, and White influence on architectural design had long since given way to modernism, or even postmodernism, and its presence was felt primarily in the splendid building the firm had designed for the academy in 1913 on the Gianicolo. Bernoudy was deeply gratified to receive this highly selective recognition from another group of professionals, and he and Gertrude had a grand time in Rome.[36] Bernoudy was further pleased when the Garden Club of America invited him to report on his stay at the American Academy. He wrote that working in that creative atmosphere, with its fine accommodations, the many rich examples of art and architecture immediately at hand, and the company of stimulating colleagues, was akin to his apprenticeship at Taliesin. He believed that this type of experience "imparts to the conscious and more importantly, to the sub-conscious, more than any other form of education."[37]

Bernoudy's four last major works brought his career to an interesting conclusion. In 1982 Mary and James Beggs commissioned Bernoudy Associates to design an addition to their large, comfortable house in Bethesda, Maryland, and to remodel a basement family room. Mr. and Mrs. Beggs, who had lived in St. Louis and been friends of the Bernoudys, had moved to the Washington, D.C., area in 1981 when he became administrator of NASA. The family room project included a luminous ceiling and light columns incorporated in the case work of boxed steel columns, integral light fixtures of the kind used in the Johnson house addition of 1974–1976, both recalling the first Mutrux-Bernoudy project, the Talbot house (Fig. 5–59).

5–59. Beggs house, family room.

5–60. Beggs house, Columbia room addition.

The new addition filled in a space between the garage and the pool house. Opening off the kitchen, it functioned as both a sitting room and a breakfast room (Fig. 5–60). NASA's shuttle program was just getting underway at this time, and the Bernoudys both were avid fans. It was Bernoudy's idea to name the new room Columbia, in honor of the first shuttle to fly successfully in space. For the plan of the Columbia room, Bernoudy used the most traditional of all church plans—a barrel-vaulted central nave separated by columns from aisles on both sides, with the long axis of the nave terminating in a projecting apse. It is a plan that has been used for churches since early Christian times right down to the present, sometimes in very large buildings, but also in countless small churches and chapels, many no larger than the Columbia room. In the Columbia room, both the vaulted ceiling and the walls are of glass. Glass had been used in a similar way in several modern churches designed by architects Bernoudy knew, including the Thorncrown Chapel in Arkansas by Fay Jones and the Wayfarer's Chapel in California by Lloyd Wright, Frank Lloyd Wright's son. Certainly architectural space had spiritual qualities for Bernoudy. It is easy to believe that for these clients and with the opportunity to dedicate a building to light and space, the idea of a chapel, named for the celestial craft Columbia, could well have occurred to him.[38]

Two very large houses, built with generous budgets, stand as final examples of the evolution of the Wright tradition in Bernoudy's work. As early as the Guthrie house of 1955–1956, this evolution had tended toward a more formal and traditional expression with strong symmetries and an axial organization, and toward more sumptuous and elegant details and finishes. The house completed in 1984 for Mr. and Mrs. James A. Schneithorst occupies a large rolling lot, as does the Guthrie house, its near neighbor in Huntleigh, but it has a more commanding presence. Its two-story central block is made distinctive by the introduction of large cylindrical motifs echoed in curved balconies on both the front side for stairs and the garden side for fireplaces and a chimney (Fig. 5–61). Low-pitched hip roofs mount up from the one-story wings to the left and right, to a half level, and then to their crowning two-story height at the center. Familiar materials and forms used in the interior include light shelves, paneled ceiling patterns achieved through the application of wood trim, and custom furnishings (Figs. 5–62, 5–63). But there are subtle differences from earlier houses in the level of finish or, more tellingly, in the use of traditional molding profiles, as on the fascias of the light shelves, an equivalent at the level of small detail to the more traditional axial organization of the principal rooms.

5–61. Schneithorst house, garden side.

The Schneithorsts signed an agreement with Bernoudy in August 1982 and one with Higginbotham Brothers, Inc., the general contractor, the following March. The construction contract stipulated a cost of $584,132, but by the time the project was completed more than a year later the cost had risen by more than $200,000. Bernoudy and his associates were also involved in choosing the furnishings for the house, and they turned to dealers with whom they were well acquainted, including Edward Fields at the Merchandise Mart in Chicago for custom carpets and the McGuire Company in San Francisco for Chinese-style furniture. On the conclusion of the project, Bruce Higginbotham wrote Bernoudy:

In reviewing the Schneithorst home today it became very apparent again what a truly delightful experience this construction job has been. Jim and Caro [Schneithorst] seem to be most pleased with the results of the combined efforts of all involved. Working with you on their home couldn't have been nicer. You are most cooperative on all areas of the construction program and the completed home is one of which you can be very proud.[39]

5–63. Schneithorst house entry, plant stand.

5–62. Schneithorst house, living room.

5–64. McLaughlin house, entrance gate.

J. C. McLaughlin, for whom Bernoudy Associates designed a house in Muttontown on Long Island, New York, was a nephew of the Guthries.[40] McLaughlin first visited St. Louis in the 1970s at the age of nineteen, when he was sent there by the family following the deaths of the Guthries to get their house in shape for putting it on the market. He realized he was dealing with no ordinary house, found out that Bernoudy was the architect, and received a characteristically generous response when he called on him for help. McLaughlin and Bernoudy went through the house together, preparing not only a detailed list of the work that needed to be done but also a list of contractors and craftsmen qualified to do the work. Bernoudy then invited McLaughlin to dinner, and the dinner lasted all night. McLaughlin, who became a devoted friend of the Bernoudys and visited them often, resolved that when he could, he would build a Bernoudy house. He signed the agreement for his house with Bernoudy Associates in December 1982, and the project was completed, with extensive participation by the architects in the acquisition of furnishings, in 1985.

The house occupies a large level lot and with its pool, guest house, and gardens forms a self-contained composition that looks inward (Figs. 5–64, 5–65). The house is organized very strictly along a central axis, starting at a walled entry court, which leads to an entry hall from which the living room is approached down three steps on either side of an axially positioned fireplace, which in form recalls the fireplace of the Guthrie house. The axis continues to the long swimming pool in the garden to the rear, beyond which it finally terminates in the guest house (Figs. 5–66, 5–67, 5–68). A strong cross axis within the house is given visual continuity through hinged shoji that can be opened (Figs. 5–69, 5–70). When asked about the symmetry, McLaughlin simply answered, "Bill wanted it balanced." The character and finish of the details are similar to those in the Schneithorst house. The carpets are custom-designed, and the furniture and furnishings, which Bernoudy helped to select, have an Oriental quality. Again Bernoudy turned to the McGuire firm in San Francisco, and he and the client together visited Lloyd Paxton–Works of Art in Dallas, Texas. The house contains Bernoudy art-glass panels as well (Fig. 5–71). The ultimate tribute to Gertrude Bernoudy came with the assembly of a collection of early modern abstract painting and sculpture for the house, a collection obviously shaped by the example of her collection. The Bernoudys traveled to New York for a party in the new McLaughlin house in the fall of 1985. When Bernoudy returned to St. Louis, he entered the hospital with heart problems.

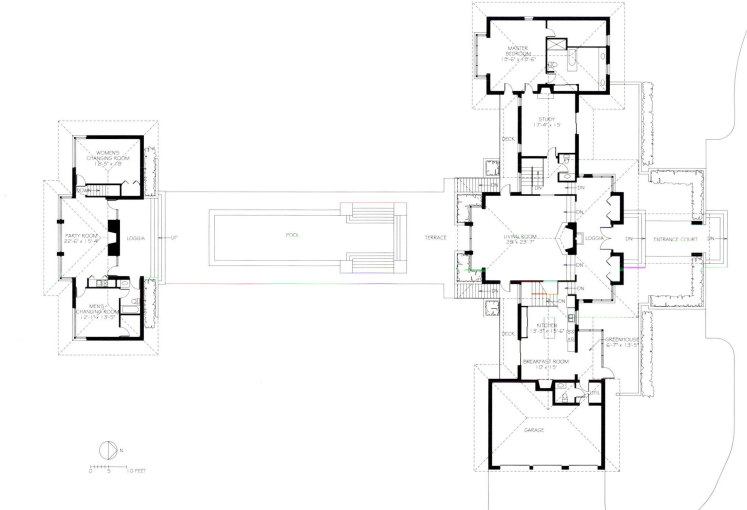

5–65. McLaughlin house, plan.

5–66. LEFT. McLaughlin house, living room.

5–67. RIGHT. McLaughlin house, swimming pool and house.

5–68. LEFT. McLaughlin house, from the southeast.

5–69. BELOW. McLaughlin house, view from the living room looking toward the kitchen and breakfast room.

5–70. RIGHT. McLaughlin house, view from the kitchen looking toward the living room and the study beyond.

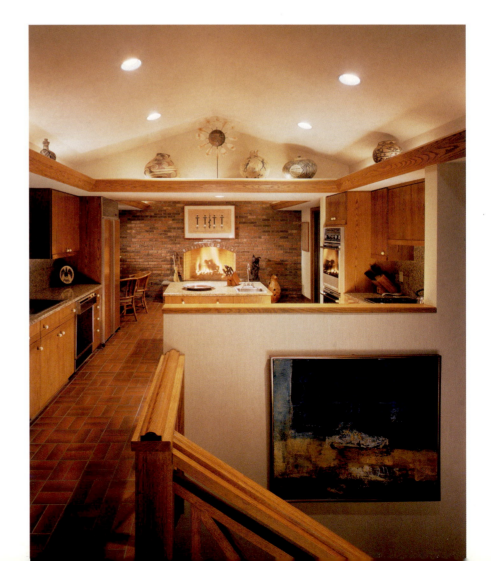

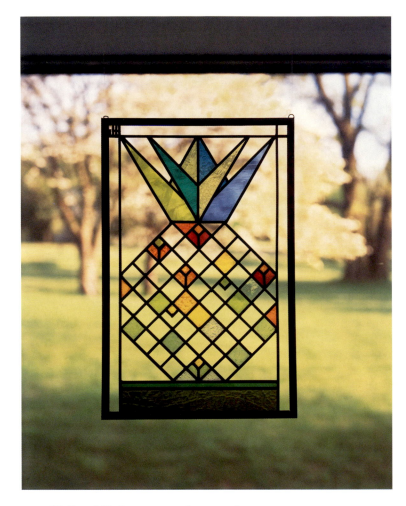

5–71. McLaughlin house, art-glass panel.

Bernoudy's final project, begun in 1985, was a Caribbean vacation house, named Aslantic House, for Mr. and Mrs. Charles Scudder Sommer of St. Louis, which was built on a spectacular site on Tortola in the British Virgin Islands (Figs. 5–72, 5–73). Two perennial themes in Bernoudy's work sum up the principal characteristics of this project: the landscape is always primary, and the architecture should defer to the vernacular context (Fig. 5–74). Bernoudy developed the basic conception on site and quickly sketched it out on a sheet of hotel stationery (Figs. 5–75, 5–76). The house consists of a series of five closely placed buildings, each one story high and under its own gable-on-hip roof. The roofs, with their deep eaves, are not unlike those often seen on Bernoudy's houses, but here they are made of dull red-orange corrugated sheet metal. Two pairs of the five buildings adjoin, and the whole comprises four bedrooms, a living room with a kitchen, and an open pavilion adjoining a swimming pool (Figs. 5–77, 5–78). The structures step up and down the site with that sure sense for joining building and landscape that was always at the heart of Bernoudy's design talent. Moving through the complex, one enjoys a carefully orchestrated experience of different spaces and outlooks, from the sweeping views of the dramatic setting with the ocean beyond, to the terraces surrounding the buildings, to the shade of the roof overhangs, to the sheltered interiors (Figs. 5–79, 5–80). The construction is basic and native, from the metal roofs with their exposed framing on the interior, to the white stuccoed walls, to the terrace walls that echo a local drywall stone-laying tradition. The doors and windows have simple wood shutters; the arched openings of the pavilion were intended to have louvered shutters.

5–72. Sommer house, aerial view from the northwest.

5-73. LEFT. Sommer house, general view from the north.

5-74. RIGHT. Sommer house, detail of stonework and vernacular materials.

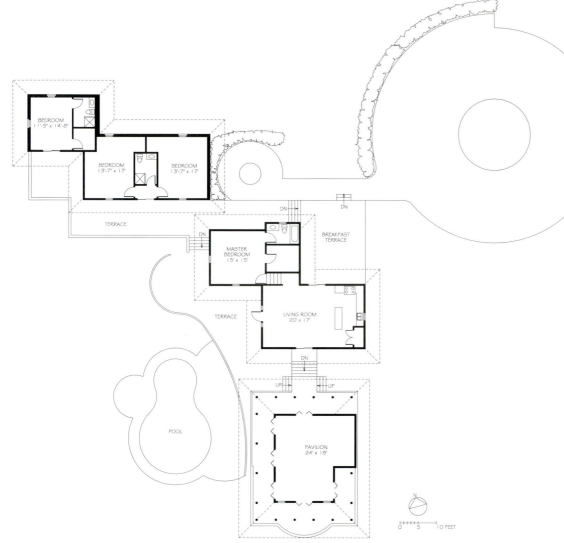

BEDROOM
11'-5" x 14'-8"

BEDROOM
13'-7" x 17'

BEDROOM
13'-7" x 17'

TERRACE

DN

DN

MASTER
BEDROOM
15' x 15'

BREAKFAST
TERRACE

TERRACE

LIVING ROOM
20' x 17'

DN

POOL

UP   UP

PAVILION
24' x 18'

N

0   5   10 FEET

5–75. LEFT. Sommer house, plan.

5–76. BELOW. Sommer house, aerial view
from the southwest.

5–77. RIGHT. Sommer house, pool.

5–78. Sommer house, pool pavilion.

5–79. Sommer house, dining area and living room.

The Bernoudys and their good friends Tom and Mary Hall, for whom Bernoudy had designed the summer house in Maine, spent four blissful days together at Aslantic House just a few months before Bill's death. Following the visit, Mary Hall wrote to the Bernoudys, "I keep thinking, Bill, of what you said about space. We loved just walking and looking beyond—and within—your house—from every different level—*feeling* the space—the circle and the square—feeling so high and yet secure on our firm rock. It is truly a masterpiece."[41]

A major retrospective of Bernoudy's work, organized by Jim Harris, the associate dean of the School of Architecture at Washington University, was held at the Steinberg Gallery on the university campus, from November 2 through December 7, 1986 (Fig. 5–81). The exhibition presented a survey of his architectural work with photographs and drawings for fifteen houses and five public buildings. Also included were examples of his decorative art: two freestanding three-panel art-glass screens, six hanging art-glass panels, two cast-aluminum planters, a low enameled-wood coffee table, and a set of round coffee tables of stainless steel, brass, and plate glass. The exhibition attracted wide interest and was the subject of a lengthy review by Frank Peters in the *Post-Dispatch*.[42] Bernoudy was seriously ill when the exhibition was in preparation, and Harris was concerned that it might prove to be a memorial event. But Bernoudy was able to be present for the opening and sat in a wheelchair greeting the large number of people who turned out. After seeing the exhibition, his friend and client Stanley J. Goodman wrote Bernoudy:

> In your art there is no posturing by the artist, not the slightest suggestion that the house exists as an expression of the architect's psyche rather than an instrument for fulfilling the life of a client . . . I have long felt that deep inside you are a philosopher. You derive deep satisfaction out of approaching design as a challenge to see how well the living environment you create can bring serenity, interrelated beauties, and creative stimulation to your clients, who often become your friends. This is what makes your art distinctive, lasting, and worthy of its place in the highest reaches of architecture.[43]

5–81. Bernoudy's former partners—from the left, Ed Mutrux, Hank Bauer, and Tom Saunders—at the opening of the retrospective at Washington University. Bernoudy Trust Archive.

5–80. Sommer house.

William Adair Bernoudy died on Tuesday, August 2, 1988, at the age of seventy-seven. He had closed his office on North Lindbergh Boulevard in 1986 and moved his practice back to Clayton, where he shared office space with Tom Saunders, his former employee. He suffered from heart disease throughout his last years, and although he rallied somewhat in early 1988, he finally succumbed to it. On August 4, a memorial service was held at Temple Emanuel, that much admired work of the Bernoudy-Mutrux-Bauer firm, at which Joseph Pulitzer Jr., Perry Rathbone, and Howard Baer offered eulogies. At the time of Bernoudy's death, the Halls were in Maine, at the summer house he had designed for them. Mary Hall hurried back to St. Louis to be with Gertrude, but Tom remained in Maine. In a private, profoundly eloquent meditation, he wrote to Gertrude:

> Bill was unique; no one resembled him, even remotely. His life was like a subtle work of art—controlled, complex, original, universal, profound, and to those who knew him infinitely rewarding.
>
> He understood us with all our differences and spoke to each of us in distinct and meaningful ways. He taught the magic of gentleness and composure. Each time we met him, he quietly led us to unanticipated realms of delight. Intolerant of mediocrity, his negative judgments were without rancor—and were often amusing. He could demolish what deserved demolition in a gentle aside. Who ever heard Bill raise his voice? . . .
>
> Perhaps there are, in some sense, two modes of human living. One mode is undistinguished, improvisatory and unreflective. The other mode treats everything with an eye on what is important, universal, and eternal. Bill lived, as the philosophers used to say, *sub specie aeternitatis*—that is, in constant awareness of what is eternally true and real. Let me give an example.
>
> In his creative work Bill's concern was with space—which he understood not merely geometrically but metaphysically. In your use of space, Bill, you captured for us what is ultimately true and real; you linked us with what is eternal. We shall try to take comfort in the thought that you are a part, now, of the space that you understood so deeply.[44]

Gertrude Bernoudy maintained a full and active schedule until her death on April 3, 1994. Again, there was a memorial service at Temple Emanuel. She had directed that her estate be liquidated to establish a charitable and educational foundation in her and her husband's memory. Her trustees sold her art collection at auction at Christie's in New York. Seven of her most important works—a landscape by Ernst Ludwig Kirchner, three paintings by Paul Klee, two still lifes by Giorgio Morandi, and a bronze sculpture by Henri Matisse—were included with other important works at the evening sale on November 9, 1994. The balance of the collection—including many more important works, such as a late Paul Cézanne watercolor landscape, three works by Pablo Picasso, and works by Jacques Lipchitz, Juan Gris, Georges Braque, Marino Marini, and many others—was sold the next day in a session devoted entirely to her collection.[45] The remaining contents of her house on Litzsinger Road were auctioned at Selkirk's in St. Louis.

Prior to her death, Gertrude Bernoudy had arranged for one of the most important pieces from their collection, the *Birth of the Muses* by Jacques Lipchitz, done in his undulant, rhythmical, expressive late style (Fig. 5–82), to stay in St. Louis. Lipchitz was a good friend of the Bernoudys and had consulted closely with them on the creation of the piece and its installation outside their house. It was a favorite of Bill's, so much so that Gertrude thought he spent an inordinate amount of time looking at it. She left the *Birth of the Muses* to the Missouri Botanical Garden in St. Louis. There, prominently displayed in a landscaped setting, it serves as a testament to Gertrude Bernoudy's remarkable artistic judgment and as a memorial to the architect she loved and admired.

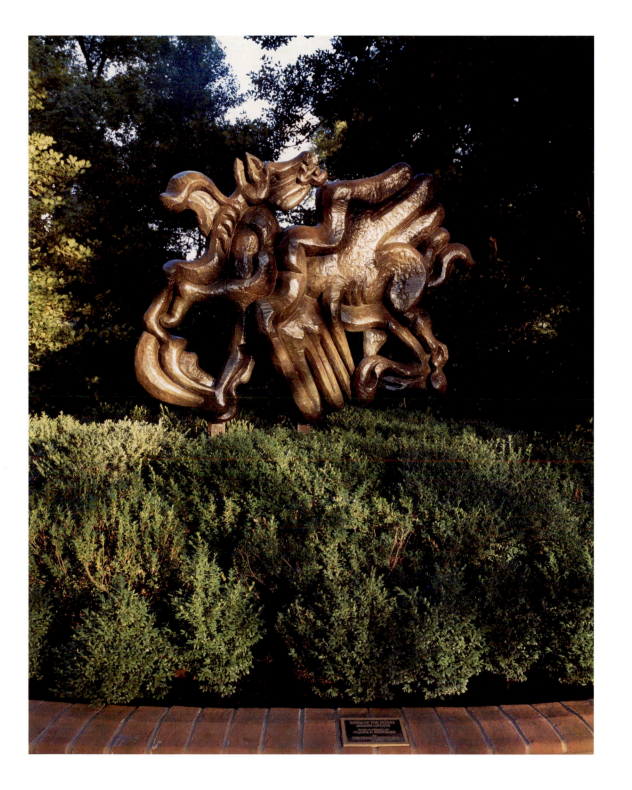

5–82. *Birth of the Muses* by Jacques Lipchitz, in the Missouri Botanical Garden. Gift of Gertrude Bernoudy in memory of William Bernoudy.

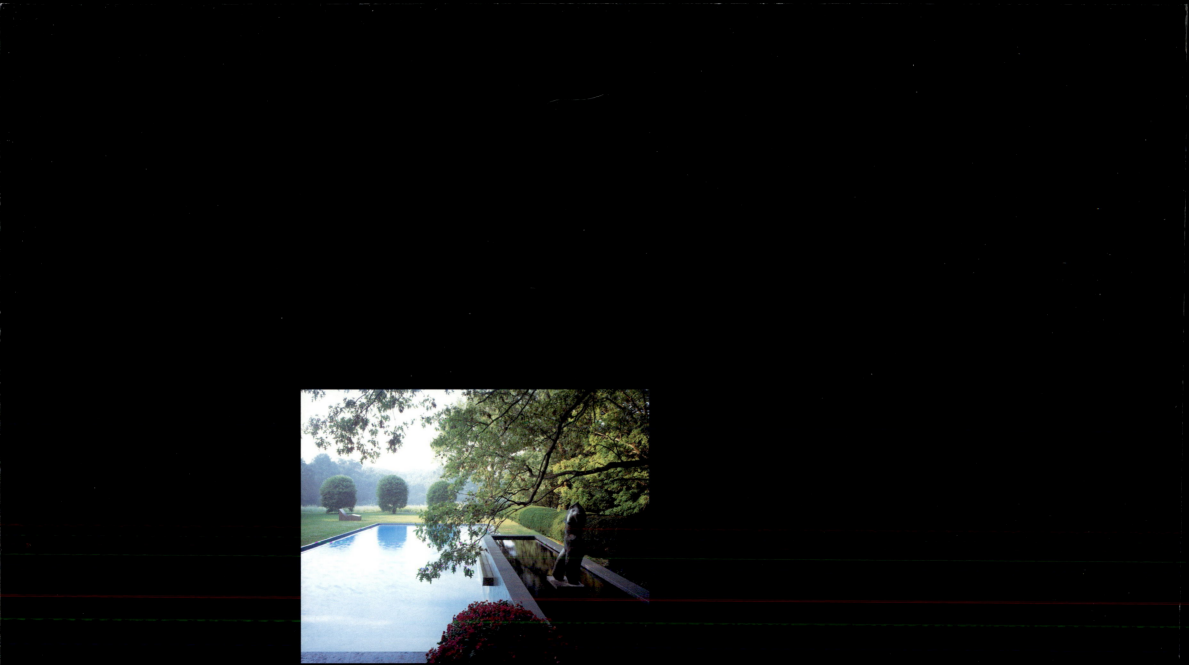

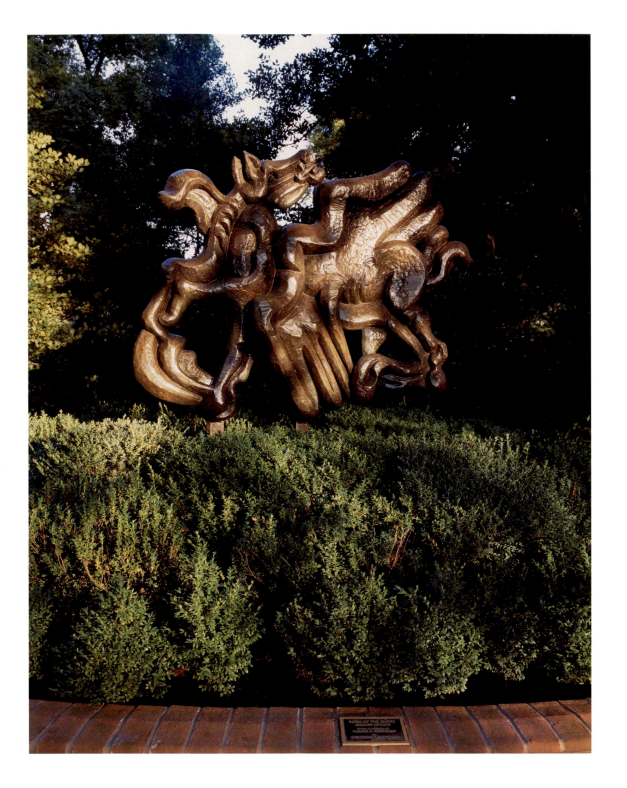

5–82. *Birth of the Muses* by Jacques Lipchitz, in the Missouri Botanical Garden. Gift of Gertrude Bernoudy in memory of William Bernoudy.

Catalog of Projects Discussed

Entries include major works photographed for this book and discussed in it. They are arranged chronologically. Although many houses were built over several years, the dates used here are those from the completion of the design, taken from project files, dated drawings, and occasionally building permits. When such complete information does not survive, the best available information—usually from dated construction drawings—has been used.

1939
Dr. and Mrs. C. Hudson Talbot, a residence at 4 Sumac Lane, St. Louis.

1940
Mr. and Mrs. Charles Lee Doris, a residence at 12501 Maret Drive, St. Louis.

1941
Dr. and Mrs. Robert Elman, a residence in St. Louis; not built.

1946
Mr. and Mrs. Wayne Leeman, a residence in St. Louis; not built.
Landon Martin, a residence in St. Louis; not built.

1947
Bernoudy-Mutrux architectural office, 7 Forsythe Walk, St. Louis; demolished.
Edgar Kaufmann Jr., garden project, New York City; not built.

1948
Mrs. Lucille W. Butler, a residence at 232 N. McKnight Road, St. Louis.
Mr. and Mrs. Donald Grant, a residence at 430 Dielman Road, St. Louis; enclosed porch addition for Marjorie Hankins, 1972.
Mr. and Mrs. Julius Klyman, a residence at 440 Dielman Road, St. Louis.
Mr. and Mrs. Joseph Pulitzer Jr., a pool and pavilion, St. Louis.

1950
Elizabeth Bernoudy, a residence at 9590 Litzsinger Road, St. Louis; addition for William and Gertrude Bernoudy, 1956.
Mary Coleman, a residence at 1863 Cliff Drive, Columbia, Missouri; enlarged 1962–1963 and extensively altered.
Mr. and Mrs. Rudolph Czufin, a residence at 24 Dielman Road, St. Louis; remodeled and enlarged, 1965–1967.
Robert Detchemendy, a residence at 1829 Cliff Drive, Columbia, Missouri.
Betty and Frank Hudak, a residence at 18 Pine Lake Drive, Collinsville, Illinois; addition, 1982.
Morris and Marilyn Moscowitz, a residence at 9255 Clayton Road, St. Louis.
Mr. and Mrs. Edouard Mutrux, a residence at 2 Sumac Lane, St. Louis.
Geneva Mutrux, a residence at 5 Sumac Lane, St. Louis.
Helen and David Pinkney, a residence at 1844 Cliff Drive, Columbia, Missouri.
Dorothy Pollock and Janice Janes, a residence at 1859 Cliff Drive, Columbia, Missouri.
Ruth and Frank Schweiss, a residence at 4 Daniel Road, St. Louis.

1952

Mr. and Mrs. George Eichelsbach, a residence at 5084 Lake Tishomingo Road, Hillsboro, Missouri.

George Lueders, a residence at 164 Flamingo Drive, St. Louis.

Dr. and Mrs. Frank W. Simms, a residence at 3 Sumac Lane, St. Louis.

Thomas Jefferson School, a gymnasium addition, St. Louis.

Robert and Suzanne Wolfson, a residence at 6 Fordyce Lane, St. Louis.

1953

Mr. and Mrs. Theron Catlin, a residence at 34 Brentmoor Park, St. Louis.

Mr. and Mrs. Robert M. Close, a residence at 801 Kent Road, St. Louis.

1954

Henry and Mary Guhleman, a residence at 2018 Green Berry Road, Jefferson City, Missouri.

Lawrence and Jane Kahn, a residence at 8 Robin Hill Lane, St. Louis.

Mr. and Mrs. Harry Tenenbaum, a residence at 1 Apple Tree Lane, St. Louis; demolished.

1955

Mr. and Mrs. William S. Friedman, a residence at 17 Brazillian Court, St. Louis.

Mr. and Mrs. Cecil M. Guthrie, a residence at 11 Squires Lane, St. Louis.

1956

Mr. and Mrs. Frank Bush, a residence at 4 Vista Brook Lane, St. Louis.

Robert Detchemendy, a residence at 301 McNab, Columbia, Missouri.

Mr. and Mrs. Joseph Grand, a residence at 821 Cella Road, St. Louis.

Mr. and Mrs. Thomas Hall, a summer residence at Northeast Harbor, Maine.

Alden J. Perrine, a residence at 1114 S. Perrine Street, Centralia, Illinois.

Mr. and Mrs. Leo Phelan, alterations and additions to a residence at 10810 Kennerly Road, St. Louis.

A residence in Ladue.

Mr. and Mrs. Ben Roth, an addition to a residence at 1140 Lay Road, St. Louis.

James W. and Nancy Singer, a terrace at 31 Crestwood Drive, St. Louis.

1957

Harry Lenart, Scottsdale office building, Phoenix, Arizona, not built.

Mr. and Mrs. Edward J. Walsh Jr., a residence at 319 Wolfrum Road, St. Charles, Missouri.

1958

Mrs. Jay C. Hormel, a residence at 630 Nimes Road, Bel Aire, California.

Dr. and Mrs. C. M. Waggoner, a residence at 712 Hilltop, Columbia, Missouri.

1959

Mr. and Mrs. John Childress, a residence at 2 Deer Creek Hill Drive, St. Louis.

1960

First Methodist Church, a new church, chapel, and education and office wing at 1001 Third Street (at Kent), East Alton, Illinois.

Mr. and Mrs. John J. Horan, a residence at 13428 Conway Road, St. Louis.

Dr. and Mrs. Alex H. Kaplan, a residence at 11 Winding Brook Lane, St. Louis.

Mr. and Mrs. Roswell Messing, a residence at 30 Westwood Country Club, St. Louis.

Mr. and Mrs. Fred O. Tietjen, a residence at 2503 Green Tree, Jefferson City, Missouri.

1961

Mr. and Mrs. Dan J. Forrestal, a residence at 17 Bellerive Country Club Grounds Drive, St. Louis.

Mr. and Mrs. Clarence H. King, a residence at 9052 Clayton Road, St. Louis.

Mr. and Mrs. Fristoe Mullins, a country residence at Highway WW, Eolia, Missouri.

Mr. and Mrs. Stuart Symington Jr., a residence at 745 Cella Road, St. Louis.

Temple Emanuel, a new synagogue and educational wing at 12166 Conway Road, St. Louis.

1962

Mr. and Mrs. Arthur Monsey, a residence at 446 N. Warson Road, St. Louis.

1963

William and Nina Elder, a residence at 2105 Rock Quarry Road, Columbia, Missouri.

Dr. and Mrs. Walter Graul, a residence at 22 West Sherwood Drive, St. Louis.

Mr. and Mrs. Maurice Hirsch, a residence at 25 Balcon Estates, St. Louis.

Irvin and Sara Larner, a residence at 16 Villa Coublay Drive, St. Louis.

Paul W. and Gertrude Mathews, a residence at 2101 Rock Quarry Road, Columbia, Missouri.

Ramada Inns, a motel, Clayton Square Motor Lodge, at 216 North Meramec, St. Louis.

Mr. and Mrs. John T. Rogers, a residence at 1 Deer Creek Hill Dr., St. Louis.

304 Corporation, a commercial building, University Tower Apartments, Galveston, Texas; not built.

1964

Mr. and Mrs. Erwin Bry, a residence at 15 Upper Barnes Road, St. Louis.

1965

Jack and Loraine Conreux, a residence at 12901 Thornhill Drive, St. Louis.

Allan and Ruth Gallup, a residence at 2 Sherwyn Lane, St. Louis.

Dr. and Mrs. Bert H. Klein, a residence at 8 Deacon Lane, St. Louis.

Mr. and Mrs. Joseph Pulitzer Jr., a house and museum project at 24 Westmoreland Place, St. Louis; not built.

Robert and Ethel Wolfson, a residence at 6 Upper Barnes Road, St. Louis.

1966

Mr. and Mrs. George Hoblitzelle, a residence at Osage Ridge Road, Augusta, Missouri.

St. Louis Art Museum, interior gallery alterations and master planning, Forest Park, St. Louis; gallery alterations subsequently remodeled, master plan not carried out.

St. Louis Zoological Park, Kiener Memorial Entrance gate, Forest Park, St. Louis.

Mr. and Mrs. Harry O. Schloss, an addition to a residence at 8 Middlebrook Drive, St. Louis.

Washington University, the Beaumont Pavilion on the Washington University campus, St. Louis.

Mrs. Eugene (Marie) Williams, a residence at 32 Glen Eagles Drive, St. Louis.

1967

Stanley and Alice Goodman, an addition to a residence at 35 Briarcliff Drive, St. Louis.

1968

City of St. Louis, redecoration of the mayor's office; subsequently remodeled.

Mr. and Mrs. Robert Phillips, a residence at 8970 Moydalgan Road, St. Louis.

Seven-Up Corporation, an exterior plaza and fountain for a Clayton office building, 121 S. Meramec, St. Louis; demolished.

1969

Eddie and Margo Albert, a studio addition to their residence at 719 Amalfi Drive, Pacific Palisades, California; not built.

1970

Marie Aull, a residence at Color Cove near Sedona, Arizona; not built.

Memorial Home, a garden chapel for a retirement center at Grand and Magnolia Avenues in St. Louis; not built.

1971

Haskins and Sells, interior finishing of offices on the sixth floor of the Equitable Building, 10 S. Broadway, St. Louis; subsequently remodeled.

Mr. and Mrs. Allen J. Portnoy, a residence at 935 Barnes Road, St. Louis.

Mr. and Mrs. Charles Yalem, a garden pavilion in St. Louis County, Missouri.

1974

United Missouri Bank of Ferguson, a bank building at 10751 Old Halls Ferry Road, St. Louis.

1975

Mr. and Mrs. Michael Pulitzer, a residence at Crown C Ranch, Patagonia/Sonoita, Arizona.

1976

Mr. and Mrs. John Fouke, a residence at Seabrook Island, Charleston, South Carolina; altered in construction.

Mr. and Mrs. James L. Johnson Jr., an addition to a residence at 8921 Moydalgan Road, St. Louis.

1977

Mr. and Mrs. Earl Millard, a residence at 7409 Concordia Church Road, Belleville, Illinois.

Lawrence K. Roos, a swimming pool at 943 Tirrill Farms Road, St. Louis.

Mr. and Mrs. J. A. Van Sant, an addition to a residence at 17 Picardy Lane, St. Louis.

1981

Fielding L. Holmes, a pergola and spa at 43 Glen Eagles Drive, St. Louis.

1982

Robert E. Kresko, a swimming pool and pavilion at 36 Glen Eagles Drive, St. Louis.

Mr. and Mrs. James A. Schneithorst, a residence at 5 Squires Lane, St. Louis.

1983

James and Mary Beggs, an addition to a residence at 5408 Falmouth Road, Bethesda, Maryland.

J. C. McLaughlin, a residence at 461 Muttontown-Eastwoods Road, Muttontown, New York.

Dr. and Mrs. Michel M. Ter-Pogossian, a swimming pool at 2 Brentmoor Park, St. Louis.

1985

Mr. and Mrs. Charles Scudder Sommer, a vacation residence at Little Bay, Tortola, British Virgin Islands.

Notes

The majority of the Bernoudy office records are preserved at the Missouri Historical Society in St. Louis, where the private files and correspondence of the Bernoudys have also been lodged. These are identified in the notes as William Bernoudy papers and Bernoudy Trust Archive, respectively. Specific information about individual buildings comes from the project files in the William Bernoudy papers unless indicated otherwise.

Chapter 1   "How I Might Study Architecture"

1. William Adair Bernoudy to Frank Lloyd Wright, ca. September 1932. Unless otherwise noted, correspondence to or from Taliesin (Frank Lloyd Wright, Olgivanna Lloyd Wright, Karl E. Jensen, or Eugene Masselink) is held by the Frank Lloyd Wright Foundation, Taliesin West, Scottsdale, Arizona, and is quoted by permission. All of the letters from Frank Lloyd Wright and his office quoted herein are copyright 1999 The Frank Lloyd Wright Foundation, Scottsdale, Arizona (hereafter cited as Frank Lloyd Wright Foundation).

2. "Wright Apprentices," *Time,* September 5, 1932, p. 33. For identifying obscure references such as this and for other help, I am indebted to Stephanie Parrish, who served as a research assistant for this book while enrolled in the course on modernism in St. Louis architecture that I led as a visiting professor at Washington University in spring 1996.

3. The certificate of birth and a certified copy of the birth record for William Adair Bernoudy both survive in the Bernoudy Trust Archive. The information is also recorded in the "Birthday Book" kept by Elizabeth Bernoudy, also in the Bernoudy Trust Archive.

4. I am indebted to Esley Hamilton for this information. Letter of March 25, 1997.

5. Information about the wedding and the young couple is preserved in a detailed scrapbook, prepared by Jerome Bauduy Bernoudy at the time, in the Bernoudy Trust Archive.

6. The diaries, in the Bernoudy Trust Archive, are detailed, concise, and factual. The elder Bernoudy died on September 18, 1948.

7. I am indebted to Wallace Klein, who in retirement from University City High School serves as the school's archivist and historian. He provided a copy of Bernoudy's transcript, copies of pages from the University City High School yearbook, the *Dial,* for 1929, and information about the school, its faculty, and some of Bernoudy's classmates. Interview, January 17, 1996.

8. Academic record of William Adair Bernoudy issued by the Office of the University Registrar, Washington University.

9. Interview with Joanne Kohn, January 16, 1996.

10. Introduction to a lecture given to the Kirkwood Garden Club, April 20, 1936.

11. Bernoudy Trust Archive.

12. Carolyn Hewes Toft, Esley Hamilton, and Mary Henderson Gass, *The Way We Came: A Century of the AIA in St. Louis,* ed. George McCue (St. Louis: Patrice Press, 1991), 60–61.

13. Pat Kirkham, *Charles and Ray Eames, Designers of the Twentieth Century* (Cambridge: MIT Press, 1995), 12–13.

14. Frank Lloyd Wright, *Modern Architecture, Being the Kahn Lectures for 1930* (Princeton: Princeton University Press, 1931). The lectures were reprinted in *The Future of Architecture* (New York: Horizon Press, 1953). *An Autobiography* (London, New York, and Toronto: Longmans, Green, 1932). The work was reprinted, revised, and enlarged several times, first in 1943. The most recent edition is New York: Horizon Press, 1977.

15. Jerome Bauduy Bernoudy diary, April 10, 1930, Bernoudy Trust Archive.

16. Karl E. Jensen to Bernoudy, October 11, 1932, Frank Lloyd Wright Foundation.

17. Entry in the diary of Jerome Bauduy Bernoudy, Bernoudy Trust Archive.

18. John Lloyd Wright, *My Father Who Is on Earth,* new ed., with comments by Frank Lloyd Wright, introduction by Narciso G. Menocal, and postscript by Elizabeth Wright Ingraham (Carbondale and Edwardsville: Southern Illinois University Press, 1994); Meryle Secrest, *Frank Lloyd Wright: A Biography* (New York: Alfred A. Knopf, 1992; rpt. New York: HarperCollins, 1993).

19. See, for example, Edgar Tafel, *Apprentice to Genius: Years with Frank Lloyd Wright* (New York: McGraw-Hill, 1979), reprinted as *Years with Frank Lloyd Wright: Apprentice to Genius* (New York: Dover, 1985); Randolph C. Henning, ed., *"At Taliesin"* (Carbondale and Edwardsville: Southern Illinois University Press, 1992); Tobias S. Guggenheimer, *A Taliesin Legacy: The Architecture of Frank Lloyd Wright's Apprentices* (New York: Van Nostrand Reinhold, 1995); Curtis Besinger, *Working with Mr. Wright: What It Was Like* (Cambridge and New York: Cambridge University Press, 1995).

20. For the term *Prairie Style,* see H. Allen Brooks, *The Prairie School* (Toronto: University of Toronto Press, 1972), 8–13.

21. Neil Levine, *The Architecture of Frank Lloyd Wright* (Princeton: Princeton University Press, 1996), 62–63; Secrest, *Frank Lloyd Wright,* 159–61.

22. Secrest, *Frank Lloyd Wright,* 157–59.

23. Levine, *Frank Lloyd Wright,* 27.

24. Mary Jane Hamilton with Anne E. Biebel and John O. Holzheuter, "Frank Lloyd Wright's Madison Networks," in *Frank Lloyd Wright and Madison: Eight Decades of Artistic and Social Interaction,* ed. Paul E. Sprague (Madison: Elvehjem Museum of Art, University of Wisconsin-Madison, 1990). *The Wisconsin Badger,* 1932, Jack Thompson, editor-in-chief; *The 1933 Badger,* senior class, University of Wisconsin, Arthur Churchill Benkert, editor; in the University of Wisconsin Archives, University Library, Madison.

25. "Frank Lloyd Wright," *Wendingen* 7, nos. 3–9; reprinted as *The Life-Work of the American Architect Frank Lloyd Wright* (Santpoort, Holland: C. A. Mees, 1925); the book was reprinted by Horizon Press in 1965 and by Dover in 1992.

26. John Howe collection, State Historical Society of Wisconsin, Madison.

27. Edgar Tafel to Bernoudy, November 28, 1933, Bernoudy Trust Archive.

28. Philip Holliday to Bernoudy, November 29, 1933, Bernoudy Trust Archive.

29. "Taliesin Fellowship," *American Magazine of Art* 26 (December 1933): 552–53.

30. Henning, ed., *"At Taliesin,"* 10.

31. It served as a masthead for the "At Taliesin" newspaper articles the fellowship began writing in 1934 and was the inspiration for a Taliesin Fellowship project under Fyfe's leadership to decorate the Celebrity Room of the Blue Parrot Patio Restaurant in Chicago for Grace Pebbles, a friend and former client of Wright's. There the silhouettes were of Oak Park buildings Wright had designed. Henning, ed., *"At Taliesin,"* 10–11, 16–17.

32. Typescript, Bernoudy Trust Archive.

33. Henning, ed., *"At Taliesin,"* 16–17.

34. Howe collection, State Historical Society of Wisconsin.

35. One hundred twelve of the 285 columns have been reprinted in Henning, ed., *"At Taliesin."*

36. "At Taliesin" article by Alfred Bush, in ibid., 29.

37. Bernoudy journal, William Bernoudy papers.

38. It is not clear if Bernoudy is referring to the languorous trio of the second movement, the Andante, or the brilliant third movement, the Allegro Assai, although the reference to "a magnificent structure" suggests the latter.

39. Fifteen drawings in Bernoudy Trust Archives.

40. Interview with Herbert Fritz and Georgia Eloise Fritz at their home adjoining Taliesin, August 16, 1996.

41. Secrest, *Frank Lloyd Wright,* 53, 197, 215.

42. "At Taliesin" articles, May 24 and June 7, 1934, in the Howe scrapbook, Howe Collection, State Historical Society of Wisconsin.

43. J. B. Bernoudy diary, Bernoudy Trust Archive.

44. This was a leading example of a common activity among artists in the period; see James Gordon Rogers Jr., *The Ste. Genevieve Artists' Colony and Summer School of Art, 1932–1941* (Ste. Genevieve, Mo.: Foundation for Restoration, 1998).

45. Bernoudy to George and Helen Beal, September 20, 1934, MS133:B3:1–17, part of the Taliesin Collection, Department of Special Collections, Kenneth Spencer Research Library, University of Kansas Libraries, Lawrence (hereafter cited as Taliesin Collection, University of Kansas).

46. Undated letter, Taliesin Collection, University of Kansas. The letter was probably written on October 13; his father's diary notes that he went to the opera that night, and in the letter he wrote, "Tonight I am going to hear Madame Butterfly in the Dress Circle."

47. *The Disappearing City* (New York: William Farquar Payson, 1932). As with other publications by Wright, this volume went through subsequent revisions and new editions, republished in 1945 as *When Democracy Builds* and in 1958 as *The Living City.*

48. The most richly anecdotal account is Eugene Masselink's "At Taliesin" article of February 10, 1935; see Henning, ed., *"At Taliesin,"* 106–10.

49. See *Frank Lloyd Wright: The Phoenix Papers,* Herberger Center for Design Excellence, Arizona State University, 1995, especially John Meunier, "A Model for the Decentralized City: An Interview with Cornelia Brierly," 1:32–46.

50. Undated letter with the return address of La Hacienda, Chandler, Arizona, with a note added by the Beals that they answered it on March 14, 1935, Taliesin Collection, University of Kansas.

51. The "At Taliesin" column for March 22, 1935, reported in detail on the Los Angeles trip; see Henning, ed., *"At Taliesin,"* 118–20. Bernoudy's snapshots survive in the Bernoudy Trust Archive.

52. Discussed in "At Taliesin," August 30, 1934; see Henning, ed., *"At Taliesin,"* 72–73. A copy of the first number is in the Howe Collection, State Historical Society of Wisconsin, Madison.

53. Henning, ed., *"At Taliesin,"* 123.

54. J. B. Bernoudy to Frank Lloyd Wright, June 15, 1935, Frank Lloyd Wright Foundation.

55. Henning, ed., *"At Taliesin,"* 140–43.

56. Letter from Bernoudy to George and Helen Beal, August 16, 1935, Taliesin Collection, University of Kansas.

57. Olgivanna Lloyd Wright to Bernoudy, November 14, 1935, Bernoudy Trust Archive and Frank Lloyd Wright Foundation.

58. Bernoudy to Helen and George Beal, November 7, 1935, Taliesin Collection, University of Kansas.

59. George S. Parker to Bernoudy, December 30, 1935, Bernoudy Trust Archive.

60. Olgivanna Lloyd Wright to Bernoudy, December 29, 1935, Bernoudy Trust Archive and Frank Lloyd Wright Foundation.

61. Undated letter from Bernoudy to Wright, written fall 1935. Frank Lloyd Wright Foundation.

62. Frank Lloyd Wright, "Apprenticeship-Training for the Architect," *Architectural Record* 80 (September 1936): 207–10.

63. This was Wright's own version of his stay at the University of Wisconsin, which historians have subsequently shown to be not quite factual. See, for example, Secrest, *Frank Lloyd Wright.*

64. Typescript text of the talk, Bernoudy Trust Archive.

Chapter 2   The Making of the Architect, 1935–1946

1. Laura P. Carpenter to Wright, April 3, 1936, Frank Lloyd Wright Foundation.

2. Wright to Bernoudy and to Laura P. Carpenter, April 14, 1936, Frank Lloyd Wright Foundation.

3. Bernoudy to Wright, April 17, 1936, Frank Lloyd Wright Foundation.

4. Wright to Bernoudy, April 24, 1936, Frank Lloyd Wright Foundation.

5. Bernoudy to Wright, April 30, 1936, Frank Lloyd Wright Foundation.

6. Bennett Champ Clark to Bernoudy, January 4, 1936, Bernoudy Trust Archive.

7. Bernoudy to Helen and George Beal, April 20, 1936, Taliesin Collection, University of Kansas.

8. Both manuscript rough draft and typed final draft, Bernoudy Trust Archive.

9. Wright's fourth Princeton lecture, "The Cardboard House," deals with themes in Bernoudy's lecture; see *The Future of Architecture,* 129–48. *Architectural Record* published fourteen short articles by Wright between May 1927 and December 1928 that comprise one of the fullest statements of his approach to architecture in his own words. Extensive typed copies of these survive in the Bernoudy Trust Archive. They have been reprinted in *In the Cause of Architecture, Frank Lloyd Wright,* ed. Frederick Gutheim (New York: Architectural Record, 1975), 53–232.

10. Bernoudy to Wright, August 28, 1936, Frank Lloyd Wright Foundation.

11. Wright to Bernoudy, September 3, 1936, Frank Lloyd Wright Foundation.

12. Bernoudy to Helen Beal, September 14, 1936, Taliesin Collection, University of Kansas.

13. Bernoudy to *House and Garden,* undated but written shortly after the Garden Club lecture, Bernoudy Trust Archive.

14. Bernoudy Trust Archive.

15. Lazer Grossman, Educational Director, the Jewish Center of Saint Louis, to Bernoudy, September 23, 1936, Bernoudy Trust Archive.

16. Bernoudy to Mr. and Mrs. Wright, Christmas 1936, Bernoudy Trust Archive.

17. Secrest, *Frank Lloyd Wright,* 450.

18. Olgivanna Lloyd Wright to Bernoudy, January 15, 1936, Bernoudy Trust Archive and Frank Lloyd Wright Foundation.

19. Fyfe to Bernoudy, postmarked June 30, 1937, Bernoudy Trust Archive.

20. Fyfe to Bernoudy, March 1, 1937, Bernoudy Trust Archive.

21. Philip Holliday to Bernoudy, March 23, 1937, Bernoudy Trust Archive.

22. James Drought to Bernoudy, April 1937, Bernoudy Trust Archive.

23. Bernoudy to Helen and George Beal, January 5, 1938, Taliesin Collection, University of Kansas.

24. Harold Wescott to Bernoudy, April 13, 1937, Bernoudy Trust Archive.

25. Invoice in Bernoudy Trust Archive.

26. Bernoudy to Helen and George Beal, July 31, 1937, Taliesin Collection, University of Kansas.

27. Bernoudy to Helen and George Beal, January 5, 1938, Taliesin Collection, University of Kansas.

28. Bernoudy Trust Archive.

29. Bernoudy to Helen and George Beal, July 31, 1937, and January 5, 1938, Taliesin Collection, University of Kansas.

30. For information about Cobblestone Gardens and Bernoudy's experience there, I am indebted to Michael J. Murphy, who wrote an excellent paper on the subject for a course on modernism in St. Louis architecture that I led while a visiting professor at Washington University in St. Louis in spring 1996.

31. Dorothy May Anderson, *Women, Design, and the Cambridge School* (Mesa, Ariz.: PDA Publishers, 1980); Leslie Rose Close, "A History of Women in Landscape Architecture," in Judith B. Tankard, *The Gardens of Ellen Biddle Shipman* (Sagaponack, N.Y.: Sagapress, 1996).

32. As indicated in the application for Missouri registration as an architect that Bernoudy filed in 1946, copy in the Bernoudy Trust Archive.

33. Drought to Bernoudy, May 18, 1938, Bernoudy Trust Archive.

34. Interview with Edouard Mutrux and his wife, Elsa Krull Mutrux, September 21, 1995.

35. See "The Mutrux Family of Washington University," *Washington University Alumni Bulletin,* December 1949.

36. E. Bénézit, *Dictionnaire des peintres, sculpteurs, dessinateurs et graveurs,* new ed. (n.p.: Librairie Gründ, 1950), 3:221.

37. For the catalog to the exhibition see Henry-Russell Hitchcock and Philip Johnson, *The International Style,* in the 1966 edition with a new foreword and appendix by Hitchcock (New York: W. W. Norton). Originally published in 1932 under the title *The International Style: Architecture since 1922.*

38. "St. Louis, Mo.: Office and Residence Integrated in One Structure," *Architectural Record* 86 (July 1939): 41–44.

39. Bernoudy to Wright, September 15, 1938, Frank Lloyd Wright Foundation.

40. Wright to Bernoudy, September 18, 1938, Frank Lloyd Wright Foundation.

41. See Tafel, *Apprentice to Genius.*

42. For information about Wright's visit to St. Louis and his lecture there, I am indebted to Lynn DuBard, who wrote an excellent paper on the subject for my course on modern architecture at the University of Missouri–Columbia, fall semester 1996. The principal sources are the local newspapers, the *St. Louis Star, St. Louis Globe-Democrat,* and *St. Louis Post-Dispatch,* for January 9, 10, and 11.

43. On the close relationship of the Great Hall and Sullivan's work, see Osmund Overby, "A Place Called Union Station: An Architectural History of St. Louis Union Station," in H. Roger Grant, Don L. Hofsommer, and Osmund Overby, *St. Louis Union Station, a Place for People, a Place for Trains* (St. Louis: St. Louis Mercantile Library, 1994).

44. Bernoudy to Helen and George Beal, January 1 and February 27, 1939, Taliesin Collection, University of Kansas.

45. Bernoudy to Helen and George Beal, January 1 and February 27, 1939, Taliesin Collection, University of Kansas.

46. Unpublished typescript with Bernoudy's handwritten corrections, Bernoudy Trust Archive.

47. Bernoudy to Helen and George Beal, December 15, 1939, Taliesin Collection, University of Kansas.

48. For a good recent discussion of the Transcendentalist basis of Wright's thought, see William Cronon, "Inconstant Unity: The Passion of Frank Lloyd Wright," in *Frank Lloyd Wright, Architect,* ed. Terence Riley (New York: Museum of Modern Art, 1994), 8–31.

49. The scholar Jay Hambidge developed the ideas of dynamic symmetry based on his studies of ancient Greek art and architecture early in the twentieth century and began lecturing on the subject in 1917, especially in New York artists' studios. From the beginning, he saw this not only as a way to understand Greek art but also as a method for modern artists to perfect their work. He developed his theories in *Dynamic Symmetry: The Greek Vase* (New Haven: Yale University Press, 1920) and *The Parthenon and Other Greek Temples: Their Dynamic Symmetry* (New Haven: Yale University Press, 1924). Professional journals for artists and architects began to carry articles on the application of the theory, and Bernoudy probably first knew about dynamic symmetry through articles such as Claude Bragdon's "Regulating Lines," *Architecture* 64 (December 1931): 329–34. Edward B. Edwards wrote a popular handbook for artists and architects, *Dynamirhythmic Design: A Book of Structural Pattern* (New York: Century Co., 1932), republished with a new title, *Pattern and Design with Dynamic Symmetry* (New York: Dover, 1967). These theories have remained of interest to many modern architects and found another outlet later at Taliesin in the eurythmic exercises and dances learned from Gurdjieff. Knowledge of the golden section and Greek geometry predated Hambidge's work, of course, and occasionally influenced the work of artists; see, for example, R. Stanley Johnson, *Cubism and la Section d'Or:*

Reflections on the Development of the Cubist Epoch, 1907–1922 (Chicago and Düsseldorf: Klees/Gustorf Publishers, 1991).

50. See H. Allen Brooks, "Wright and the Destruction of the Box," in *Writings on Wright,* ed. H. Allen Brooks (Cambridge: MIT Press, 1981), 175–88.

51. See especially the May 1928 article on wood reprinted in *The Cause of Architecture,* ed. Gutheim, 179–86.

52. See David Van Zanten, "Schooling the Prairie School: Wright's Early Style as a Communicable System," in *The Nature of Frank Lloyd Wright,* ed. Carol R. Bolon, Robert S. Nelson, and Linda Seidel (Chicago and London: University of Chicago Press, 1988), 70–84.

53. A carefully preserved clipping of the article survives in the Bernoudy Trust Archive.

54. Interview with Nancy Smith, April 3, 1996.

55. Olgivanna Lloyd Wright to Bernoudy, October 16 and November 28, 1939, Bernoudy Trust Archive and Frank Lloyd Wright Foundation.

56. Bernoudy to Mr. and Mrs. Wright, June 11, 1940, Frank Lloyd Wright Foundation.

57. Information about Harris Armstrong is from a lecture by Andrew Raimist, April 9, 1996, in a course on American architecture and modernism in St. Louis offered by the author as a visiting professor at Washington University.

58. J. B. Bernoudy's diary, entries for December 29, 1939, and January 14, 1940, Bernoudy Trust Archive.

59. A mimeographed catalog in 250 copies was prepared by Charles E. Peterson for the exhibition, with lists of not only the works being shown but also the members of the HABS team. A copy is held by the St. Louis Public Library. Interview with Charles E. Peterson, October 15, 1995.

60. Bernoudy to Helen and George Beal, undated letter probably written October 13, 1934, Taliesin Collection, University of Kansas.

61. Bernoudy to Wright, January 5, 1942, requesting the letter of recommendation, in both Bernoudy Trust Archive and Frank Lloyd Wright Foundation. An undated note from Bernoudy to Wright thanking him for the letter of recommendation, and a letter from Wright's secretary, Eugene Masselink, to Bernoudy confirming that the recommendation had been sent, February 18, 1942, Bernoudy Trust Archive. Bernoudy to Wright, March 2, 1941, again thanking him for the recommendation and saying that he expected to be called any day now, Frank Lloyd Wright Foundation.

62. The founding of the Washington, D.C., chapter was reported in the *Journal of the Society of Architectural Historians* 2:2 (October 1942). In addition to Bernoudy, Perry T. Rathbone and Ralph Cole Hall were present, both young officers in the navy. Louise Pulitzer, whose husband, Joseph Pulitzer Jr., was also in the navy, was hostess for the founding meeting. Leicester Holland, head of the Division of Fine Arts at the Library of Congress, an architectural historian who had played a key role in the founding of HABS, presided. The sixth person present was another architectural historian, Alan Burnham, who was a civilian employee of the camouflage workshop of the War Plans Division of the U.S. Navy Bureau of Yards and Docks. Information from Marian C. Donnelly, letter

of September 9, 1997, and Charles E. Peterson, letter of September 29, 1997.

63. I am grateful to Lynn H. Nicholas for this information about Valentin, which she collected in preparing *The Rape of Europa: The Fate of Europe's Treasures in the Third Reich and the Second World War* (New York: Alfred A. Knopf, 1994).

Chapter 3   Bernoudy-Mutrux, 1946–1955

1. *House and Garden,* June 1953, pp. 72–75, 145.

2. *Progressive Architecture,* May 1960, pp. 158–61.

3. Donald Hoffmann, *Frank Lloyd Wright's Fallingwater: The House and Its History* (New York: Dover, 1978), 69–70.

4. William Bernoudy papers.

5. Ibid.

6. Typescript of the extemporaneous broadcast, Bernoudy Trust Archive.

7. Frank Peters, "Architectural Treasures of Low Profile," *St. Louis Post-Dispatch,* July 11, 1982. Correspondence in the project files confirms this general statement. Nearly all of the contracts between the architects and clients were signed by Bernoudy.

8. *Knoll Index of Contemporary Design* (New York: Knoll Associates, 1954). The full list of international designers included Franco Albini, Hans Bellman, Lewis Butler, Pierre Jeanneret, Florence Knoll, George Nakashima, Kurt Nordstrom, Abel Sorensen, Richard Stein, Ilmari Tapiovaara, plus fifteen textile designers.

9. John Luten to Bernoudy, February 9, 1957, Bernoudy Trust Archive.

10. David A. Hanks, *Innovative Furniture in America: From 1800 to the Present* (New York: Horizon Books, 1981), 119–20.

11. Interview with Richard Carney at Taliesin, August 16, 1996.

12. Bernoudy to Eugene Masselink, December 16, 1948; Masselink to Bernoudy, January 6, 1949; Frank Lloyd Wright Foundation.

13. *Bulletin, the Quarterly Newsletter of the Frank Lloyd Wright Building Conservancy* 7:1 (February 1998): 9.

14. Bernoudy to Mr. and Mrs. Wright, undated letter written fall 1946 and letters dated July 27 and August 5, 1947, Frank Lloyd Wright Foundation.

15. Bernoudy to Wright, January 20, 1948, Frank Lloyd Wright Foundation.

16. Miscellaneous correspondence between Mutrux and Wright or Masselink, 1951–1958, Frank Lloyd Wright Foundation.

17. Both the *St. Louis Post-Dispatch* and the *St. Louis Globe-Democrat* reported the lecture in their editions for November 24, 1948.

18. *Living for Young Homemakers* 4:6 (June 1951): 56–65, 107, 113.

19. Letter from Coleman to Stephen Toth, June 4, 1951, William Bernoudy papers.

20. One example is the Abby Beecher Roberts house of 1936; see William Allin Storrer, *The Frank Lloyd Wright Companion* (Chicago: University of Chicago Press, 1993), 247.

21. *Perfect Home,* February 1952, pp. 12–13.

22. Bernoudy to Mr. and Mrs. Wright, July 18, 1949; Eugene Masselink to Bernoudy, July 21, 1949; Frank Lloyd Wright Foundation.

23. Interview with Henry Herold, April 11, 1996.

24. Storrer, *Wright Companion,* 243–44, 290.

25. Thomas C. Jester, ed., *Twentieth-Century Building Materials, History, and Conservation* (New York: McGraw-Hill, 1995), 124–25, 229–33.

26. Storrer, *Wright Companion,* 292–93.

27. Herbert Jacobs to Jack and Lu Howe, July 4, 1966, Howe Collection, State Historical Society of Wisconsin.

28. *Progressive Architecture,* December 1956, pp. 96–97. An earlier (1929), larger example of a lamella roof is found in the St. Louis Arena, recently demolished, done before the economies of prefabrication as seen in the Jefferson School. E. F. Porter Jr., "The Flying Lamella and How It Turned into a Dinosaur," *St. Louis Post-Dispatch,* August 14, 1983; and Esley Hamilton, "The Lamella Barn at Faust Park, Chesterfield, Missouri," *Newsletter of the Missouri Valley Chapter of the Society of Architectural Historians* 4:4 (winter 1998): 5–6.

29. William Bernoudy papers.

30. Guggenheimer, *A Taliesin Legacy,* 56–57.

31. A discussion with George Talbot, in Madison, Wisconsin, August 17, 1996, first brought this to my attention. Talbot had interviewed Hill as part of a Frank Lloyd Wright oral history project.

32. "This House Is a Converted Swimming Pavilion," *House Beautiful* 101:6 (June 1959): 134–35, 184–85.

33. Drawings of the early versions of the Kahn house, which are held by the Washington University School of Architecture, were exhibited in a show of architectural drawings organized by Esley Hamilton at the Missouri Historical Society, St. Louis, in 1991. For the Hanna house, see Storrer, *Wright Companion,* 243–45.

34. Lawrence Kahn to Bernoudy, July 15, 1982, Bernoudy Trust Archive.

Chapter 4   Bernoudy-Mutrux-Bauer, 1955–1965

1. I am indebted to Linda M. Dougherty of Bank of America, St. Louis, a trustee of the Bernoudy Foundation, for information about Gertrude's early life gathered on a trip to Prague in May 1998. We are grateful to Eleanora Holešovská for her assistance in Prague.

2. This account is based on documents in the Bernoudy Trust Archive. It differs from the account given in the *St. Louis Post-Dispatch* obituary of April 5, 1994, which placed the marriage earlier and had her returning to Europe before World War II. The obituary also formed the basis for the brief tribute to her published in the catalog of the sale of her artworks at Christie's, New York, on November 10, 1994. The life of Gertrude Bernoudy deserves a book in itself; here it is recounted only as it contributes to an understanding of the life and architectural career of William Bernoudy.

3. Certificate of successful completion of ground instruction dated May 29, 1942; photos in flying gear; offprints of published articles, 1944 and 1946,

inscribed by Kurt Lange, M.D.; legal documents for name change, property settlement, and divorce; all Bernoudy Trust Archive.

4. New York City telephone directories show them both living at 30 Beekman Place until the divorce, then her living at that address until her move to St. Louis. Following the divorce, he is listed as a broker at 115 Broadway with a residence at 434 East Fifty-second Street. Following her move to St. Louis, he returned to the Beekman Place residence. New York Public Library, microfilm collection.

5. *New York Times,* obituary and subsequent articles about the gallery, August 21, September 10, and September 19, 1954, and about the closing of the gallery, June 8, 1955; *Newsweek,* October 18, 1954.

6. Nicholas, *The Rape of Europa,* 3–30.

7. *House and Garden,* October 1954, pp. 134–35.

8. Morton D. May to Gertrude Lenart, Bernoudy Trust Archive. The principal beneficiaries of Valentin's estate were two brothers, a sister, and a former wife. There were also important gifts to five museums, including the City Art Museum of St. Louis. Eight close friends also received bequests; Gertrude Lenart received two paintings, *Clown* by Paul Klee (1929) and *Pommes et Couteau* by Georges Braque (1927). In addition, she purchased another notable painting, *Diana,* by Paul Klee, from Valentin's estate. Photocopies of Curt Valentin estate papers, Bryan Cave LLP, St. Louis.

9. Phone conversation with Linda M. Dougherty, June 8, 1998.

10. *House and Garden,* June 1954, pp. 88–91.

11. Letter of condolence following Bernoudy's death from Benjamin Roth to Gertrude Bernoudy, August 3, 1988, Bernoudy Trust Archive.

12. Dojean Saymon, Lady Smithers, to Gertrude Bernoudy, August 7, 1988, Bernoudy Trust Archive.

13. Certificate of marriage, Bernoudy Trust Archive, and report of the marriage, *St. Louis Post-Dispatch,* June 20, 1955.

14. A particularly handsome presentation of these Japanese traditions widely read by architects was published at just this time: Norman F. Carver Jr., *Form and Space of Japanese Architecture* (Tokyo: Shokokusha Publishing Co., 1955). Carver not only wrote the text but also took the photographs and designed the book. See pp. 130 ff. for the influence of Zen Buddhism. Even Walter Gropius, creator of the Bauhaus, joined this movement with *Katsura: Tradition and Creation in Japanese Architecture,* written with Kenzo Tange, with photographs by Yasuhiro Ishimota (New Haven: Yale University Press, 1960).

15. Dozens of thank-you letters for these visits are in the Bernoudy Trust Archive.

16. Wright died on April 9, 1959, in Phoenix, and was buried in the cemetery at the family's Unity Chapel at Taliesin in Wisconsin on April 12. He was just two months shy of his ninety-second birthday. Secrest, *Frank Lloyd Wright,* 11–13.

17. Telephone interview with Henry Herold, July 11, 1998. Herold, an architect in Tiburon, Calif., carries on the Wright tradition in his work.

18. Ibid.

19. Bernoudy to David and Helene Thompson, November 6, 1961, Bernoudy Trust Archive.

20. Peters, "Architectural Treasures of Low Profile."

21. Storrer, *Wright Companion,* 400. Curtis Besinger wrote an article about the Grand house, "The Secret to Eye Comfort: Light from All Directions," *House Beautiful* (May 1960): 200–203, 256.

22. Bernoudy Trust Archive.

23. Bernoudy to Harry Lenart, Bernoudy Trust Archive.

24. Interviews with Edouard Mutrux and Elsa Mutrux, September 21, 1995, and Henry Bauer and Ann Bauer, November 30, 1995.

25. The details of the project, the people involved, and other aspects of the congregation are chronicled in a booklet issued on the twentieth anniversary of the congregation containing a "History of Temple Emanuel" by Estelle Shamski (published by Temple Emanuel, 1976).

26. See Andreas Jordahl Rhude, "Structural Glued Laminated Timber: History and Early Development in the United States," *APT Bulletin: The Journal of Preservation Technology* 29:1 (1998): 11–17.

27. The temple was pictured in the *National Jewish Post,* April 5, 1963, in an advertisement for Rilco wood products from the Weyerhaeuser Company. Rabbi Rosenbloom's description was written to accompany that advertisement. Copies preserved in the project file, William Bernoudy papers.

28. Carol Herselle Krinsky, *Synagogues of Europe: Architecture, History, Meaning* (New York: Architectural History Foundation, 1985), 21–27.

29. Interview with Howard Baer, February 8, 1996.

30. Storrer, *Wright Companion,* 400–401.

31. Meredith L. Clausen, *Spiritual Space: The Religious Architecture of Pietro Belluschi* (Seattle: University of Washington Press, 1992).

32. Albert Christ-Janer and Mary Mix Foley, *Modern Church Architecture: A Guide to the Form and Spirit of 20th Century Religious Buildings* (New York: McGraw-Hill, 1962).

33. Mary M. Stiritz, with Cynthia Hill Longwisch and Carolyn Hewes Toft, *St. Louis: Historic Churches and Synagogues* (St. Louis: St. Louis Public Library and Landmarks Association of St. Louis, 1995), 122–23.

34. These criticisms, from Lewis Mumford, one of the most ardent advocates of the modern movement, are quoted in the introduction to Thomas H. Creighton and Katherine M. Ford, *Contemporary Houses, Evaluated by Their Owners* (New York: Reinhold, 1961), 7.

35. Ibid., 7–13.

36. For the house as furnished by its new owners, Kyrle and Ann Boldt, see Christy Marshall, "Unbolted: Splash Founder Shares His Bernoudy-Designed Home," *St. Louis Homes and Lifestyles,* July–August 1998, pp. 46–52.

37. Description prepared by Bernoudy, June 19, 1963, for publication by the Washington University School of Architecture in a series featuring alumni, in this case Edouard Mutrux; Bernoudy Trust Archive.

38. William Bernoudy papers.

39. Nina Elder to Don Lehman, January 17, 1964, and Gertrude Mathews to Bernoudy and Lehman, September 23, 1964, William Bernoudy papers.

40. Maurice L. Hirsch Jr. to the author, February 5, 1998.

41. For the Wright buildings, see Storrer, *Wright Companion,* 292–93, 323, 331, 430–31, 466–67.

42. *Galveston Daily News,* February 2, 1963, front page.

43. Storrer, *Wright Companion,* 378–79.

44. Pictured in supplement to *Louisville Courier-Journal,* Sunday, March 13, 1966.

45. Bernoudy to David Wheatley, July 26, 1963, Bernoudy Trust Archive.

46. Interview with Henry Herold, November 29, 1995.

47. Telephone interview with Charles Klein, March 20, 1996.

48. Interview with Henry Bauer and Ann Bauer, November 30, 1995.

49. Charles Klein to Bernoudy, June 18, 1982, congratulating him on his election to the College of Fellows of the American Institute of Architects, Bernoudy Trust Archive.

Chapter 5   Bernoudy Associates, 1965–1988

1. *House Beautiful* 107:10 (October 1965): 220–21.

2. As told to the author by Lee Wightman, present owner of the house, November 10, 1995.

3. Unidentified letter simply addressed "Dear Gladys," October 5, 1941, Bernoudy Trust Archive.

4. *House Beautiful* 107:10 (October 1965): 227. The other five architects were Aaron Green, who had a long association with Wright, Ralph Anderson, William Kenneth Frizzell, Malcolm Wells, and John M. Johansen.

5. Robert Venturi, *Complexity and Contradiction in Architecture* (New York: Museum of Modern Art, 1966).

6. Interview, August 2, 1996, with George Talbot, who was on the architecture faculty at Washington University from 1963 to 1968.

7. See for example, in Storrer, *Wright Companion:* Neils Residence, Minneapolis, 1949, p. 326; Anthony Residence, Benton Harbor, Mich., 1949, p. 328; or Austin Residence, Greenville, S.C., 1951, p. 367.

8. Interview with Thomas H. Saunders, December 21, 1995.

9. Interview with the current owner of the house, Robert Falk, June 19, 1996.

10. Both projects were published in *Architectural Digest:* the first, winter 1969, pp. 44–57; the second, January–February 1975, front cover and pp. 72–75. The second, the pavilion project, was also published in the *St. Louis Post-Dispatch,* Home Magazine, October 3, 1971. Other information from a letter to Sam Fentress from Joseph Braswell, January 20, 1997.

11. Famous-Barr full-page advertisement, *St. Louis Globe-Democrat,* Wednesday, August 19, 1959, p. 14; *Life,* April 14, 1958.

12. Extensive correspondence with people in the arts survives in the Bernoudy Trust Archive.

13. Charles Nagel to Gertrude Bernoudy, October 23, 1958, Bernoudy Trust Archive.

14. Kenneth E. Hudson to Gertrude Bernoudy, May 26, 1959, Bernoudy Trust Archive.

15. Charles van Ravenswaay to Gertrude Bernoudy, May 22, 1958, Bernoudy Trust Archive.

16. See Osmund Overby, *The Saint Louis Art Museum: An Architectural History* (St. Louis: Saint Louis Art Museum Fall Bulletin, 1987).

17. "Zoo Reveals Plans for Mammal House," *St. Louis Globe-Democrat,* February 9, 1966.

18. Information about the Memorial Home project from an interview with Corinne Haverstick, former member of the Memorial Home board and a friend of the Bernoudys, January 18, 1996.

19. Government documents concerning the deportation and death of Gertrude's mother and father are in the Bernoudy Trust Archive. Other information about family members and the fate of Prague's Jews was collected by Linda M. Dougherty on a trip to Prague in May 1998.

20. Gertrude Bernoudy to William Bernoudy, from Berlin, March 2, 1973, from Munich, March 25, 1973, and from London, March 29, 1973, Bernoudy Trust Archive.

21. Gertrude Bernoudy to William Bernoudy, from Berlin, July 25, 1973, from Rottach-Egern, July 30, 1973, Bernoudy Trust Archive.

22. Storrer, *Wright Companion,* 296.

23. Ibid., 448–49.

24. Bettie S. Johnson to Bernoudy, June 8, 1976, Bernoudy Trust Archive.

25. *St. Louis Country Club: The First 100 Years* (St. Louis: St. Louis Country Club, 1992), 210.

26. For Wright's decorative arts, see David A. Hanks, *The Decorative Designs of Frank Lloyd Wright* (New York: Dutton, 1979).

27. The window was acquired from the New York and Paris dealer Theodore Schempp, a friend of the Bernoudys, for $500.00 shortly before the market for Wright pieces began its dramatic rise. Bernoudy to Schempp enclosing payment, May 13, 1963, Bernoudy Trust Archive.

28. Compare Hanks, *Decorative Designs of Wright,* 111–13, and Storrer, *Wright Companion,* 134–37, 175.

29. Frank Lloyd Wright, *An Autobiography,* rev. ed. (New York: Horizon Press, 1977), 248–52. For a further discussion of the analogy with music, see Narciso Menocal, "Form and Content in Frank Lloyd Wright's 'Tree of Life' Window," *Elvehjem Museum of Art Bulletin,* University of Wisconsin-Madison (1983–1984): 18–32.

30. Reviewed by Patricia Degener with photos by Robert C. Holt Jr., *St. Louis Post-Dispatch,* December 29, 1980, section 1–8D, pp. 1, 4. Other reviews by Mary King for the *Post-Dispatch,* no date, and by Michael G. Rubin, no source or date, are in the clippings file at the Greenberg Van Doren Gallery.

31. Toft, Hamilton, and Gass, *The Way We Came,* ed. McCue.

32. Copies of the nomination survive in the Bernoudy Trust Archive and the AIA Archives in Washington, D.C. Unfortunately the AIA Archives does not preserve the letters of reference sent to the AIA in support of the nomination.

33. Paul E. Sprague, "The Wainwright—Landmark Built and Saved," *Historic Preservation* 26:4 (October–December 1974): 5–11.

34. *St. Louis Post-Dispatch,* July 11, 1982, p. 5B.

35. Bradley Ray Storrer to Bernoudy, June 20, 1982, September 2, 1982, Bernoudy Trust Archive.

36. The appointment as visiting artist at the American Academy was one of the few items Bernoudy included in the brief biography of him that appeared in *Who's Who in America* in 1986–1987, the only volume in which he was included. It was probably election to the College of Fellows of the AIA that merited his inclusion in *Who's Who.*

37. Manuscript written at the request of the Garden Club of America, Bernoudy Trust Archive.

38. Mr. and Mrs. Beggs like this interpretation very much but admit they never discussed the idea with Bernoudy. Jane Beggs to the author, June 4, 1996.

39. Bruce Higginbotham to Bernoudy, May 17, 1984, Schneithorst project file, William Bernoudy papers.

40. Interview with J. C. McLaughlin at his house on Long Island, October 13, 1995.

41. Mary Hall to the Bernoudys, Bernoudy Trust Archive. The letter, which is undated and not entirely clear in its references, was explained by Mary Hall in an interview, November 16, 1995.

42. Frank Peters, "The Private Side of William Bernoudy: Homes Are Where the Architect's Heart Is," *St. Louis Post-Dispatch,* November 9, 1986.

43. Stanley J. Goodman to Bernoudy, November 10, 1986, Bernoudy Trust Archive.

44. Thomas Hall to Gertrude Bernoudy, August 4, 1988, Bernoudy Trust Archive.

45. Illustrated sale catalogue, *Property from the Collection of Gertrude Bernoudy,* for the auction held Thursday, November 10, 1994, at Christie's, 502 Park Avenue, New York, N.Y.

Index